D1571003

# LONG-TERM CARE
# AND ETHNICITY

# LONG-TERM CARE AND ETHNICITY

*Ada C. Mui,*
*Namkee G. Choi, and*
*Abraham Monk*

AUBURN HOUSE
Westport, Connecticut • London

**Library of Congress Cataloging-in-Publication Data**

Mui, Ada C., 1949–
   Long-term care and ethnicity / Ada C. Mui, Namkee G. Choi, and
Abraham Monk.
     p.    cm.
   Includes bibliographical references and index.
   ISBN 0–86569–232–7 (alk. paper)
    1. Afro-American aged—Long-term care—United States.  2. Hispanic
American aged—Long-term care—United States.  3. Frail elderly—
Long-term care—United States.  I. Choi, Namkee G., 1955–  .
II. Monk, Abraham.  III. Title.
HV1465.M84    1998
362.1'6'08900973—dc21          98–11157

British Library Cataloguing in Publication Data is available.

Library of Congress Catalog Card Number: 98–11157

ISBN: 0–86569–232–7

First published in 1998

Auburn House, 88 Post Road West, Westport, CT 06881
An imprint of Greenwood Publishing Group, Inc.

Printed in the United States of America

The paper used in this book complies with the
Permanent Paper Standard issued by the National
Information Standards Organization (Z39.48–1984).

10  9  8  7  6  5  4  3  2

# Contents

# Tables

# Preface

This book examines some of the racial and ethnic differences and similarities in the way frail older persons resort to long-term care services. Special attention is given to four aspects of such services: (1) the extent of actual needs for long-term care; (2) the rates and determinants of applications for admission to nursing home facilities; (3) modalities of in-home and community-based services and patterns of utilization of these services; and (4) how informal caregiving—that is, the services provided by relatives, friends, and neighbors—is manifested. Associated with the last named, this book examines whether informal providers experience the stress of burden and, in the affirmative, how they cope with it.

This book intends to make a modest contribution to the gerontological literature by filling a void in the existing body of knowledge about the long-term care needs of ethnic minority elders. Among its special features worth noting are the extensive empirical analysis of information contained in two major national datasets, as well as the conceptualization of long-term care as a multifaceted and complex domain of service.

Special care was taken to link research findings to policy and practice concerns. The book may therefore prove to serve as a critically important resource for the teaching of multiple disciplines, of which public health, social work, nursing, gerontology and geriatrics, and urban and social planning come immediately to mind. In addition, professional practitioners involved with senior clients or patients, agency administrators, community leaders and volunteers, public officials, legislators and, last but not least, the relatives of recipients of long-term care services, will similarly find this book informative and helpful.

The authors were fortunate to receive the expert and warm assistance of many colleagues and friends. Special thanks are extended to Professor Fred

Seidl, former Dean, and Professor Wilburn Hayen, Jr., former Associate
Dean, of the School of Social Work at the State University of New York at
Buffalo, for their constant encouragement and for providing the resources
that made the periodic consultation and meetings of the three authors possible. The authors are particularly indebted to Evelyn Pettit. They wish to
similarly thank the Inter-University Consortium for Political and Social Research for making available the datasets that constitute the very foundation
of this book. Last, but not least, they express their appreciation to Professors
Robert N. Butler, Rose C. Gibson, Terry Fulmer, Rose Dobrof, Jordan I.
Kosberg, and Fernando Torres-Gil for their insightful and most valuable
comments.

*Chapter One* _____

# Introduction

The United States is at the threshold of two very dramatic demographic changes: the aging of its population and the increasing ethnic and racial diversification of its population. The population segment that is age 65 and over (33.5 million) comprises about 12.8% of the total U.S. population now, and this proportion is expected to remain near its current level over the next 10 years. But between 2010 and 2030, the baby boomers will join this older population, and by 2030, about 20% of the total population (69.4 million) is projected to be over 65. Moreover, the most rapidly growing age group is expected to be the 85+ population, with its current size doubled by 2025 and increased fivefold by 2050—that is, from 3.6 million in 1995 to 18.2 million in 2050 (U.S. Bureau of the Census, 1996). The non-Hispanic White share of the population is projected to fall steadily from 74% in 1995 to 72% in 2000, to 64% in 2020, and to 53% in 2050. By the middle of the next century the Black population is expected to nearly double its 1995 size to 61 million. According to the Census Bureau's middle-series projection, more Blacks than non-Hispanic Whites will be added to the population each year after 2016. But the racial/ethnic groups with the highest rates of increase are expected to be those of Hispanic, Asian, and Pacific Islander origin. By 2010, that is, about 10 years from now, the Hispanic-origin population in particular is likely to become the second largest racial/ethnic group, following the non-Hispanic White population. After 2020, owing to its high birth and immigration rates, the Hispanic population is projected to add more people to the U.S. population every year than all other racial/ethnic groups combined (U.S. Bureau of the Census, 1996).

This book is about aging, ethnicity, and long-term care. Specifically, it is organized to fill the knowledge gap with respect to the long-term care needs, patterns, and determinants of formal long-term care service utilization, informal support, and caregiver burden among African American and Hispanic elders and their caregivers as compared to those of their non-Hispanic White counterparts. Despite the rapid aging of the population and the tremendous growth in ethnic and racial diversity among the elderly in this society, empirical studies on possibly heterogamous long-term care needs and service-utilization patterns of minority elders have not been numerous. Existing social epidemiological research findings have been unambiguous about the higher morbidity and mortality rates (i.e., up to a crossover point of age 85 or so) among African American elders than among White elders, with the two groups' differential socioeconomic status being a consistently important explanatory variable (Markides & Black, 1996). Beyond these findings of African American/White differences in health indicators, we do not have firmly established knowledge about long-term care arrangements among minority elders and their families. Until recently, nationally representative data sets that would allow both cross-sectional and longitudinal studies of the comparative psychological, physical, and functional health statuses especially of Hispanic elders have been lacking. The same can be said of their long-term care experiences. Because existing studies on Hispanic elders have been based on small and/or geographically limited area samples, the generalizability of the findings has been undermined. In this book, based on two nationally representative data sets, we present a comprehensive, systematic analysis and comparison of long-term care needs and service use among African American, Hispanic (primarily Mexican American, Puerto Rican, and Cuban American), and White frail elders. Although the increasing number of Asian American elders and the economic and social disadvantages of native American elders call for a study of the long-term care issues they face, we did not include these two groups in this study because of the lack of nationally representative data sets with them large enough to make it possible to conduct a meaningful multivariate analysis. There is a definite need for a large, national-level data bank to help researchers do the studies that will lead to a better understanding of the long-term care needs and patterns of service use of these two minority elderly groups.

## POPULATION AGING AND LONG-TERM CARE NEEDS

The impact of the demographic changes in American society described earlier has been felt for some time in many institutions, including those of education, employment, and health care. With increased life expectancy, however, long-term care for frail elders has begun to emerge as one of the most important familial, social, and financial issues in recent years. Long-term care essentially involves diverse sets of health, personal care, and social services for people who need assistance with their daily life because of chronic physical, functional, or mental disabilities and subsequent loss of the ability to function independently on a daily basis (see Kane & Kane, 1987; U.S. General Accounting Office [GAO], 1996). The settings of long-term care are usually divided into two types: institution based (primarily nursing homes) and home and community based (home care, visiting nurse services, nutrition programs, senior center programs, and other formal and informal services). Of the 7.3 million elders who currently need long-term care, 5.7 million live at home or in small community residential settings, such as group homes or supervised apartments, whereas 1.6 million live in nursing homes or other institutions (U.S. GAO, 1996). Since the 1970s, rising Medicaid expenditures for and concerns about the quality of nursing home care have provided the impetus for a number of research and demonstration programs geared to expanding home- and community-based long-term care services to provide less expensive alternatives to institutional care. Although the results of these programs have not proven the substitution and cost-saving effects, the programs did spur the expansion of home- and community-based programs, dramatically increasing their share of total long-term care expenditures in the past decade. In spite of the recent surge of home- and community-based components of long-term care services, however, Medicaid spending still reflects a bias toward institutional care.

Long-term care services may also be divided into two types: unpaid informal services that are chiefly provided by family members, and formal services that encompass institutional services and home- and community-based services supported by public and private funds. Whether these two types of services are compensatory/substituting or reciprocal has been debated, and the answers that have been advanced are not yet clear. What is clear and has not changed for decades, however, is that unpaid informal support from family and friends has been the most prevalent form of long-term care services. Currently, more than 90% of the noninstitutionalized long-term care beneficiaries receive some informal care, and 67% depend exclusively on family and friends for their long-term care services (National Academy on Aging, 1997). The engagement of a formal support system is prompted mainly by deterioration in the level of an elder's dependency. That is, research findings indicate that, at least among Whites, there is a strong, direct correlation between the severity of a person's disability and his or her formal service utilization (Kelman, Thomas, & Tanaka, 1994; Penning, 1995). Racial/ethnic differences in this area have to be examined further.

Previous studies have shown that a majority of the community-dwelling population age 65 and over are disability free, but existing research results have also demonstrated a strong positive association between advancing age and the prevalence of certain disabilities, as well as the linkage between some chronic diseases and subsequent disability (see Jette, 1996). The proportion of people who have difficulties with activities of daily living (ADL)—a common measure

of functional limitations and disabilities among elders—increases rapidly
with age: Only 11.8% of those between ages 65 and 74 have any ADL difficulties, but the percentage increases to 26.5% of those between ages 75 and
84 and to 57.6% for those age 85 or older (Jette, 1996). Another reflection
of the link between advancing age and disability can be found in the rates
of nursing home use in different age categories. In 1990, about 1% of persons ages 65 to 74 were in a nursing home; this compares with 6.1% of those
ages 75 to 84 and with 24% of those age 85 or older (U.S. Bureau of the
Census, 1993). Although in general the morbidity rate among older persons has been decreasing (Manton, Stallard, & Corder, 1995), the increasing life expectancy and the growing size of the older population, especially
those age 85 or older, will certainly usher in the era of increasing numbers
of disabled elderly who need assistance with the details of their daily life.
Recent projections of the number of elderly needing long-term care reach
10 million to 14 million by 2020 and 14 million to 24 million by 2060, compared with 7.3 million today (Manton, 1989; U.S. GAO, 1994). It is estimated that in 2018 there will be 3.6 million elderly persons needing nursing
home beds, up 2 million from the current figure. Since 87% of all nursing
home beds are routinely filled, there is the threat that increasing demand
will exceed available space and that the competition for nursing home beds
will become intense (National Academy on Aging, 1997). Needless to say,
an increasing number of families would also face the daunting challenge
of providing long-term care for their older relatives while juggling other
familial and job-related responsibilities.

Long-term care for frail elders is a serious issue for a majority of American families because the family is the primary source of caregiving for its
frail elderly relatives. About 80% of the long-term care provided to older
persons outside of nursing homes is presently provided by family members—spouses, adult children, siblings, and broader kin networks. The family also plays an important role in obtaining and managing services from
paid sources (Binstock, Cluff, & von Mering, 1996). Many families also continue to provide supplemental caregiving for their relatives residing in nursing homes (Aneshensel, Pearlin, Mullan, Zarit, & Whitlatch, 1995; George &
Maddox, 1989). Although many family members readily make themselves
available to care for their dependent elderly relatives out of love and a sense
of commitment, caregiving often creates physical, emotional, and financial
strains on the younger generation, because caregiving duties may conflict
with their family life and employment as well as drain individual and family
finances. Currently, about 2 million working Americans provide significant
levels of unpaid care to elderly relatives living in the community who need
assistance with everyday activities. In 1993, families and individuals also
made out-of-pocket payments that were nearly 36% of all long-term care
expenditures (U.S. GAO, 1996).

The challenge of meeting long-term care needs has also become a substantial concern for all levels of governments, primarily because of the increasing cost of care. Long-term care spending under Medicaid grew at an average rate of 13.2% annually from fiscal year 1989 to fiscal year 1993, with expenditures for home- and community-based services growing faster than those for services provided in institutions. And Medicare long-term care spending grew at a rate of 33.8% per year during the same period. In 1993, federal and state governments paid 64% of the total long-term care cost of $108 billion, of which 70% was spent for institutional care (U.S. GAO, 1996). Private long-term care insurance contributed only a minuscule proportion (0.2%) of the long-term care costs and is not expected to increase its share of payment in the near future. Government sources, mainly Medicaid and Medicare, and families and individuals, with their private out-of-pocket expenses, are expected to continue to bear the financial burden of long-term care.

## ETHNIC/RACIAL DIVERSIFICATION
## OF THE ELDERLY POPULATION

Ethnicity has been defined by Holzberg (1982) as follows:

Social differentiation based on such cultural criteria as a sense of peoplehood, shared history, a common place of origin, language, dress and free preferences, and participation in particular clubs or voluntary associations, engenders a sense of exclusiveness and self-awareness that one is a member of a distinct and bounded social group. But it is not the ethnic content (marker) per se that constitutes the diacritica of social differentiation. More important for the purposes of social distance are the feelings of shared particularity, self-identification, and membership in ethnic-exclusive associations. (p. 252)

Thus, an ethnic group may be composed of any racial or religious group whose members share a common history and common cultural norms and identities and experiences that differentiate them from other groups in the society. People of common European ancestry, Arabs, Jews, native Americans, African Americans, and different nationality groups of Hispanics and Asian Americans make up the varied ethnic/racial groups in this country. But because of the country's history of according differential treatment to different ethnic/racial groups, not all of them have been allowed equal political, economic, and social opportunity. Some groups have become more dominant in their economic, political, and social status and have enjoyed greater privileges than others, with some of the latter having become the object of collective discrimination from the dominant groups. Hence, there is the need for differentiating minority from ethnic groups, because "minority status carries with it the exclusion from full participation in the life of the society" (Wirth, 1945, p. 348). In the United States, the primary markers for unequal treatment of and discrimination against an ethnic/racial group have been their physical (notably skin pigmentation) and cultural characteristics (Wirth, 1945). People of color—native Americans, African Americans, Asian Americans, and Hispanics—who have physical and cultural characteristics that are different from those of the dominant Caucasians have thus become the minority groups. Although overt, institutionalized discrimination may have become illegal with the passage of the Civil Rights Act three decades ago, the history of institutionalized racism in all spheres of life and the continuation of subtle discrimination have left indelible marks of both absolute and relative deprivation in the economic and social life of the minorities. Being a member of a minority group is often strongly associated with facing a host of related risk factors throughout one's life, including risk of poverty and the accompanying stresses of low social class, of prejudice and discrimination, and of poor psychological and physical health as the negative consequences of low income and stress.

Some argue that, unlike their White majority counterparts, minority elders are thus likely to bear the stresses and burdens of being a minority person, on top of those associated with being an older person, which derives from the devaluation of old age found in most modern societies (Dowd & Bengtson, 1978). As a result of the interaction effect between racial and age discrimination, minorities' comparative disadvantages may become worse in old age than in young or middle ages (double jeopardy hypothesis). Others, however, argue that, to a certain extent, old age may level off, rather than exacerbate or amplify, the effect of the stratification system based on race (age-as-a-leveler hypothesis). According to this argument, this occurs because (1) the process of aging brings such basic challenges to health and functional ability that racial inequality is no longer important; (2) minority persons adopt coping strategies throughout life to deal with racial discrimination, and these help them deal with age discrimination; (3) income-maintenance and health care programs designed to help the elderly in effect reduce racial differentials; and (4) society fails to recognize the differences among older people in temperament, values, norms, and skills by lumping them together into one negative stereotype of frail, incapable older folks (for further discussion, see Ferraro & Farmer, 1996; Gelfand, 1994).

Indeed, aging is a process that everyone who lives long enough has to go through, regardless of ethnic background. But elderly members of the minority groups that have experienced the institutionalized racism and educational, residential, and social segregation that have limited their legal, economic, and social opportunities are in an especially vulnerable position. Because of their experience of discrimination per se and of other risk factors (e.g., lower economic and health statuses) that often result from discrimination, we believe that non-White minority elders and their families experience aging differently from the White majority elders and that they have different long-term care needs. In fact, many previous studies found a widening of economic and health disadvantages, although others also found such disadvantages of minority group members declining from middle to old age (see Crystal, 1996; Crystal & Shea, 1990; Ferraro, 1987; Gibson, 1991). The point is that, whether or not their comparative disadvantages have declined with aging, minority elders are likely to be exposed to a greater number of stressors and to have fewer coping resources after a lifetime of financial deprivation and systematic exclusion from access to equal opportunities. Empirical evidence shows that, compared to White elders, minority elders have a lower economic status and suffer from poorer health, both objectively and subjectively.

In addition, the cultural norms and values of the minority groups that are different from those of the White majority also contribute to shaping differences in the long-term care arrangements that the two groups make for their frail elders. For example, strong extended familism and a high degree of respect for the older generation among African Americans and Hispanics have often been cited as factors that cause the aging experience of minority elders to be different from that of White elders. The availability of larger and more supportive informal networks; an ingrained sense of "respect," bordering on veneration, for elders; and economic dislocation, migration, and urbanization factors, which may have contributed to the extension of familial supports, especially among African Americans, are factors that have been particularly cited to interpret the lower rates of utilization of formal services by African Americans and Hispanics (Aschenbrenner, 1975; Cantor, 1979; Gratton, 1987; Maldonado, 1977; Mindel & Wright, 1982; Rogler, 1978). It is therefore important for policy makers and practitioners to be equipped with knowledge of differences among diverse racial/ethnic groups in order to be able to design and implement policies and programs that are sensitive to differing needs of minority elders and their families.

In the case of Hispanic elders, the high proportion of immigrants, different national origins, and the different political, economic, and individual circumstances that led to immigration bring added complexities to the issues pertaining to aging and long-term care. For example, research has found that the level of immersion in the traditional culture of the country of origin or the level of assimilation to the host country as well as the level of English proficiency are significantly correlated with Hispanic elders' physical and mental health (Angel & Angel, 1992; Gelfand, 1994). In another example, a larger fraction of foreign-born than native-born Mexican American elders stated that they would prefer to continue living with their children in the event that they could no longer care for themselves (Angel, Angel, McClellan, & Markides, 1996). Possibly significant variations among various Hispanic national-origin groups and among those with different immigration histories make it important not to aggregate all the Hispanics in search of common traits as this may defeat the very purpose of the inquiry about cultural differentiation and sensitivity.

Thus, in addition to the need to analyze and compare differences between minority elders and majority elders, the increasing number of and internal heterogeneity among minority elders also dictate the need to examine within-group differences in each minority elder group. For one thing, social class and gender are often significant antecedent variables for within-group differences among White elders, and they may also be significantly associated with within-group differences among minority elders. Some studies have found significant effects of social class and/or gender on African American and Hispanic elders' psychological well-being, intergenerational interaction, and perceived caregiver availability (Gibson, 1991; Mendes de Leon & Markides, 1988; Mui, 1996; Mutran, 1985; Talamantes, Cornell, Espino, Lichtenstein, & Hazuda, 1996). In this book, determinants of long-term care service utilization and informal caregiving within groups of African American, Hispanic, and White frail elders are analyzed. These three groups are referred to as ethnic or racial/ethnic groups, and African American and Hispanic elders especially are referred to as ethnic minority, racial minority, ethnic/racial minority, or minority elders. The designations African American and Black are used interchangeably.

## ETHNIC/RACIAL DIFFERENCES IN UTILIZATION OF FORMAL LONG-TERM CARE SERVICES AND INFORMAL CAREGIVING

As shown in the earlier National Nursing Home Survey of 1977, both African American and Hispanic elderly are underrepresented in nursing home and other institutional services, relative to their proportion of the general population (National Center for Health Statistics, 1979). Although racial disparities in the rates of nursing home utilization have been closing in the past decades, African American elders are institutionalized at a significantly lower rate than White elders despite their generally lower physical and functional health status and even after instrumental support from informal support networks has been controlled for (Belgrave & Bradsher, 1994; Belgrave, Wykle, & Choi, 1993). An analysis of the 1990 Census data also showed that the proportion of Hispanic elders who were institutionalized was much lower that that of White elders (Himes, Hogan, & Eggebeen, 1996). Two assumptions have been that both populations of the minority group prefer family caretaking over long-term institutional care (Watson, 1990) and that family informal supports meet the need for care. Other researchers, meanwhile, have attributed the ineffectual level of utilization of formal support, including nursing homes, to the caregivers' perceived lack of availability or access to services (Aronson & Lipkowitz, 1981; Mace & Rabins, 1984). Factors that may contribute to such perceptions include lack of knowledge, difficulties in access, poor linkage between services, negative attitudes toward the use of formal support services, and financial constraints. Frail elders and their families may be further deterred from service utilization, even when they know about existing services, if they are not able to associate them with their own particular needs. For instance, although adult day care centers in the United States are highly effective in terms of the skill of care administered, the dementia population has been found to be largely underserved (Mace & Rabins, 1984). In other instances, perceived lack of cultural sensitivity of a program and its service providers, a general suspicion of unknown cultures, or past negative experiences with persons from other cultures may function as barriers to service utilization. Because today's minority elders have lived so much of their lives with overt discrimination, it is not surprising that cultural differences and past experiences have been found to inhibit service use (Yeatts, Crow, & Folts, 1992). Moreover, the policy reforms brought about by Medicare's diagnostic related groups (DRGs) in the early 1980s and the prospective payment system (PPS) may have exerted a negative effect on minorities' applications to nursing homes. As many seniors are being released from hospitals still feeble and convalescing, the number of elders who need posthospitalization care in nursing homes has increased, and the wait lists for nursing home admission have grown. Under the circumstances, minority elders, who are more often than not Medicaid beneficiaries, are likely to have been shunned by profit-conscious nursing homes in favor of private-pay White applicants.

With respect to racial differences in the utilization of formal home and community-based long-term care services, previous studies report mixed findings. Earlier studies (e.g., Mindel & Wright, 1982) reported a significantly lower likelihood of service use among Blacks than among Whites, but more recent studies based on nationally representative sample surveys did not find race to be a significant predictor (Miller et al., 1996; Norgard & Rodgers, 1997). According to these studies, one of the significant predictors of use of formal home and community-based services is living arrangement, indicating that elders who live alone are more likely than those living with spouse or others to use and depend on formal services. Frail elders' living arrangement is indeed a key dimension in long-term care service delivery, because many elders who live alone move in with others, mostly their adult children, or have relatives move in with them following the onset of disability or as their disability progresses significantly (Choi, 1997). African American and Hispanic elders are significantly more likely than White elders to live in a multigenerational household regardless of their health status. Minority elders, especially African Americans, are also more likely to live with nonrelatives. Thus, it appears that frail minority elders are likely to receive proportionately more informal support from coresiding relatives or nonrelatives, which may have a substitution effect on formal services.

Aside from the problems of possible biases in sampling minority elders for national surveys, which may have led to biased findings with regard to racial differences or lack thereof, the real issue regarding formal home- and community-based services is that of underutilization of the services by frail minority elders and their caregivers. Despite frail minority elders' high need for such formal services, as indicated by their physical and functional health problems vis-à-vis the size of their informal social support networks, studies have consistently found that community-residing minority elders underutilize long-term care services that are designed to enhance their health status and quality of life and, in some instances, to prevent further deterioration of their health and alleviate the caregiving burden on their families (Kart, 1991; Miller et al., 1996).

Empirical data about service-utilization patterns among minority elders and their caregivers are very limited (Kulys, 1990). There is, however, a growing awareness about cultural differentiation among aged ethnic and racial subgroups on issues regarding attitude toward illness, social support networks, and the complementarity and/or supplantation between informal supports and formal services. For instance, in their study of families of African American and Hispanic dementia patients, Monk, Lerner, McCann-Oakley, and Cox (1989) found that the stigma associated with mental problems, a greater acceptance of abnormal behavior among the aged, and the reluctance to take such problems outside the family domain may partially account for the underutilization of formal services by minority caregivers. Studies have also shown that the extended social support networks of African American and Hispanic elders are larger than those of White elders and that these groups' bonds of filial obligation and normative expectations to assist frail elderly relatives are also stronger (Chatters & Taylor, 1990; Connell & Gibson, 1997; Johnson & Barer, 1990; Markides & Mindel, 1987; Watson, 1990). As to the relationship between informal support and formal support, Miner (1995) found, based on data from the 1984 Supplement on Aging Survey, that receiving formal services was not associated with lower use of informal support, but that informal support reduced the likelihood of receiving formal support among African American elders, whereas formal and informal supports had a full substitution effect among White elders. Since underutilization of services is likely to lead to unmet need and increased caregiver burden, these issues related to cultural differentiation beg for more precise and reliable information, an essential prerequisite for the formulation of more adequate and better targeted public policies governing the provision of services.

Providing care for a loved one in his or her last stage of life can be a rewarding experience. Yet caregiving frequently consumes an individual's energy, leading to physical and emotional exhaustion and conflicts with the caregiver's other interests (Older Women's League, 1989). In many cases, caregiving is also a responsibility that stretches over a period of several years and requires an increasingly intensive and more difficult array of tasks as the care recipient's condition continues to deteriorate. Much of the burden usually falls on the primary caregiver, often a woman with other family responsibilities and, increasingly, one employed outside the home as well. Thus, more often than not, caregiving stress reverberates and encroaches upon other aspects of a caregiver's life, compromising his or her well-being.

The considerable physical, emotional, and financial tolls that caregiving exacts from families and friends of frail elders have been widely studied. The frequently used conceptual framework for studying caregiver burden originates from stress and coping theories (see Lawton, Moss, Kleban, Glickman, & Rovine, 1991; Pearlin, Mullan, Semple, & Skaff, 1990). That is, the studies of caregiver burden often examined how an individual's well-being as an outcome is affected by the process in which the psychosocial and financial stressors that the individual experiences as a caregiver are mediated by her/his coping resources. A review and analysis of empirical studies of racial differences in caregiver burden among caregivers of dementia patients concludes that, as compared with White caregivers, African American caregivers generally report a lower level of caregiver stress and burden and are more likely to use prayer, faith, and religion as coping mechanisms (Connell & Gibson, 1997). Comparative studies of African American and White caregivers in general found lower levels of stress among the African Americans (see Fredman, Daly, & Lazur, 1995). However, studies of Hispanic caregivers of dementia patients found that they reported levels of psychological burden or depression similar to or higher than those reported by White caregivers (Aranda & Knight, 1997). These racial differences or similarities tend to be interpreted, again, as cultural derivatives. But within the African American and Hispanic caregiver subgroups, what factors account for internal heterogeneity in the level of caregiver stress? For Hispanics, are the findings from caregivers of dementia patients generalizable to caregivers of other frail elders? Answers to these questions, yet to be found, are needed to provide a basis for the formulation of culturally sensitive policies and programs for frail elder and their caregivers.

## ORGANIZATION OF THE BOOK

Chapter 2 introduces two national databases that are used in this book and presents profiles of the samples. Chapter 3 provides a comparative analysis of psychological symptomatology among African American, Hispanic, and White frail elders, and Chapter 4 analyzes perceived health, financial strain, and psychological distress among Mexican American, Cuban American, and Puerto Rican elders. Chapter 5 compares frail elders who have applied for nursing home admission with those who have not in an effort to find out predictors of such application. Chapter 6 analyzes predictors of nursing home application among African American and White frail elders. Chapter 7 analyzes patterns and determinants of in-home and community-based services among African American, Hispanic, and White frail elders, and Chapter 8 analyzes the same among the three national origin groups of Hispanic elders. Chapter 9 examines the relationship between elders' living arrangements and their utilization of formal services and racial/ethnic differences thereof. Chapter 10 analyzes racial/ethnic differences in the size of informal support network and caregiver burden among primary caregivers of African American, Hispanic, and White frail elders. Chapter 11 summarizes the findings and presents policy and practice implications of the findings.

## REFERENCES

Aneshensel, C. S., Pearlin, L. I., Mullan, J. T., Zarit, S. H., & Whitlatch, C. J. (1995). *Profiles in caregiving: The unexpected career.* San Diego: Academic Press.

Angel, J. L., & Angel, R. J. (1992). Age at migration, social connections and well-being among elderly Hispanics. *Journal of Aging and Health, 4,* 480–499.

Angel, J. L., Angel, R. J., McClellan, J. L., & Markides, K. S. (1996). Nativity, declining health, and preferences in living arrangements among elderly Mexican Americans: Implications for long-term care. *The Gerontologist, 36,* 464–473.

Aranda, M. P., & Knight, B. G. (1997). The influence of ethnicity and culture on the caregiver stress and coping process: A sociocultural review and analysis. *The Gerontologist, 37,* 342–354.

Aronson, M. K., & Lipkowitz R. (1981). Senile dementia, Alzheimer's type: The family and the health care delivery system. *Journal of the American Geriatric Society, 29,* 568–571.

Aschenbrenner, J. (1975). *Lifelines: African-American families in Chicago.* New York: Holt, Rinehart, & Winston.

Belgrave, L. L., & Bradsher, J. E. (1994). Health as a factor in institutionalization: Disparities between African Americans and Whites. *Research on Aging, 16,* 115–141.

Belgrave, L. L., Wykle, M. L., & Choi, J. M. (1993). Health, double jeopardy, and culture: The use of institutionalization by African-Americans. *The Gerontologist, 33,* 379–385.

Binstock, R. H., Cluff, L. E., & von Mering, O. (1996). Issues affecting the future of long-term care. In R. H. Binstock, L. E. Cluff, & O. von Mering (Eds.), *The future of long-term care: Social and policy issues* (pp. 3–18). Baltimore: Johns Hopkins University Press.

Cantor, M. H. (1979). The informal support system of New York's inner city elderly: Is ethnicity a factor? In D. E. Gelfand & A. J. Kutzik (Eds.), *Ethnicity and aging: Theory, research, and policy* (pp. 153–174). New York: Springer.

Chatters, L. M., & Taylor R. J. (1990). Social integration. In Z. Harel, E. A. McKinney, & M. Williams (Eds.), *Black aged: Understanding diversity and service needs* (pp. 82–99). Newbury Park, CA: Sage.

Choi, N. G. (1997, November). No longer independent: Dynamics of care arrangements among frail elderly parents. Paper presented at the 51st Annual Scientific Meeting of the Gerontological Society of America, Cincinnati, Ohio.

Connell, C. M., & Gibson, G. D. (1997). Racial, ethnic, and cultural differences in dementia caregiving: Review and analysis. *The Gerontologist, 37*, 355–364.

Crystal, S. (1996). Economic status of the elderly. In R. H. Binstock & L. K. George (Eds.), *Handbook of aging and the social sciences* (pp. 388–409). San Diego: Academic Press.

Crystal, S., & Shea, D. (1990). Cumulative advantages, cumulative disadvantage, and inequality among elderly people. *The Gerontologist, 30*, 437–443.

Dowd, J. J., & Bengtson, V. L. (1978). Aging in minority populations: An examination of the double jeopardy hypothesis. *Journal of Gerontology, 33*, 427–436.

Ferraro, K. F. (1987). Double jeopardy to health for Black older adults? *Journal of Gerontology, 42*, 528–533.

Ferraro, K. F., & Farmer, M. M. (1996). Double jeopardy, aging as a level, or persistent health in equality? A longitudinal analysis of White and Black Americans. *Journal of Gerontology, 51B*, S319–S328.

Fredman, L., Daly, M. P., & Lazur, A. M. (1995). Burden among White and Black caregivers to elderly adults. *Journal of Gerontology, 50B*, S110–S118.

Gelfand, D. E. (1994). *Aging and ethnicity: Knowledge and services.* New York: Springer.

George, L. K., & Maddox, G. (1989). Social and behavioral aspects of institutional care. In M. Ory & K. Bond (Eds.), *Aging and health care: Social science and health perspectives* (pp. 116–141). London: Rutledge.

Gibson, R. C. (1991). Age-by-race differences in the health and functioning of elderly persons. *Journal of Aging and Health, 3*, 335–351.

Gratton, B. (1987). Familism among the black and Mexican-American elderly: Myth or reality? *Journal of Aging Studies, 1*, 19–32.

Himes, C. L., Hogan, D. P., & Eggebeen, D. J. (1996). Living arrangements of minority elders. *Journal of Gerontology, 51B*, S42–S48.

Holzberg, C. (1982). Ethnicity and aging: Anthropological perspectives on more than just minority elderly. *The Gerontologist, 22*, 249–257.

Jette, A. M. (1996). Disability trends and transitions. In R. H. Binstock & L. K. George (Eds.), *Handbook of aging and the social sciences* (pp. 94–116). San Diego: Academic Press.

Johnson, C. L., & Barer, B. M. (1990). Families and networks among older inner-city Blacks. *The Gerontologist, 30*, 726–733.

Kane, R. A., & Kane, R. L. (1987). *Long-term care: Principles, programs, and policies.* New York: Springer.

Kart, C. S. (1991). Variation in long-term care service use by aged Blacks. *Journal of Aging and Health, 3*, 511–526.

Kelman, H. R., Thomas, C., & Tanaka, J. S. (1994). Longitudinal patterns of formal and informal social support in an urban elderly population. *Social Science and Medicine, 38*, 905–914.

Kulys, R. (1990). The ethnic factor in the delivery of social services. In A. Monk (Ed.), *Handbook of gerontological services* (2d ed., pp. 629–661). New York: Columbia University Press.

Lawton, M. P., Moss, M., Kleban, M. H., Glickman, A., & Rovine, M. (1991). A two-factor model of caregiving appraisal and psychological well-being. *Journal of Gerontology, 46*, P181–P189.

Mace, N. L., & Rabins, P. V. (1984). *The 36-hour day: A family guide to caring for persons with Alzheimer's disease, related dementing illness, and memory loss in later life.* Baltimore: Johns Hopkins University Press.

Maldonado, J. D. (1977). La familia Mexico Americana and the elderly. *Research Utilization Report, 4,* 18.

Manton, K. (1989). Epidemiological, demographic, and social correlates of disability among the elderly. *Milbank Quarterly, 67* (suppl. 2, pt. 1), 13–58.

Manton, K., Stallard, E., & Corder, L. (1995). Changes in morbidity and chronic disability in the U.S. elderly population: Evidence from the 1982, 1984, and 1989 National Long-Term Care Surveys. *Journal of Gerontology, 50B,* S194–S204.

Markides, K. S., & Black, S. A. (1996). Race, ethnicity, and aging: The impact of inequality. In R. H. Binstock & L. K. George (Eds.), *Handbook of aging and the social sciences* (pp. 153–170). San Diego: Academic Press.

Markides, K. S., & Mindel, C. H. (1987). *Aging and ethnicity.* Newbury Park, CA: Sage.

Mendes de Leon, C. F., & Markides, K. S. (1988). Depressive symptoms among Mexican Americans: A three generations study. *American Journal of Epidemiology, 127,* 159–160.

Miller, B., Campbell, R. T., Davis, L., Furner, S., Giachello, A., Prohaska, T., Kaufman, J. E., Li, M., & Perez, C. (1996). Minority use of community long-term care services: A comparative analysis. *Journal of Gerontology, 51B,* S70–S81.

Mindel, C. H., & Wright, R. (1982). The use of social services by African-American and White elderly: The role of social support systems. *Journal of Gerontological Social Work, 4,* 107–125.

Miner, S. (1995). Racial differences in family support and formal service utilization among older persons: A nonrecursive model. *Journal of Gerontology, 50B,* S143–S153.

Monk, A., Lerner, J., McCann-Oakley, A., & Cox, C. (1989). *Families of African American and Hispanic dementia patients: Their use of formal and informal support services.* Final report to the AARP-Andrus Foundation. New York: The Institute on Aging, Columbia University, School of Social Work, 220 pp.

Mui, A. C. (1996). Correlates of psychological distress among Mexican, Cuban, and Puerto Rican elders living in the USA. *Journal of Cross-Cultural Gerontology, 11,* 131–147.

Mutran, E. (1985). Intergenerational family support among Blacks and Whites: Response to culture or to socioeconomic differences. *Journal of Gerontology, 40,* 382–389.

National Academy on Aging. (1997). *Facts on long-term care.* Washington, DC: Author.

Norgard, T. M., & Rodgers, W. L. (1997). Patterns of in-home care among elderly Black and White Americans. *Journal of Gerontology, 52B,* 93–101.

Older Women's League. (1989). *Failing America's caregivers: A status report on women who care.* Washington, DC: Author.

Pearlin, L. I., Mullan, J. T., Semple, S. J., & Skaff, M. M. (1990). Caregiving and the stress process: An overview of concepts and their measures. *The Gerontologist, 30,* 583–594.

Penning, M. (1995). Health, social support and the utilization of health services among older adults. *Journal of Gerontology, 50B,* S330–S339.

Rogler, L. H. (1978). Help patterns, the family, and mental health: Puerto Ricans in the United States. *International Migration Review, 12,* 248–259.

Talamantes, M. A., Cornell, J., Espino, D. V., Lichtenstein, M. J., & Hazuda, H. P. (1996). SES and ethnic differences in perceived caregiver availability among

    young–old Mexican Americans and non-Hispanic Whites. *The Gerontologist,*
    *36,* 88–99.

U.S. Bureau of the Census. (1993). *Nursing home population, 1990.* CPH-L-137. Wash-
    ington, DC.: U.S. Government Printing Office.

U.S. Bureau of the Census. (1996). *Population projections of the United States by age, sex,*
    *race, and Hispanic origin: 1995 to 2050.* Current Population Reports, P24-
    1130. Washington, DC: U.S. Government Printing Office.

U.S. General Accounting Office (GAO). (1994). *Long-term care: Diverse, growing*
    *population includes millions of Americans of all ages.* GAO/HEHS-95-26. Wash-
    ington, DC: U.S. Government Printing Office.

U.S. General Accounting Office (GAO). (1996). *Long-term care: Current issues and*
    *future directions.* GAO/HEHS-95-109. Washington, DC: U.S. Government
    Printing Office.

Watson, W. H. (1990). Family care, economics, and health. In Z. Harel, E. A.
    McKinney, & M. Williams (Eds.), *Black aged: Understanding diversity and service*
    *needs* (pp. 50–68). Newbury Park, CA: Sage.

Wirth, L. (1945). The problem of minority groups. In R. Linton (Ed.), *The science of*
    *man in the world crisis* (pp. 347–372). New York: Columbia University Press.

Yeatts, D. E., Crow, T., & Folts, E. (1992). Service use among low-income minority
    elderly: Strategies for overcoming barriers. *The Gerontologist, 32,* 24–32.

# Chapter Two

# Data Sources and Profiles
# of the Samples

## DATA SOURCES

This book is based on two national databases: the National Long-Term Care Channeling Demonstration, 1982–1984; and the National Survey of Hispanic Elderly People, 1988. Channeling was a national experiment, initiated by the U.S. Department of Health and Human Services, to test whether an expanded, publicly financed home- and community-based care program would help to reduce the long-term care costs associated with nursing home expenditures and would improve the well-being of frail elderly persons and their families. Channeling was implemented in 10 communities through case-management agencies (Phillips et al., 1986).

The target population was frail elderly people at risk of institutionalization, defined as those who had severe impairments in terms of ADL and/or instrumental activities of daily living (IADL). Under the functional disability criterion, an elderly person must have exhibited one of the following conditions: two moderate disabilities in performing ADL, three severe impairments in his or her ability to perform IADL, or one severe ADL disability and two severe IADL impairments. Cognitive or behavioral difficulties that affected an individual's ability to perform ADL could count as one of the severe IADL impairments. The second criterion (the existence of unmet needs) was fulfilled if needs for two or more services were not expected to be met for a period of at least six months. A fragile informal support system that was having difficulty continuing to meet the elderly person's needs also provided evidence of unmet needs (Phillips et al., 1986).

Potential participants were referred by family members and service providers and interviewed, usually by telephone, to determine eligibility. Overall, 5,626 elderly persons completed the baseline interviews, with 73.6% non-Hispanic Whites, 22.7% African Americans, and 3.7% Hispanics. Enrollees were then randomly assigned to either a treatment group, which received "channeling" services (outreach, screening, comprehensive needs assessment, care planning, service arrangement, monitoring, and reassessment), or a control, which continued to rely on existing long-term care services (Stephens & Christianson, 1986). Both groups received an initial standardized baseline assessment and follow-up interviews that included information on demographics, living arrangement, personal finances, medical conditions, physical and psychological functioning, informal supports, formal service utilization, and attitudes toward current living situation and institutionalization.

The original data were collected through both baseline and follow-up interviews, but for the purpose of this book, only the baseline (preintervention) data were analyzed. Consequently, our analysis does not include the follow-up measures, nor does it reflect the experimental effects of the demonstration.

In addition to the elderly sample surveys, another survey was conducted of individuals identified by the elders as their primary informal caregivers—that is, the family members or friends who provided the greatest amount of unpaid assistance to the elderly person in terms of caretaking, helping with personal affairs, or performing household chores (Stephens & Christianson, 1986). Of the 2,552 primary caregivers who entered the demonstration program between November 1982 and May 1983, a total of 1,940 primary caregivers fully or partially completed the preintervention interviews, with a response rate of 76% (Phillips et al., 1986). Nonreponse caregiver data were not available. However, the older persons whose caregivers were not interviewed generally were not significantly different from those whose caregivers did complete interviews (Stephens & Christianson, 1986).

The entire channeling demonstration included 10 participating states and local agencies, a technical assistance contractor, and a national evaluation contractor. Although the sample was not a random sample of the elderly population, the 10 sites—Baltimore, Houston, Cleveland, Miami, Philadelphia, Eastern Kentucky, Southern Maine, Middlesex (New Jersey), Rensselaer (New York), and Greater Lynn (Massachusetts)—did represent a broad range of the nation's noninstitutionalized frail elderly.

The National Survey of Hispanic Elderly People, 1988, a part of the Commonwealth Fund Commission's project on elderly people living alone (Commonwealth Fund Commission on Elderly People Living Alone, 1989), used a telephone survey to obtain a profile of the health, economic, and social circumstances of Hispanic people aged 65 and over. Between August and October 1988, trained bilingual interviewers gathered information on living arrangements, length of time the respondent had lived in the United States, economic resources, health and functional status, social network, family support, and psychological well-being (Davis, 1990).

Selection of the screening sample was conducted in several stages. The first step was the identification of telephone exchanges in the entire United

States (including Alaska and Hawaii) in which Hispanic households constituted 30% or more of the total. Then, using random-digit dialing, 48,183 households were screened for Hispanics aged 65 and over, resulting in completed interviews with 2,299 older Hispanics. The survey provides a nationally representative sample of Hispanics aged 65 and over, living within telephone exchanges that have at least a 30% concentration of Hispanic residents in three geographic areas: New England and the Middle Atlantic; Florida; and the balance of the country. The overall response rate was 80%, and 87% of the interviewees chose to be interviewed in Spanish. The analyses presented in Chapters 3, 6, and 7 of this book are based on a subsample of Mexican Americans ($n$ = 773), Cuban Americans ($n$ = 714), and Puerto Ricans ($n$ = 368). Other Hispanic groups were not included because their numbers were limited. With respect to these national-origin groups, this survey used as strict a self-classification procedure as the Census Bureau. The respondents determined which Hispanic subgroup they belonged to after the interviewer read the five subgroups to them (Mexican Americans/Chicano; Cuban Americans; Puerto Ricans; Hispanic/Spanish Americans, and other).

## PROFILE OF THE SAMPLES

### The National Long-Term Care Channeling (1982–1984) Sample

Tables 2.1 and 2.2 present profiles of the three racial/ethnic groups in the sample. Hispanic elders were the oldest (63% were 80 years of age or older), and the highest proportion of currently unmarried elders were African Americans (73.6%), followed by Whites. African Americans had low mean incomes ($464 per month), but Hispanics had even less ($406 per month), and they were more likely to receive Medicaid (64.9%). As shown in Table 2.2, a higher percentage of Hispanic elders were also severely impaired, both functionally (34.6%) and cognitively (19.8%). This group also reported the highest mean number of depressive symptoms.

Table 2.3 presents data on use of the three types of long-term care services and informal supports. Whites had the highest percentage of regular home health care use (30.3%), Hispanics used mobile meal services more than African Americans, and the latter had the highest church and social center participation (15.8%). Whites reported significantly more nursing home use during the preceding six (10.1%) and two (61.6%) months and more nursing home applications (5.2%), whereas African Americans and Hispanics reported more informal helpers.

Table 2.4 presents the elderly persons' sense of control and confidence in problem solving. White elders reported lower life satisfaction and more sense of control than either African Americans or Hispanics. A possible explanation is that White elders may have higher expectations in life. On the other

**Table 2.1**
**Sociodemographic Characteristics of Frail Elders by Ethnicity**

| Characteristics | African American $\underline{n} = 1,272$ (%) | White[a] $\underline{n} = 4,133$ (%) | Hispanic $\underline{n} = 211$ (%) |
|---|---|---|---|
| **Age****** | | | |
| 65 to 69 | 14.5 | 10.7 | 9.9 |
| 70 to 74 | 18.5 | 15.4 | 16.6 |
| 75 to 79 | 20.6 | 22.1 | 10.4 |
| 80 to 84 | 22.6 | 23.3 | 30.3 |
| 85 to 89 | 13.7 | 18.2 | 19.4 |
| >= 90 | 10.1 | 10.2 | 13.3 |
| **Gender** | | | |
| Female | 70.7 | 71.9 | 69.2 |
| Male | 29.3 | 28.1 | 30.8 |
| **Marital status****** | | | |
| Married | 26.4 | 33.0 | 40.8 |
| Not married | 73.6 | 67.0 | 59.2 |
| **Education****** | | | |
| None or elementary | 71.3 | 57.5 | 75.4 |
| Some secondary | 14.0 | 13.9 | 2.4 |
| Completed high school | 8.0 | 16.8 | 12.3 |
| Completed college | 5.7 | 9.5 | 5.7 |
| Postcollege | 0.9 | 2.2 | 4.3 |
| **Living arrangement****** | | | |
| Alone | 31.2 | 39.7 | 23.2 |
| With spouse | 25.2 | 32.3 | 39.3 |
| With children | 23.5 | 20.1 | 26.1 |
| With others | 20.1 | 7.9 | 11.4 |
| **Income** (per month)[b]***** | | | |
| < $500 | 75.4 | 38.6 | 61.5 |
| $500 to $999 | 16.9 | 42.0 | 23.1 |
| >=$1000 | 7.7 | 19.4 | 15.4 |
| **Medicaid receipt****** | 35.1 | 16.7 | 64.9 |

Data Source: National Long-Term Care Channeling Demonstration, 1982–1984.
Note: Chi-square statistics were used.
[a]None was of Hispanic origin.
[b]The mean monthly income, excluding imputed missing data, was $463.95 for African American elders ($n = 1,178$), $406.11 ($n = 198$) for Hispanic elders, and $594.32 ($n = 3,600$) for White elders.
****$p < 0.0001$.

**Table 2.2**
**Health and Mental Health Status of Frail Elders by Ethnicity**

|  | African American $\underline{n} = 1,272$ (%) | White[a] $\underline{n} = 4,133$ (%) | Hispanic $\underline{n} = 211$ (%) |
|---|---|---|---|
| **Perceived health status*** | | | |
| Excellent | 2.6 | 2.8 | 1.9 |
| Good | 15.3 | 15.1 | 8.5 |
| Fair | 31.0 | 29.7 | 38.9 |
| Poor | 51.1 | 52.5 | 50.7 |
| **ADL impairment****** | | | |
| Mild or none | 15.4 | 20.9 | 19.9 |
| Moderately severe | 23.3 | 22.7 | 11.9 |
| Very severe | 33.7 | 35.2 | 33.7 |
| Extremely severe | 27.7 | 21.2 | 34.6 |
| **Cognitive impairment***** | | | |
| Mild or none | 47.2 | 51.0 | 44.1 |
| Moderate | 38.4 | 32.4 | 36.1 |
| Severe | 14.4 | 16.6 | 19.8 |

*Data Source*: National Long-Term Care Channeling Demonstration, 1982–1984.
*Note*: Chi-square statistics were used.
*$p < 0.05$; ***$p < 0.001$; ****$p < 0.0001$.

hand, Hispanic elders reported less confidence about dealing with problems and getting needed services and more concern about whom to turn to for necessary help. Even though family interaction and contact did not differ among the three groups of elders, they seemed to have different concerns in their lives. Family contact did not seem to sufficiently meet the needs of the minority elders.

## The National Survey of Hispanic Elderly People (1988) Sample

Table 2.5 presents a descriptive profile of the three groups of Hispanic elderly people. About one-fifth of the Mexican and Cuban Americans were 80 years of age or older, which means that these groups were somewhat older than the Puerto Ricans. But nearly two-thirds of Puerto Rican elders were unmarried (compared to less than half of the other groups) and nearly twice as many of the Puerto Ricans lived alone (36.7% compared to 22.1% of the Mexican Americans and 21% of the Cuban Americans). There were no differences in the use of Supplemental Security Income (SSI) among the three

**Table 2.3**
**Formal and Informal Support of Frail Elders by Ethnicity**

| Characteristics | African American $\underline{n} = 1,272$ (%) | White[a] $\underline{n} = 4,133$ (%) | Hispanic $\underline{n} = 211$ (%) |
|---|---|---|---|
| **In-home service use** | | | |
| Home health care | 28.0 | 30.3 | 25.2 |
| Meals on Wheels**** | 11.8 | 17.5 | 17.1 |
| **Community-based service use** | | | |
| Congregate meals | 3.4 | 4.5 | 5.3 |
| Health program | 0.8 | 2.1 | 1.6 |
| Social center/church*** | 15.8 | 12.0 | 10.1 |
| Counseling* | 3.6 | 5.1 | 8.6 |
| **Nursing home use** | | | |
| Nursing home use in preceding 6 months* | 4.0 | 10.1 | 3.8 |
| Nursing home use in preceding 2 months* | 42.4 | 61.6 | 40.0 |
| Nursing home application**** | 2.6 | 5.2 | 3.4 |
| **Informal support** | | | |
| Informal helper (mean)**** | 2.2 | 1.9 | 2.0 |

*Data Source*: National Long-Term Care Channeling Demonstration, 1982–1984.
*Note*: Chi-square and *t* statistics were used.
*$p < 0.05$; ***$p < 0.001$; ****$p < 0.0001$.

groups, whereas fewer Puerto Ricans had private insurance. Cuban Americans had the least facility with English-language skills.

Table 2.6 shows that Cuban American elders are in better physical and functional health than their Mexican American and Puerto Rican counterparts. A larger percentage of Cuban Americans reported being in either excellent or good health, and they were the least impaired in ADL and IADL.

Table 2.7 presents sources of social support, including the two types of formal service use (in home and community based) and informal network variables for the three subgroups. Puerto Rican elders reported much higher use of homemaker services (16%) and regular visiting nurses (17.9%) than the other two groups and they had also used more transportation and senior center services during the preceding year. Mexican Americans, on the other hand, reported greater use of mobile meals and church programs, and they also reported having more living children and more frequent contact with children each week.

**Table 2.4**
**Psychosocial Characteristics of Frail Elders by Ethnicity**

| Characteristics | African American $\underline{n}$ = 1,272 (%) | White[a] $\underline{n}$ = 4,133 (%) | Hispanic $\underline{n}$ = 211 (%) |
|---|---|---|---|
| **Life satisfaction****** | | | |
| Completely satisfying | 23.9 | 16.2 | 18.5 |
| Somewhat satisfying | 44.3 | 35.8 | 43.7 |
| Not very satisfying | 31.7 | 48.1 | 37.8 |
| **Sense of choice/control**** | | | |
| A great deal of choice | 28.2 | 32.5 | 21.9 |
| Some choice | 26.3 | 22.2 | 34.2 |
| Not very much choice | 45.5 | 45.3 | 43.9 |
| **Confident of ability to deal with problems****** | | | |
| Very confident | 44.0 | 32.5 | 28.1 |
| Somewhat confident | 34.3 | 37.4 | 32.5 |
| Not very confident | 21.7 | 30.1 | 39.4 |
| **Worried about not knowing whom to turn to for help****** | | | |
| Not very much | 57.1 | 44.5 | 26.3 |
| Some | 17.8 | 21.8 | 35.1 |
| A lot | 25.1 | 33.9 | 38.6 |
| **Confident of ability to get services when needed****** | | | |
| Very confident | 40.7 | 33.9 | 17.4 |
| Somewhat confident | 33.0 | 35.8 | 44.0 |
| Not very confident | 26.3 | 30.0 | 38.5 |
| **Contact during preceding week with friends/family who live apart** | | | |
| Once a day or more | 54.7 | 55.2 | 58.1 |
| 2-6 times | 29.8 | 28.3 | 29.9 |
| Once | 6.4 | 7.3 | 6.8 |
| Not at all | 9.1 | 9.2 | 5.1 |

*Data Source*: National Long-Term Care Channeling Demonstration, 1982–1984.
**$p < 0.01$; ****$p < 0.0001$.

**Table 2.5**
**Sociodemographic Characteristics of Three Groups of Hispanic Elders**

| Characteristics | Mexican American<br>n = 773[a]<br>(%) | Cuban American<br>n = 714[a]<br>(%) | Puerto Rican<br>n = 368[a]<br>(%) |
|---|---|---|---|
| **Age****** | | | |
| 65 to 69 | 37.7 | 32.3 | 39.9 |
| 70 to 74 | 23.0 | 23.9 | 24.2 |
| 75 to 79 | 18.6 | 22.7 | 19.6 |
| 80 to 84 | 13.7 | 12.8 | 9.5 |
| >=85 | 7.0 | 8.3 | 6.8 |
| **Gender** | | | |
| Female | 62.5 | 62.5 | 66.6 |
| **Marital status****** | | | |
| Married | 51.1 | 53.1 | 34.2 |
| Not married | 48.9 | 46.9 | 65.8 |
| **Education****** | | | |
| Grade school or less | 81.6 | 59.2 | 84.0 |
| High school | 15.3 | 23.0 | 12.2 |
| College or more | 3.1 | 17.8 | 3.8 |
| **Living arrangement****** | | | |
| Alone | 22.1 | 21.0 | 36.7 |
| With others | 77.9 | 79.0 | 63.3 |
| **Financial source and**<br>**medical insurance** | | | |
| SSI | 12.2 | 13.2 | 16.5 |
| Private Insurance****** | 27.9 | 31.8 | 16.3 |
| **English language skills** | | | |
| Able to speak****** | 46.3 | 36.7 | 51.4 |
| Able to read****** | 56.3 | 43.4 | 51.9 |
| Able to write****** | 44.9 | 34.5 | 41.0 |

*Data Source*: 1988 National Survey of Hispanic Elderly People.
*Note*: Chi-square statistics were used.
[a]Unweighted *Ns*.
****$p < 0.0001$.

**Table 2.6**
**Physical and Psychological Status of Three Groups of Hispanic Elders**

| Characteristics | Mexican American $n = 773^a$ (%) | Cuban American $n = 714^a$ (%) | Puerto Rican $n = 368^a$ (%) |
|---|---|---|---|
| **Perceived health status (%)****** | | | |
| Excellent | 12.4 | 16.6 | 10.4 |
| Good | 30.3 | 37.4 | 24.3 |
| Fair | 44.8 | 37.1 | 51.1 |
| Poor | 12.5 | 8.9 | 14.2 |
| **Mean (SD)** | $2.57(0.86)^a$ | $2.38(0.86)^b$ | $2.69(0.84)^c$ |
| **Physical functioning Mean (SD)** | | | |
| ADL impairment | $1.14(1.10)^a$ | $0.82(1.00)^b$ | $1.39(1.45)^c$ |
| IADL impairment | $1.36(1.21)^a$ | $0.98(1.11)^b$ | $1.41(1.71)^a$ |
| **Psychological distress variable (%)** | | | |
| Restless**** | 23.7 | 22.3 | 36.9 |
| Remote*** | 25.2 | 22.6 | 33.2 |
| Bored**** | 26.8 | 23.9 | 37.5 |
| Depressed* | 29.1 | 27.7 | 35.9 |
| Upset* | 11.8 | 8.1 | 11.7 |
| Lonely | 23.8 | 21.6 | 26.9 |
| Anxious* | 42.2 | 37.5 | 45.7 |
| **Mean (SD)** | $1.83(1.91)^a$ | $1.64(1.81)^a$ | $2.28(2.15)^b$ |

*Data Source*: 1988 National Survey of Hispanic Elderly People.
*Note*: Chi-square statistics were used to test the proportion differences. ANOVA statistics with post hoc multiple group comparisons were used to test the differences among means.
[a, b, c]Means with the different letters are significantly different at less than the 0.05 level in the same variable.
$*p < 0.05; ***p < 0.001; ****p < 0.0001$.

## REFERENCES

Commonwealth Fund Commission on Elderly People Living Alone. (1989). *Poverty and poor health among elderly Hispanic Americans*. New York: The Commonwealth Foundation.

Davis, K. (1990). *National survey of Hispanic elderly people, 1988*. Ann Arbor, MI: Interuniversity Consortium for Political and Social Research.

**Table 2.7**
**Formal and Informal Support of Three Groups of Hispanic Elders**

| Characteristics | Mexican American $n = 773$ | Cuban American $n = 714$ | Puerto Rican $n = 368$ |
|---|---|---|---|
| **Use of in-home services (%)[a]** | | | |
| Homemaker service**** | 6.7 | 4.8 | 16.0 |
| Visiting nurse**** | 8.9 | 9.5 | 17.9 |
| Home health aide | 4.1 | 5.7 | 6.8 |
| Meals on Wheels**** | 8.5 | 3.4 | 3.5 |
| **Community-based service use (%)[a]** | | | |
| Transportation**** | 8.9 | 18.1 | 22.6 |
| Senior center**** | 12.0 | 9.4 | 19.8 |
| Congregate meals** | 14.9 | 10.2 | 15.8 |
| Telephone checks | 4.7 | 3.5 | 4.1 |
| Church programs**** | 8.4 | 2.7 | 5.4 |
| **Informal support network[b]** | | | |
| No. of children (mean)* | 4.6 | 2.0 | 3.8 |
| Frequency of children contact per week (mean)* | 2.5 | 1.6 | 1.3 |

*Data Source*: 1988 National Survey of Hispanic Elderly People.
[a]Chi-square statistics were used.
[b]ANOVA statistics were used to test the differences between means.
*$p < 0.05$; **$p < 0.01$; ****$p < 0.0001$.

Phillips, B. R., Stephens, S. A., Cerf, J. J., Ensor, W. T., McDonald, A. E., Moline, C. G.,
    Stone, R. T., & Wooldridge, J. (1986). *The evaluation of the national long term care
    demonstration survey data collection design and procedures*. Report prepared for
    the Department of Health and Human Services. Princeton, NJ: Mathematica
    Policy Research, Inc.
Stephens, S. A., & Christianson, J. B. (1986). *Informal care of the elderly*. Lexington, MA:
    Lexington Books.

# Psychological Symptomatology among African American, Hispanic, and White Frail Elders

Based on the National Long-Term Care Channeling Demonstration data, this chapter examines the quality-of-life issues among African American, Hispanic, and White frail elders. Racial/ethnic minority elderly persons have not benefited from the use of mental health services in the same proportion as the overall older population (Butler, Lewis, & Sunderland, 1991). Many racial/ethnic elders, particularly those who immigrated from other countries, harbor norms and beliefs that may have influenced their adjustment to old age as well as their ability to cope with frailty and chronic life stresses in ways that contrast with those of the majority of White elders. It is important to note that in 1980 approximately 10% (2.5 million) of the elderly population were members of a racial/ethnic minority group. By 2025, 15% of the elderly population are expected to be nonwhite, and by 2050, the projection climbs to 20% (American Association of Retired Persons, 1985). Despite the rapid growth in older racial/ethnic minorities, little is known about their prevailing health and mental health status and how these differ from the majority culture's profile (Jackson, 1989).

There is substantial research literature concerning the sources of depression and psychological distress among the older population, as well as the roles chronic health problems, life stresses, and social supports play in both majority and minority elderly (e.g., Arling, 1987; Blazer, 1980; Krause, 1986; Norris & Murrell, 1984). Many researchers have compared the psychological well-being and distress of older African Americans and older Whites (e.g., Husaini, Castor, Linn, Moore, Warren, & Whitten-Stovall, 1990; Smallegan, 1989; Ulbrich & Warheit, 1989), but few studies have explored the depression and other mental health issues racial/ethnic minority elders experience by examining the differences between as well as the similarities among these groups.

There is, however, a growing sensitivity to cultural differentiation among ethnic and racial groups of older adults on issues such as health and mental health status and informal supports, as well as the rate of utilization of organized, formal services. Research evidence tends to indicate that racial/ethnic minorities experience more psychological distress than majority Americans (Kemp, Staples, & Lopez-Aqueres, 1987; Kessler & Neighbors, 1986; Linn, Hunter, & Perry, 1979). Racial/ethnic minority status is particularly associated with low income, minimal education, substandard housing, and lack of opportunity (Markides & Mindel, 1987). It is not surprising that racial/ethnic minority elders living under these conditions not only experience more strain and stress but often have fewer social and psychological coping resources at hand (Kulys, 1990).

This chapter aims to further explore the correlates of self-reported depressive symptoms among non-Hispanic African American and Hispanic elders from a sociocultural perspective. It also includes non-Hispanic Whites as a reference group.

## PREVIOUS RESEARCH ON DEPRESSION

Social support and coping resources have been hypothesized to exert direct and indirect influences on the psychological health of the elderly, but research findings have proven inconclusive. Some inquiries found no relationship between coping resources and depression (Warheit, Vega, Shimizu, & Meinhardt, 1982). Others found instead that social support systems can mediate and reduce the impact of stress among the elderly (Arling, 1987; Husaini, Moore, Castor, Whitten-Stovall, Linn, & Griggin, 1991; Krause, 1986; Norris & Murrell, 1984). A third set of studies indicates that family supports can be a source of psychological distress rather than the hypothesized relief (see Rook, 1984).

Whether the traditional stress-coping paradigm for explaining depression is applicable to the racial/ethnic older population has yet to be seen. Limited studies on minority elders similarly have yielded conflicting results regarding the availability of coping resources and their role in predicting depressive symptoms. Some research on older Hispanics found that health problems and family-support variables were associated with depression (Kemp et al., 1987; Mahard, 1988). On the other hand, Markides and Krause (1985) concluded that high levels of family interaction were associated with greater depression among older Mexican Americans. Studies on older African Americans indicate that family help has a positive buffering effect on psychological distress (Husaini et al., 1991; Ulbrich & Warheit, 1989).

Hispanic elders, according to Cantor's study (1979), enjoy consistently higher levels of interaction with their offspring than either African American or White elders. Compared to White elders, both African American and Hispanic elders are disproportionately poor and underserved by mental health services (Butler et al., 1991; Mui & Burnette, 1994). Some differences in family support and service utilization among racial minority groups can be attributed to culture, socioeconomic status, and immigration patterns (Linn et al., 1979; Markides & Mindel, 1987). Moreover, family supports and formal-service use may vary greatly depending on the degree of acculturation (Vaux, 1985). This may be especially true among Hispanic elders, more than 50% of whom, according to the 1980 Census, are natives of other countries (Biafora & Longino, 1990). Given that the life experience and immigration history of the two racial/ethnic groups in reference are different, the meaning and centrality attached to both informal supports and formal services use may also vary (Vaux, 1985).

From a clinical standpoint, depression is a disease category with predictable symptoms and treatment response (Grau & Padgett, 1988). From a sociocultural perspective, depression can be defined as both a disease and a set of feelings and behaviors expressed within a particular culture (Grau & Padgett, 1988; Smith, 1985). The expression of depressive symptoms, definition of the illness, and the response to the illness may be shaped by cultural values and norms governing perception, interpretation, meaning, and valuation of the discomforting experience (Berkanovic & Telesky, 1985; Kleinman, Eisenberg, & Good, 1978; Mui, 1992). In addition, because of differences in migration, acculturation, length of stay in the United States, language ability, and other social circumstances, Hispanic as well as African American elders may have different ways of coping with difficulties and differing preferences for informal or formal assistance.

The following research questions are examined in this chapter: (1) Do African American, Hispanic, and White elders differ in terms of their self-reported depressive symptoms? (2) If they do, what are the predictors of depression for the three groups?

## METHODOLOGY

### Data Source and Sample

The data for this chapter were drawn from the National Long-Term Care Channeling Demonstration, 1982–1984, which was initiated in 1980 by the U.S. Department of Health and Human Services. As described in Chapter 2, this demonstration encompassed a study sample of 5,626 frail older persons at high risk of institutionalization. (See Chapter 2 for a detailed description of the data set.)

### Measurement of Variables

The dependent variable, self-reported depressive symptoms among the African American, Hispanic, and White elders, is conceptualized and hypothesized to correlate with three sets of independent variables: (1) life-strain variables (including ADL or IADL impairments, chronic medical problems, self-rated health status, perceived unmet needs, involuntary relocation, and loss of a significant other); (2) coping resources (including sense of control in life, social contacts, number of informal helpers, and number of formal care providers); and (3) sociodemographic variables (including race/ethnicity, gender, income, and living arrangements). These measures indicate the amount of psychological and social support available to the frail elders. The concept of life strain is more appropriate than the more traditional, neutral concept of life events in examining depressive symptoms because it captures the enduring and chronic nature of a frail elderly person's health and functional impairments (Arling, 1987). The life-strain concept has been used in other studies (Mui, 1993; Pearlin, Menaghan, Lieberman, & Mullan, 1981) to conceptualize the chronic health problems, economic deprivation, and ADL impairments of frail elders and is a powerful predictor of depression. Some studies have, in fact, shown that chronic medical problems, functional disability, and self-rated health status were highly correlated with depressive symptoms among the noninstitutionalized elderly population (Aneshensel, Frerichs, & Huba, 1984; Hall, 1983; Linn et al., 1979).

Self-reported depressive symptoms were operationally defined by eight dichotomously coded items (Table 3.1), and a factor analysis was conducted to create a depressive-symptom composite score. One factor structure was identified. This composite score covers a range of depressive symptomatology with five items comparable to the Multidimensional Functional Assessment Questionnaire (MFAQ) developed by the Older Americans Resources and Services (OARS) Program at Duke University (Duke University Center for the Study of Aging and Human Development, 1978) and seven items comparable to the Center for Epidemiologic Studies Depression (CES-D) scale (Radloff, 1977).

Life strain was operationally defined by means of seven items: impairments in ADL, impairments in IADL, number of medical problems, self-rated health, perceived unmet needs (ADL and IADL), loss of a significant other, and involuntary relocation. Impairment in ADL was measured by asking the elderly respondents if they had received help during the preceding week in these five areas: eating, bathing, dressing, toileting, and getting out of bed or a chair. Impairment in IADL was measured by asking the elderly respondents if they had received help during the preceding week in these nine areas: meal preparation, housekeeping, shopping, taking medicine, indoor mobility, outdoor mobility, transportation, money management, and telephone use.

Chronic medical problems were measured by self-reports of the following conditions: anemia, high blood pressure, heart disease, stroke, diabetes, arthritis, cancer, Parkinson's disease, respiratory problems, skin problems, paralysis, orthopedic problems, vision or hearing problems, or other health problems.

**Table 3.1**
**Item-Total Correlation of Depressive Symptoms**

| Symptoms | Correlation with composite scale[a] |
|---|---|
| Depressed feeling[b,c] | .69**** |
| Sleep problems[b,c] | .60**** |
| Shortness of breath[b] | .56**** |
| Constant fatigue[b,c] | .64**** |
| Crying spells[c] | .62**** |
| Poor appetite[c] | .47**** |
| Lonely feeling[b,c] | .59**** |
| Concentration problems[c] | .49**** |

*Data Source*: National Long-Term Care Channeling Demonstration, 1982–1984.
*Note*: For each item answered yes, score 1 point. Thus total scores range from 0 to 8.
[a]Alpha coefficient = 0.74 for the whole sample; alpha was 0.71 for the African American sample, 0.72 for the Hispanic sample, and 0.73 for the White sample.
[b]Comparable to items used in the OARS instrument (Duke University).
[c]Comparable to items used in the CES-D.
****$p < 0.0001$.

Elderly respondents rated their perceived health status on a four-point scale ranging from excellent (1) to poor (4). Perceived unmet needs were assessed by asking elderly persons if they needed more help in those ADL and IADL areas. Loss of a significant other was measured by asking respondents if any friends or family members they felt close to had died within the preceding year. Involuntary relocation was defined by asking respondents if they had had to move when they did not want to within the preceding year.

Coping resources were operationally defined by four items: feeling of control in life, social contacts, number of informal helpers, and number of formal care providers. Feeling of control in life was a composite score of the following five questions: (1) "In general, how satisfying do you find the way you're spending your life these days? Would you call it completely satisfying, pretty satisfying, or not very satisfying?" (2) "Day to day, how much choice do you have about what you do and when you do it? Would you say a great deal of choice, some choice, or not very much choice?" (3) "How confident are you of figuring out how to deal with your problems? Would you say you feel very confident, somewhat confident, or not very confident?" (4) "How much do you worry about not knowing who to turn to for help? Would you say you worry a lot, some, or not very much?" (5) "How confident are you of getting services when you need them? Would you say you feel very confident, somewhat confident, or not very confident?" These questions were rated on a three-point scale, with a high score indicating an unfavorable rating. To summarize the data and to avoid the problem of multicollinearity, a principal components analysis with varimax rotation was also performed on the data, yielding one component. These five items were highly correlated, with factor loadings ranging from .56 to .71, and scores were added to form the "feeling of control in life" composite (alpha coefficient = .74).

Social contacts, another dimension of social resources, were measured by asking respondents the frequency of contacts, in person or by phone, with family and friends during the preceding week. Responses were categorized as not at all, once a week, two to six times a week, and once a day or more. The category of informal caregivers included all the family and friends who provided them unpaid help. The value used for formal care providers consisted of the reported number of helpers sent by social service agencies to provide ADL and IADL assistance. Several sociodemographic variables (sex, income, and living arrangements) were subsequently included as controls.

### Methods of Analysis

The preliminary analysis indicated that some of the independent variables had differential effects on the depressive symptoms reported by the African American, Hispanic, and White elders. Therefore, separate parallel ordinary least squares (OLS) regression analyses for the three groups were conducted.

### RESULTS

A higher percentage of Hispanic elderly reported having more problems with each individual item of the depressive scale than their African American counterparts. The distribution of depressive symptom scores indicated that 96.6% of the Hispanics as compared with 93.1% of the Whites and 86.6% of the African Americans reported at least one depressive symptom (Table 3.2). The mean score of depressive symptoms for Hispanic elderly was 4.10 ($SD$ = 2.18), as compared to 3.74 ($SD$ = 2.32) for White elderly; both Hispanic and White elders reported significantly more depressive symptoms than the African American elders' 3.03 ($SD$ = 2.19) score (Table 3.3).

**Table 3.2**
**Distribution of Self-Reported Depressive Symptoms**

|  | African American $\underline{n} = 1,272$ (%) | White $\underline{n} = 4,133$ (%) | Hispanic $\underline{n} = 211$ (%) |
|---|---|---|---|
| **Percentage reporting each depressive symptom** |  |  |  |
| Depressed feeling**** | 43.9 | 57.6 | 61.0 |
| Sleep problems**** | 42.9 | 52.4 | 50.4 |
| Shortness of breath**** | 30.2 | 38.7 | 44.5 |
| Constant fatigue**** | 51.0 | 62.0 | 61.2 |
| Crying spells**** | 28.7 | 39.2 | 40.7 |
| Poor appetite**** | 22.1 | 33.1 | 41.2 |
| Lonely feeling**** | 53.4 | 64.1 | 71.3 |
| Concentration problems* | 35.3 | 34.0 | 45.7 |
| **Distribution of the composite depressive symptoms**** |  |  |  |
| 0 | 13.4 | 6.9 | 3.4 |
| 1 | 16.9 | 11.4 | 10.9 |
| 2 | 15.8 | 13.8 | 12.6 |
| 3 | 14.4 | 14.1 | 15.1 |
| 4 | 12.9 | 15.4 | 14.3 |
| 5 | 9.6 | 15.0 | 11.8 |
| 6 | 9.1 | 11.6 | 16.8 |
| 7 | 6.1 | 8.3 | 9.2 |
| 8 | 1.8 | 3.6 | 5.9 |

*Data Source*: National Long-Term Care Channeling Demonstration, 1982–1984.
*$p < 0.05$; ****$p < 0.0001$.

Table 3.3 also shows the means and standard deviations of the predictor variables, and, as noted, there were more differences than similarities among the three racial/ethnic groups. They were similar on IADL impairments, self-rated health, involuntary relocation, and frequency of social contact, but compared to the African Americans and Whites, the Hispanics reported more ADL impairments and medical problems and fewer informal helpers. They also reported fewer unmet needs and a lower sense of control over their lives.

## Factors Associated with Depressive Symptoms

Table 3.4 shows that the model for the African Americans explained 35% of the variance in the depressive symptoms score. For White elders, the

Table 3.3
**Means and Standard Deviations of Composite Depressive Symptom Scale, Life-Strain Factors, and Coping Resources by Racial and Ethnic Groups**

|  | African American $\underline{n} = 1,272$ | White $\underline{n} = 4,133$ | Hispanic $\underline{n} = 211$ |
|---|---|---|---|
| **Depressive Symptoms** | 3.03[a] | 3.74[b] | 4.10[c] |
| **Life strain factors** |  |  |  |
| ADL impairment | 1.84[a] | 1.63[b] | 2.18[c] |
| IADL impairment | 3.26[a] | 3.21[a] | 3.05[a] |
| No. of medical conditions | 4.90[a] | 4.75[b] | 5.51[c] |
| Perceived health | 3.31[a] | 3.32[a] | 3.38[a] |
| Loss of significant other | 0.43[a] | 0.36[b] | 0.33[c] |
| Unmet ADL & IADL needs | 4.63[a] | 3.87[b] | 3.41[c] |
| Involuntary relocation | 0.09[a] | 0.06[a] | 0.08[a] |
| **Coping resources** |  |  |  |
| Feeling of loss of control in life | 9.00[a] | 9.64[b] | 10.32[c] |
| Social contact | 1.70[a] | 1.71[a] | 1.59[a] |
| No. of informal helpers | 2.18[a] | 1.90[b] | 1.97[c] |
| No. of formal helpers | 0.90[a] | 1.10[b] | 0.76[c] |

*Data Source*: National Long-Term Care Channeling Demonstration, 1982–1984.
*Notes*: All scales were scored so that higher scores indicate less favorable ratings except for the number of formal and informal helpers.
ANOVA statistics with post hoc multiple group comparisons were used to test the differences among means.
[a, b, c]Means with the different letters are significantly different at less than the .05 level in the same variable. Means with the same letters are not different statistically.

model explained 36% of the variance, and for the Hispanic group, the model explained 51% of the variance in the depressive symptoms score. Women across the three groups reported higher levels of depressive symptoms, other things being equal, than did the men. The common predictors of depressive symptoms for the three groups were being female, suffering more physical illnesses, perceiving their health as poor, feeling that more of their needs were not attended to, and experiencing less control over their lives. Unique predictors for the African American elders were a higher level of IADL impairments, involuntary relocation, and fewer formal care providers. For the Hispanic elders, the unique predictor was having fewer informal helpers, and for the White elders, the two unique predictors were living alone and having more ADL impairments.

**Table 3.4**
**Depressive Symptoms Models for African American, White, and Hispanic Elders**

| Predictors | Unstandardized regression coefficients (SE) | | |
|---|---|---|---|
|  | African American | White | Hispanic |
| **Sociodemographic factors** | | | |
| Sex | -0.32(.16)* | -0.36(.09)**** | -1.38(.35)**** |
| Income | -0.00(.00) | -0.00(.00) | -0.00(.00) |
| Living alone | 0.21(.15) | 0.29(.08)*** | -0.53(.39) |
| **Life strain factors** | | | |
| No. of ADL impairments | -0.06(.06) | -0.08(.03)** | -0.08(.13) |
| No. of IADL Impairments | 0.14(.04)**** | 0.03(.02) | -0.00(.09) |
| No. of medical conditions | 0.24(.04)**** | 0.19(.02)**** | 0.22(.07)** |
| Perceived health | 0.50(.09)**** | 0.58(.05)**** | 0.57(.23)* |
| Loss of significant other | 0.49(.14)*** | 0.26(.08)*** | -0.22(.34) |
| Unmet needs (ADL & IADL) | 0.08(.03)** | 0.06(.02)**** | 0.18(.06)** |
| Involuntary relocation | 0.71(.26)** | 0.27(.01) | 0.62(.52) |
| **Coping resources factors** | | | |
| Feelings of control in life | 0.26(.03)**** | 0.27(.02)**** | 0.27(.06)**** |
| Friend/family contact | -0.05(.07) | -0.09(.03) | -0.11(.20) |
| No. of informal helpers | 0.01(.06) | 0.04(.03) | -0.31(.15)* |
| No. of formal helpers | -0.13(.07)* | -0.03(.03) | -0.26(.18) |
| $R^2$ | 0.35 | 0.36 | 0.51 |
| Adjusted $R^2$ | 0.33 | 0.35 | 0.45 |

*Data Source*: National Long-Term Care Channeling Demonstration, 1982–1984.
*Note*: Standard error in parentheses. All scales were scored so that higher scores indicate
more unfavorable ratings except the number of formal and informal helpers.
*$p < 0.05$; **$p < 0.01$; ***$p < 0.001$; ****$p < 0.0001$.

## DISCUSSION

The foregoing report of findings examined differences in the life-strain
and resource correlates of depressive symptoms among the three groups of
frail elderly who were at risk for nursing home placement. The data showed
both commonalities of and differences in predictors for the three groups.
The differential rates and varying correlates of depressive symptoms offer
preliminary support for the hypothesis that cultural factors play a role in the
psychological well-being of individual elders.

The overall results indicate that women reported more depressive symptoms than men and that Hispanics expressed more depressive symptoms
than African Americans and Whites. One possible explanation of women's
reporting more depressive symptoms than men is that the help they receive
is qualitatively poorer. Another possibility is that the gender difference results from the men's underreporting or denying their support deficits (Mui,

1995; Vaux, 1985). Moreover, these observed differences in self-reported depressive symptoms may be attributed to both varying interpretations of their depressive condition and ways of coping with it (Mui, 1993).

There are several possible specific explanations for the Hispanic elders' higher manifestation of depressive symptomatology. Some researchers link it to such cultural factors as a more somber, fatalistic perspective on life pervading the Spanish culture (Torres-Gil, 1982). Others suspect that the research instruments need to be better adapted to the Hispanic group and their statistical norms need to be calibrated differently (Cox & Monk, 1990; Mui, 1993). Previous research has also shown that Hispanic elders experience a more negative psychosocial adjustment, as in the case of Cuban Americans who were displaced from their native country because of political and ideological circumstances (Linn et al., 1979). This is a plausible finding because almost 50% of the Hispanic sample in the channeling study under scrutiny were Floridian Cuban American elders (Phillips et al., 1986). On the other hand, the noted racial disparities in the report of depressive symptoms may not constitute a substantive difference, but rather may reflect cultural variations in the way symptoms are expressed among the three groups (Mui, 1992; 1993).

Overall, the African American elders appeared to be more affected by life-strain factors than their Hispanic counterparts (the analysis shows that African Americans contributed significantly to the explanation of the variance in depression on six of seven events, compared to three of seven factors in the case of the Hispanics). It should be noted that the strong association between physical illness, perceived health, and depressive symptoms noted among the three groups is consistent with the literature (Burnette & Mui, 1994; Husaini et al., 1991; Kemp et al., 1987; Tran, Wright, & Chatters, 1991). However, the covariation of depression with physical illness is complex (Ouslander, 1982), and depressive symptoms may well be natural responses to physical illness. Furthermore, some of the symptoms in question, such as sleep disturbance and fatigue, can also be manifestations of underlying physical illness or reactions to drug treatments for those illnesses. It is not surprising then that a wide variety of physical illnesses can be accompanied by depressive symptoms in the elderly (Ouslander, 1982; Reifler, 1991). The three groups of frail elderly discussed in this chapter were very impaired functionally, exhibiting multiple chronic health problems, facts that may explain, at least partially, the extremely high prevalence of depressive symptoms among them (86.6% of the African Americans, 93.1% of the Whites, and 96.6% of the Hispanics reported at least one depressive symptom).

The loss of a sense of control in life constituted a strong predictor of depression for all three groups. Having control over one's life may encourage active problem solving, which may in turn decrease the risk of depression (Mui, 1993; Ross & Mirowsky, 1989). It follows, on the other hand, that the sense of losing control may lead to feelings of helplessness and powerlessness and, ultimately, to depression. It is understandable that frail elders, especially racial minorities, would experience a progressive loss of control over their lives because of coping difficulties and multiple chronic medical and functional impairments.

For White frail elders, as noted, living alone was just one of the singular predictors of their depression, which may result from the fact that almost 40% of them lived alone (see Chapter 1) and were unable to easily reconcile their wish to remain independent with the realization that they could not manage without substantial assistance in their daily lives (Burnette & Mui, 1994).

The minority elders were probably the selective survivors of their respective groups who tried to cope with life's challenges with culturally and socially acceptable means and options. For the African American elders, depressive symptoms were associated with fewer formal care providers, whereas for the Hispanic group, having fewer informal helpers was the unique predictor. The association between formal care providers and the level of depressive symptoms among African American elders may thus reflect their greater willingness to receive formal services and their choice of formal care to supplement their informal support systems (Mui & Burnette, 1994). It is also likely that African Americans are more inclined to receive formal care because they have significantly more unmet needs than both White and Hispanic elders.

On the other hand, Hispanic elders may choose to rely almost exclusively on their informal support networks. This finding lends some support to Torres-Gil's (1982) idea that the expectation of filial assistance remains strong among Hispanics, but the Hispanic elders' preference for informal help may also reflect the absence of alternatives and/or the presence of barriers impeding their access to formal services. This finding may also be indicative of differences in acculturation within these two racial/ethnic minority groups concerning the acceptability of formal service providers. Furthermore, since most elderly Hispanics were born outside the United States and may not speak English well, they may find informal supports to be the most viable and expeditious way of meeting their needs. Because the majority of African American elders are, of course, native born, language is not an issue for them. They may therefore feel freer to use formal services to supplement the help they receive from relatives and friends.

Cultural explanations of these findings must, however, be considered with caution. First, Hispanic elderly do not constitute a homogeneous group, as they encompass many sources of diversity (nationality, migration experiences, acculturation process, and others). Second, because this chapter rests on a secondary data analysis, qualitative, cultural variables such as health-related attitudes, ways of coping, and attitudes toward the use of formal and informal supports that were not tapped in the original study could not be examined.

As a consequence, an in-depth and comprehensive cultural interpretation of the data does not appear feasible.

## IMPLICATIONS AND CONCLUSIONS

The sociocultural perspective applied in this chapter, which includes cultural determinants of depression, is sharply different from the disease model of depression (Grau & Padgett, 1988). This framework provides a broader perspective for explaining depressive symptoms among frail elders of different racial/ethnic backgrounds. The stress-coping paradigm is useful in accounting for the impact of chronic life strains/stresses and coping resources on the psychological well-being of the racial/ethnic minority elders. The findings point to clusters of frail minority elders who are vulnerable and at risk of psychological distress. A major issue is how to develop or validate culturally sensitive and cross-culturally valid measures of depression. Such validation of measures must be part of a future agenda of research on minorities (Mui, 1993).

Another issue is to determine whether the different ways of coping demonstrated by the African American and Hispanic elders are a reflection of underlying problems or cultural preferences. For example, the African American elders may not have been initially more receptive to formal services, but may have had to turn to them if their informal supports proved to be inadequate. By the same token, the Hispanic elders may have had problems accessing the organized formal services and, therefore, had to depend on informal help to cope, regardless of its quality or sufficiency. Further research is needed to understand the contributions of such qualitative variables as attitude toward receiving formal and informal help, quality and adequacy of informal and formal supports, cultural barriers in service use, and other coping strategies in predicting depressive symptoms. Future research should examine not only the effects of race, ethnicity, and culture, but also of class, discrimination, and accessibility of formal services, on the psychological distress of frail minority elders. Further research is needed to improve rates of detection of depression in frail elders who have multiple physical illnesses. More data should be collected with longitudinal studies to examine how depressive symptoms change over time and to determine the eventual outcomes of depression in such areas as functional performance and institutionalization of frail older persons. There is a need to respond clinically and in terms of health policy to the findings on the course of depression, including culturally acceptable interventions and outreach programs.

The findings of this chapter also point to a need for comprehensive long-term care policies and programs to support frail elderly persons and their families as they contend with the elders' chronic physical illnesses and functional impairments. Multifaceted long-term care programs are needed to provide adequate, available, accessible, affordable, and culturally sensitive programs to meet the special needs of frail elderly people and their families of all racial/ ethnic groups. The data also point to important implications for the training of professional and paraprofessional service providers so that they can dispense high-quality, culturally acceptable interventions to minority elders. Such educational programs must be designed to train bicultural or even multicultural care providers to identify, understand, and appreciate the special concerns of different racial or ethnic groups of elders and their families.

## REFERENCES

American Association of Retired Persons. (1985). *A profile of older minorities.* Washington, DC: Author.

Aneshensel, C., Frerichs, R., & Huba, G. (1984). Depression and physical illness: A multiwave, nonrecursive, casual model. *Journal of Health and Social Behavior, 25*, 350–371.

Arling, G. (1987). Strain, social support, and distress in old age. *Journal of Gerontology, 42*, 107–113.

Berkanovic, E., & Telesky, C. (1985). Mexican-American, African-American, and White-American differences in reporting illnesses, disability and physician visits for illnesses. *Social Science Medicine, 20*, 567–577.

Biafora, F. A., & Longino, C. F. (1990). Elderly Hispanic migration in the United States. *Journal of Gerontology, 45*, S212–219.

Blazer, D. (1980). Life events, mental health functioning and the use of health care services by the elderly. *American Journal of Public Health, 70*, 1174–1179.

Burnette, D., & Mui, A. C. (1994). Determinants of self-reported depressive symptoms by frail elderly persons living alone. *Journal of Gerontological Social Work, 22*, 3–19.

Butler, R. N., Lewis, M. I., & Sunderland, T. (1991). *Aging and mental health: Positive psychological and biomedical approaches.* New York: Macmillan.

Cantor, M. H. (1979). The informal support system of New York's inner city elderly: Is ethnicity a factor? In D. E. Gelfand & A. J. Kutzik (Eds.), *Ethnicity and aging: Theory, research, and policy* (pp. 153–174). New York: Springer.

Cox, C., & Monk, A. (1990). Minority caregivers of dementia victims: A comparison of Black and Hispanic families. *Journal of Applied Gerontology, 9*, 340–354.

Duke University Center for the Study of Aging and Human Development. (1978). *Multidimensional functional assessment: The OARS methodology.* Durham, NC: Author.

Grau, L., & Padgett, D. (1988). Somatic depression among the elderly: A sociocultural perspective. *International Journal of Geriatric Psychiatry, 3*, 201–207.

Hall, R. C. (1983). Psychiatric effects of thyroid hormone disturbance. *Psychomatics, 24*, 7–117.

Husaini, B. A., Castor, R. S., Linn, G., Moore, S. T., Warren, H. A., & Whitten-Stovall, R. (1990). Social support and depression among the African-American and White elderly. *Journal of Community Psychology, 18*, 12–18.

Husaini, B. A., Moore, S. T., Castor, W. N., Whitten-Stovall, R., Linn, G., & Griggin, D. (1991). Social density, stressors, and depression: gender differences among the African-American elderly. *Journal of Gerontology, 46*, 236–242.

Jackson, J. S. (1989). Methodological issues in survey research on older minority adults. In M. P. Lawton & A. R. Herzog (Eds.), *Special research methods for gerontology* (pp. 137–161). Amityville, NY: Baywood.

Kemp, B. J., Staples, F., & Lopez-Aqueres, W. (1987). Epidemiology of depression and dysphoria in an elderly Hispanic population: Prevalence and correlates. *Journal of American Geriatric Society, 35*, 920–926.

Kessler, R. C., & Neighbors, H. W. (1986). A new perspective on the relationships among race, social class, and psychological distress. *Journal of Health and Social Behavior, 27*, 107–115.

Kleinman, A., Eisenberg, L., & Good, B. (1978). Culture, illness, and care: Clinical lessons from anthropologic and cross-cultural research. *Annals of Internal Medicine, 88*, 251–258.

Krause, N. (1986). Social support, stress, and well-being among older adults. *Journal of Gerontology, 41*, 512–519.

Kulys, R. (1990). The ethnic factor in the delivery of social services. In A. Monk (Ed.), *Handbook of gerontological services* (2d ed., pp. 629–661). New York: Columbia University Press.

Linn, M. W., Hunter, K. I., & Perry, P. R. (1979). Differences by sex and ethnicity in the psychosocial adjustment of the elderly. *Journal of Health and Social Behavior, 20*, 273–281.

Mahard, R. E. (1988). The CES-D as a measure of depressive mood in elderly Puerto Rican population. *Journal of Gerontology, 43*, P24–P25.

Markides, K. S., & Krause, N. (1985). Intergenerational solidarity and psychological well-being among older Mexican Americans: A three-generations chapter. *Journal of Gerontology, 40*, 390–392.

Markides, K. S., & Mindel, C. H. (1987). *Aging and ethnicity.* Newbury Park, CA: Sage.

Mui, A. C. (1992). Caregiver strain among Black and White daughter caregivers: A role theory perspective. *The Gerontologist, 32*, 203–212.

Mui, A. C. (1993). Self-reported depressive symptoms among Black and Hispanic frail elders: A sociocultural perspective. *Journal of Applied Gerontology, 12*, 170–187.

Mui, A. C. (1995). Caring for frail elderly parents: A comparison of adult sons and daughters. *The Gerontologist, 35*, 86–93.

Mui, A. C., & Burnette, J. D. (1994). Long-term care service use by frail elders: Is ethnicity a factor? *The Gerontologist, 34*, 190–198.

Norris, F. H., & Murrell, S. A. (1984). Protective function of resources related to life events, global stress, and depression in older adults. *Journal of Health and Social Behavior, 25*, 424–437.

Ouslander, J. G. (1982). Physical illness and depression in the elderly. *American Geriatrics Society, 30*, 593–599.

Pearlin, L. I., Menaghan, E. G., Lieberman, M. A., & Mullan, J. T. (1981). The stress process. *Journal of Health and Social Behavior, 22*, 337–356.

Phillips, B. R., Stephens, S. A., Cerf, J. J., Ensor, W. T., McDonald, A. E., Moline, C. G., Stone, R. T., & Wooldridge, J. (1986). *The evaluation of the national long term care demonstration survey data collection design and procedures.* Princeton, NJ: Mathematica Policy Research, Inc.

Radloff, L. S. (1977). The CES-D Scale: A self-reported depression scale for research in the general population. *Applied Psychological Measurement, 1*, 385–401.

Reifler, B. (1991). Depression: Diagnosis and comorbidity. Paper presented at NIH Consensus Development Conference, National Institutes of Health, Washington, D.C.

Rook, K. S. (1984). The negative side of social interaction: Impact on psychological well-being. *Journal of Personality and Social Psychology, 46,* 1097–1108.

Ross, C. E., & Mirowsky, J. (1989). Explaining the social patterns of depression: Control and problem solving—support and talking? *Journal of Health and Social Behavior, 30,* 206–219.

Smallegan, M. (1989). Level of depressive symptoms and life stresses for culturally diverse older adults. *The Gerontologist, 29,* 45–50.

Smith, E. M. J. (1985). Ethnic minorities: life stress, social support, and mental health issues. *Counseling Psychologist, 13,* 537–579.

Torres-Gil, F. (1982). *Politics of aging among older Hispanic.* Washington, DC: University Press of America.

Tran, T. V., Wright, R., Jr., & Chatters, L. (1991). Health, stress, psychological resources, and subjective well-being among older African-Americans. *Psychology and Aging, 8,* 100–108.

Ulbrich, P. M., & Warheit, G. J. (1989). Social support, stress, and psychological distress among older African-American and White adults. *Journal of Aging and Health, 1,* 286–305.

Vaux, A. (1985). Variations in social support associated with gender, ethnicity, and age. *Journal of Social Issues, 41,* 89–110.

Warheit, G., Vega, W., Shimizu, D., & Meinhardt, K. (1982). Interpersonal coping network and mental health problems among four race-ethnic groups. *Journal of Community Psychology, 10,* 312–324.

# Chapter Four

# Perceived Health, Financial Strain, and Psychological Distress among Mexican American, Cuban American, and Puerto Rican Elders

This chapter utilizes data from the 1988 National Survey of Hispanic Elderly People to examine the correlates of physical, financial, and psychological well-being among older Mexican Americans, Cuban Americans, and Puerto Ricans. Its first objective is to determine the roles that health-related and family stresses and coping resources play in predicting well-being. The second objective is to determine whether these relationships differ among Hispanic nationality groups. This chapter therefore consists of an inquiry similar to that of the preceding one, but focuses in more detail on a separate and more recent data set of Hispanic elderly.

Chapter 3 treated all Hispanic elders as a single, undifferentiated entity. Its limited sample size simply did not allow probing for the subgroups subsumed under the Hispanic designation. This chapter acknowledges that Hispanic elders in the United States are not a homogeneous group and that they differ by country or region of origin, cultural background, degree of acculturation, socioeconomic class, educational level, immigration history, and political ideology.

## PREVIOUS STUDIES

Most researchers have until recently ignored the diverse cultural, historical, demographic, and ecological conditions of Hispanic subnational groups in the United States (Aguirre & Bigelow, 1983), merging Mexican Americans, Cuban Americans, and Puerto Ricans into one "Hispanic" category, but recent large national studies of Hispanic elders that used inferential statistical models to examine differences among and within Hispanic subgroups revealed substantial group variations. These variations were also associated with differential patterns of family dynamics, service needs, and expressed preferences for formal service use (Starrett, Todd, & De Leon, 1989; Starrett, Wright, Mindel, & Tran, 1989).

A substantial body of research centered around the role of informal support systems, particularly family members, and their impact on the mental and physical well-being of racial/ethnic minority elders (Cantor, 1979; Lubben & Becerra, 1987). Findings are mixed, however. Several studies found that social support systems can mediate the impact of stress among the elderly (Arling, 1987; Husaini, Moore, Castor, Whitten-Stovall, Linn, & Griggin, 1991; Norris & Murrell, 1984). Other evidence indicated that, in itself, family support can turn into a source of psychological distress among the elderly (e.g., Rook, 1984). For example, some research on Hispanic elders indicated that health problems and increased family support were associated with depression (Kemp, Staples, & Lopez-Aqueres, 1987; Mahard, 1988). Markides and Krause (1985) found that high levels of family interaction were associated with greater depression among older Mexican Americans.

By and large, studies on Hispanic family support have shown consistently that Hispanic elders have stronger bonds with family members and higher levels of interaction and support from children than either African American or White elders, after gender and social class are controlled for (Cantor, 1979; Lubben & Becerra, 1987). Furthermore, there is a strong sense of family obligation that often supersedes the personal needs of individual family members. Hispanic elders also expect their family to assist them in their old age and to treat them with respect (Markides & Krause, 1985).

Yet some evidence has suggested that family support varies among Hispanic subgroups. Older Cuban Americans have generally sought the help only of their children and not that of other family members (Escovar & Kurtines, 1983). Among Mexican Americans, there has been a high level of exchange and reciprocity between generations of children and grandchildren (Markides & Krause, 1986). Puerto Rican elders, unlike their Mexican American, Cuban American, and other Hispanic counterparts, have relied on themselves and their friends for assistance more than on family members (Lacayo, 1980). Association between Hispanic elders and their family members may not always be beneficial for the elders. Research has indicated that increased association of older Mexican Americans with their children was related to an increase in the elders' depression (Markides & Krause, 1985; 1986). These findings suggest that family contact is not uniformly positive and could, in some circumstances, turn into a source of stress.

This chapter addresses the impact of health-related and family stresses on the physical, financial, and psychological well-being of Hispanic elders, utilizing a stress-and-coping framework (Aldwin, 1994; Lazarus & Folkman, 1984) that acknowledges the effects that personal and environmental adverse circumstances such as family conflicts have on elders' overall well-being

(Aldwin, 1994; Mui, 1993). Coping resources for overcoming stress at the individual level usually include physical, psychological, spiritual, and social skills as well as social supports (Burnette & Mui, 1995; Lazarus & Folkman, 1984; Mui, 1993). Theoretically, there are at least two possible ways in which coping can affect well-being outcomes. First, there may be direct effects on measures of well-being. Second, the coping strategies may moderate or buffer the effect of stress on well-being outcomes (Aldwin, 1994). In this chapter, both additive and interactive effects of stress and coping resources were tested. In addition, three hypotheses were tested concerning the group differences among Hispanic nationality groups:

$H_1$: Stress factors and coping resources have significant direct effects on the physical, financial, and psychological well-being of Hispanic elders.

$H_2$: Coping resources moderate the effects of stress factors on the well-being of Hispanic elders.

$H_3$: The nationalities of Hispanic elders have significant independent effects on these well-being measures when sociodemographics, stresses, and coping resources are controlled for.

## METHODOLOGY

### Data Sources and Sample

As stated earlier, this chapter is based on data from the 1988 National Survey of Hispanic Elderly People. Part of the Commonwealth Fund Commission's project on elderly people living alone (Commonwealth Fund Commission on Elderly People Living Alone, 1989), the study used a telephone survey to obtain a profile of the health, economic, and social circumstances of Hispanic people aged 65 and over. Between August and October 1988, trained bilingual interviewers gathered information on living arrangements, length of time lived in the United States, economic resources, health and functional status, social network, family support, and psychological well-being (Davis, 1990).

The survey provided a nationally representative sample of Hispanics aged 65 and over, living within telephone exchanges that had Hispanic concentrations of at least 30% in three geographic areas in the United States. Using random-digit dialing, 48,183 households were screened for Hispanics aged 65 and over, resulting in completed interviews of 2,299 older Hispanics. The overall response rate was 80%, and 87% of interviewees chose to be interviewed in Spanish. The analyses presented in this paper are based on a subsample of Mexican Americans ($n = 773$), Cuban Americans ($n = 714$), and Puerto Ricans ($n = 368$). Other Hispanic groups were not included because their numbers were limited.

### Measurement of Variables

*Outcome Variables.*    Perceived health status was rated by Hispanic elders on a four-point scale ranging from excellent (1) to poor (4) health. Self-rated health has been documented to be a valid measure of a respondent's physical health status because it has been highly correlated with physicians' ratings in many samples of elderly persons (Mui, 1992; 1993). Financial strain was a composite score of two items regarding financial difficulties: (1) not having enough money to live on and (2) having too many medical bills. These two items were factor analyzed with factor loadings of .83 and .89.

Psychological distress was assessed by self-reported experiences in the preceding few weeks of feeling restless, remote from other people, bored, depressed, upset, worried, and/or lonely (each coded dichotomously). A principal-components analysis with varimax rotation was performed, and the five items were summed to create a composite score of psychological distress (Cronbach alpha = .76). The first five items are comparable to the negative affect items in the Affective-Balance Scale (Bradburn, 1969).

*Independent Variables.*    Based on the stress and coping framework, the independent variables were conceptualized and categorized into sociodemographics, health-related stresses, personal and family stresses, and coping resources. Their coding schemes are presented in Table 4.1.

With regard to sociodemographic variables, education was used as a proxy measure of social class standing (Krause & Goldenhar, 1992). Receipt of public assistance was treated as a proxy measure of income because the income variable was not usable due to excessive missing data. Two dummy variables, Mexican American and Puerto Rican, were created in order to examine subgroup differences, with persons of Cuban ancestry serving as the reference group (Burnette & Mui, 1995; Krause & Goldenhar, 1992).

### Methods of Analysis

Descriptive statistics were used to generate a sociodemographic profile of the three groups of Hispanic elders. Hierarchical regression analyses were conducted to test the three hypotheses using separate models for each of the three well-being measures. For the first two hypotheses, a simple additive model and a model with additive and interactive effects were used to test the direct and moderating effects of stress and coping factors on well-being of Hispanic elders. For the third hypothesis, another hierarchical regression was conducted, with sociodemographic factors entered first, followed by stress factors, then coping resources, and finally national-origin group variables (Bass, Looman, & Ehrlich, 1992; Burnette & Mui, 1995). The national-origin variable was entered into the regression model last to determine if there were differences among nationality groups in the outcome measures, when the other variables were controlled for. Zero-order correlations of the 23 variables in the model ranged from .07 to .38, indicating that collinearity was not a problem.

## RESULTS

Table 4.2 shows that Cuban American elders are in better physical health and have less financial strain than their Mexican American and Puerto Rican counterparts. In addition, Cuban American and Mexican American elders had less psychological distress than Puerto Rican elders.

Table 4.3 presents the means and standard deviations of all stress and coping resource variables. Among the stress factors, Cuban American elders were the least impaired on ADL and IADL. They also reported fewer unmet service needs, caregiving responsibilities, and family conflicts. In terms of coping resources, including the two types of formal service use (in home and community based) and informal network variables for the three subgroups, Puerto Rican elders reported a much higher use of in-home and community-based services than the other two groups. Mexican American elders reported having more living children and more frequent contact with their offspring each week.

The results of the statistical analyses indicated that the interaction models were not significant; that is, the interactions between stress and coping factors did not yield a significant increase in the explained variance of the well-being measures. Tables 4.4, 4.5, and 4.6 present the results of the additive models of perceived health, financial strain, and psychological distress of Hispanic elders.

### Factors Associated with Perceived Health Status

The additive model was significant ($p < 0.0001$), explaining 32% of the variance in perceived health. Among the four categories of independent variables, health-related and family stresses had the greatest effect on the perceived health status of Hispanic elders, as indicated by the amount of unique explained variance (24%). Other significant predictors of perceived health included being younger and having lower income (as indicated by being on public assistance). After controlling for other differences in the model, being Puerto Rican or Mexican American had an independent effect on self-rated health. In other words, older Cuban Americans reported better health status than either older Puerto Ricans or Mexican Americans.

### Factors Associated with Financial Strain

Eleven predictor variables were significantly associated with the sense of financial strain among Hispanic elders: younger age; lower income; more

**Table 4.1**
**Variables and Measures**

| Variables | Code |
|---|---|
| **Outcomes** | |
| Psychological distress (Cronbach alpha=.76)[a] | Actual number of symptoms (including feeling restless, remote, bored, depressed, upset, lonely, and anxious) |
| Financial strain (sum score of two items) | 1=Not having enough money to live on; 1=having too many medical bills |
| Perceived health | 1=Excellent to 4=poor |
| **Predictors** | |
| **Sociodemographics** | |
| Age | Actual age |
| Gender | 0=Female; 1=male |
| Education | Level of education |
| Living arrangements | 1=Alone; 0=Living with others |
| Length of stay in the United States | Actual years |
| Receipt of public assistance (proxy of income) | 1=Food Stamps; 1=SSI; 1=Medicaid |
| **Health-related stresses** | |
| ADL impairments (Cronbach alpha=.86)[a] | No. of impairments (including bathing, dressing, eating, getting into and out of bed, walking, getting outside, using toilet) |
| IADL impairments (Cronbach alpha=.82)[a] | No. of impairments (including preparing meals, managing money, using telephone, grocery shopping, doing heavy or light work) |
| Doctor visits (proxy of medical needs) | No. of visits during the preceding 12 months |
| Hospital use (proxy of severity of illness) | In the hospital during preceding 12 months; 1=yes; 0=no |
| Unmet service needs (Cronbach alpha=.86)[a] | Total number of in-home and community-based services needed |

48

**Personal and Family Stresses**

Fear of dependence — 1=Having to depend too much on other people
Caregiving duty — 1=Having to take care of sick spouse or relative
Family problems and conflicts — 1=Have too many problems or conflicts in the family

**Coping Resources**

English-language ability (Cronbach alpha=.82)[a] — 1=Able to speak English; 1=able to read English; 1=able to write English
No. of children (proxy of network size) — Actual number
Children contact — Frequency each week
Social contacts — 1=Friends/neighbors contact or 1=church contact
In-home service use — No. of services used (including Meals on Wheels, homemaker, home health aide, visiting nurse)
Community-based service use — No. of services (including senior center, congregate meals, transportation, church, telephone assurance program)

**National origin**

Puerto Rican; Mexican American; Cuban American — Binary variable, with Cuban American as a reference group

*Data Source:* 1988 National Survey of Hispanic Elderly People.
[a]Measures were validated with factor analyses, and Cronbach alphas were calculated using the source data.

Table 4.2
**Physical, Financial, and Psychological Strain of Three Groups of Hispanic Elders**

|  | Mexican American $\underline{n}$ = 773 | Cuban American $\underline{n}$ = 714 | Puerto Rican $\underline{n}$ = 368 |
|---|---|---|---|
| **Perceived health status\*\*\*\*** |  |  |  |
| Excellent | 12.4% | 16.6% | 10.4% |
| Good | 30.3 | 37.4 | 24.3 |
| Fair | 44.8 | 37.1 | 51.1 |
| Poor | 12.5 | 8.9 | 14.2 |
| **Mean (SD)** | 2.57 (0.86)[a] | 2.38 (0.86)[b] | 2.69 (0.84)[c] |
| **Financial strain** |  |  |  |
| Not enough money\*\*\* | 42.6% | 33.8% | 41.9% |
| Having too many medical bills\*\*\* | 37.4 | 18.2 | 24.2 |
| **Mean (SD)** | 0.80 (0.80)[a] | 0.52 (0.70)[b] | 0.66 (0.75)[c] |
| **Psychological distress variables** |  |  |  |
| Restless\*\*\*\* | 23.7% | 22.3% | 36.9% |
| Remote\*\*\* | 25.2 | 22.6 | 33.2 |
| Bored\*\*\*\* | 26.8 | 23.9 | 37.5 |
| Depressed\* | 29.1 | 27.7 | 35.9 |
| Upset\* | 11.8 | 8.1 | 11.7 |
| Lonely | 23.8 | 21.6 | 26.9 |
| Anxious\* | 42.2 | 37.5 | 45.7 |
| **Mean (SD)** | 1.83 (1.91)[a] | 1.64 (1.81)[a] | 2.28 (2.15)[b] |

*Data Source*: 1988 National Survey of Hispanic Elderly People.
*Note*: Chi-square statistics were used to test the proportion differences. ANOVA statistics with post hoc multiple comparisons were used to test the differences among means.
[a,b,c]Means with the different letters are significantly different at a level less than the 0.05 level in the same variable.
\*$p < 0.05$; \*\*\*$p < 0.001$; \*\*\*\*$p < 0.0001$.

doctor visits; more hospital use; higher levels of unmet service need; fear of depending too much on others; more psychological distress; having caregiving responsibility; having family conflicts; a higher level of community-based service use; and being a Mexican American elder. Among the stressors, fear of depending too much on other people had the strongest impact (beta = 0.31; $p < 0.0001$) on financial strain, followed by family conflicts (beta = 0.18; $p < 0.0001$). Mexican American elders had higher levels of financial strain than Cuban American counterparts, other things being equal. Stress factors, as a set, also had the strongest influence on Hispanic elders' financial strain (unique $R^2$ = 0.32).

Table 4.3
**Means and Standard Deviations of Stress and Coping Resource Variables**

|  | Mexican American<br>n = 773 | Cuban American<br>n = 714 | Puerto Rican<br>n = 368 |
|---|---|---|---|
| **Health-related and family stresses** | | | |
| ADL impairments | 1.14(1.10)[a] | 0.82(1.00)[b] | 1.39(1.45)[c] |
| IADL impairments | 1.36(1.21)[a] | 0.98(1.11)[b] | 1.41(1.71)[a] |
| Doctor visits | 6.39(7.53)[a] | 8.03(9.99)[b] | 11.65(16.3)[c] |
| Hospital use | 0.21(0.41)[a] | 0.23(0.42)[a] | 0.30(0.45)[b] |
| Unmet needs | 2.13(2.14)[a] | 1.35(2.10)[b] | 2.11(2.10)[a] |
| Fear of dependence | 0.32(0.46)[a] | 0.26(0.43)[b] | 0.27(0.44)[b] |
| Caregiving duty | 0.21(0.40)[a] | 0.16(0.36)[b] | 0.20(0.40)[a] |
| Family conflicts | 0.22(0.41)[a] | 0.17(0.37)[b] | 0.25(0.43)[c] |
| **Coping resources** | | | |
| English ability | 1.47(1.22)[a] | 1.15(1.31)[b] | 1.44(1.28)[a] |
| No. of children | 4.64(3.26)[a] | 2.05(1.68)[b] | 3.81(2.88)[c] |
| Children contact | 2.51(1.80)[a] | 1.58(1.58)[b] | 1.31(0.83)[b] |
| Social contact | 0.74(0.32)[a] | 0.69(0.58)[b] | 0.63(0.49)[b] |
| In-home service use | 0.28(0.18)[a] | 0.23(0.19)[a] | 0.44(0.30)[b] |
| Community-based use | 0.49(0.36)[a] | 0.43(0.37)[a] | 0.68(0.31)[b] |
| Public assistance | 0.62(0.82)[a] | 0.99(0.89)[b] | 1.06(1.00)[c] |

*Data Source*: 1988 National Survey of Hispanic Elderly People.
*Note*: ANOVA statistics with post hoc multiple comparisons were used to test the differences among means.
[a,b,c]Means with the different letters are significantly different at a level less than the 0.05 level in the same variable.

## Factors Associated with Psychological Distress

This model also explained a significant amount of the variation in psychological distress ($R^2 = 0.39$, $p < 0.0001$). Predictors of psychological distress included being female; having more ADL impairments; having perceived poor health; having more unmet service needs; having high levels of financial strain; being afraid of depending too much on others; having family conflicts; and having caregiving responsibility. None of the coping resources, in terms of formal and informal support, made any difference in predicting psychological distress. Neither the acculturation variable (English-language ability variable) nor the nationality variable had any independent effect on the psychological distress score, suggesting that among elderly Hispanics, psychological distress is not inherently related to national origin or English-language ability. Family conflicts and problems comprise the strongest predictor of psychological distress (beta = 0.20; $p < 0.0001$).

### Table 4.4
### Correlates of Perceived Health among Hispanic Elders

| | Unstandardized regression coefficients (SE) | Standardized regression coefficients (beta) |
|---|---|---|
| **Sociodemographics** | | |
| Age | -.01(.01)** | -.09** |
| Gender | -.12(.06) | -.05 |
| Education | -.06(.05) | -.01 |
| Living alone | -.21(.15) | -.03 |
| Length of stay in the United States | .00(.00) | .00 |
| Receipt of public assistance | .07(.03)** | .08** |
| $R^2$ at this step | | .06 |
| **Health-related/personal and family stresses** | | |
| ADL impairments | .07(.02)**** | .15**** |
| IADL impairments | .10(.02)**** | .18**** |
| Doctor visits | .01(.00)** | .08** |
| Hospital use | .17(.08)** | .08** |
| Unmet service needs | .01(.01) | .03 |
| Financial strain | .02(.03) | .02 |
| Fear of dependence | .16(.06)** | .08** |
| Psychological distress | .08(.01)**** | .17**** |
| Caregiving duty | .08(.06) | .04 |
| Family conflicts | .03(.06) | .01 |
| Incremental to $R^2$ at this step | | .24 |
| **Coping resources** | | |
| English ability | .00(.02) | .00 |
| No. of children | -.01(.01) | -.01 |
| Children contact | .00(.01) | .01 |
| Social contact | -.07(.05) | -.04 |
| In-home service use | -.01(.02) | -.01 |
| Community-based service | -.01(.03) | -.01 |
| Incremental to $R^2$ at this step | | .002 |
| **Nationality** | | |
| Puerto Rican | .14(.06)** | .09** |
| Mexican American | .18(.07)** | .12** |
| Incremental to $R^2$ at this step | | .02 |
| Total $R^2$ | | .32 |

*Data Source*: 1988 National Survey of Hispanic Elderly People.
**$p < 0.01$; ****$p < 0.0001$.

## Table 4.5
## Correlates of Financial Strain among Hispanic Elders

|  | Unstandardized regression coefficients (SE) | Standardized regression coefficients (beta) |
|---|---|---|
| **Sociodemographics** | | |
| Age | -.02(.00)**** | -.13**** |
| Gender | .03(.05) | .05 |
| Education | .01(.04) | .03 |
| Living alone | -.54(.12) | -.02 |
| Length of stay in the United States | .00(.00) | .02 |
| Receipt of public assistance | -.08(.04)* | -.05* |
| $R^2$ at this step | | .03 |
| **Health-related/personal and family stresses** | | |
| ADL impairments | -.02(.02) | -.06 |
| IADL impairments | -.03(.03) | -.01 |
| Perceived health | .01(.02) | .02 |
| Doctor visits | .01(.00)* | .06* |
| Hospital use | .13(.04)** | .08** |
| Unmet service needs | .05(.01)**** | .14**** |
| Fear of dependence | .54(.06)**** | .31**** |
| Psychological distress | .04(.01)*** | .10*** |
| Caregiving duty | .29(.06)**** | .13**** |
| Family conflicts | .30(.07)**** | .18**** |
| Incremental to $R^2$ at this step | | .32 |
| **Coping resources** | | |
| English ability | -.03(.02) | -.05 |
| No. of children | -.01(.01) | -.03 |
| Children contact | -.01(.01) | -.03 |
| Social contact | -.01(.03) | -.01 |
| In-home service use | -.02(.04) | -.04 |
| Community-based service | .11(.03)*** | .08*** |
| Incremental to $R^2$ at this step | | .02 |
| **Nationality** | | |
| Puerto Rican | .08(.07) | .01 |
| Mexican American | .30(.08)**** | .13**** |
| Incremental to $R^2$ at this step | | .02 |
| Total $R^2$ | | .39 |

*Data Source*: 1988 National Survey of Hispanic Elderly People.
*$p < 0.05$; **$p < 0.01$; ***$p < 0.001$; ****$p < 0.0001$.

**Table 4.6**
**Correlates of Psychological Distress among Hispanic Elders**

| | Unstandardized regression coefficients (SE) | Standardized regression coefficients (beta) |
|---|---|---|
| **Sociodemographics** | | |
| Age | -.01(.01) | -.05 |
| Gender | -.41(.14)**** | -.09**** |
| Education | .00(.02) | .03 |
| Living alone | .35(.32) | .04 |
| Length of stay in the United States | .00(.00) | .01 |
| Receipt of public assistance | -.01(.02) | -.01 |
| $R^2$ at this step | | .04 |
| **Health-related/personal and family stresses** | | |
| ADL impairments | .09(.04)* | .08* |
| IADL impairments | .09(.07) | .03 |
| Perceived health | .35(.06)**** | .15**** |
| Doctor visits | .00(.01) | .03 |
| Hospital use | .05(.06) | .01 |
| Unmet service needs | .16(.03)**** | .18**** |
| Financial strain | .25(.07)*** | .10*** |
| Fear of dependence | .84(.12)**** | .19**** |
| Caregiving duty | .20(.12)*** | .06*** |
| Family conflicts | .84(.12)**** | .20**** |
| Incremental to $R^2$ at this step | | .35 |
| **Coping resources** | | |
| English ability | .01(.04) | .01 |
| No. of children | -.05(.03) | -.02 |
| Children contact | .02(.03) | .02 |
| Social contact | -.05(.04) | -.01 |
| In-home service use | -.01(.03) | -.01 |
| Community-based service | .14(.08) | .01 |
| Incremental to $R^2$ at this step | | .001 |
| **Nationality** | | |
| Puerto Rican | .16(.13) | .05 |
| Mexican American | .15(.15) | .04 |
| Incremental to $R^2$ at this step | | .001 |
| Total $R^2$ | | .39 |

*Data Source*: 1988 National Survey of Hispanic Elderly People.
*$p < 0.05$; ***$p < 0.001$; ****$p < 0.0001$.

## DISCUSSION

Using a national probability sample of Hispanic elders, this chapter extends current knowledge about the roles of health-related and family stresses and of coping resources in predicting physical, financial, and psychological well-being among Mexican Americans, Cuban Americans, and Puerto Ricans. The first and the third hypotheses presented earlier in this chapter were partially supported. A majority of health-related, personal, and family stresses had a significant effect on the physical, financial, and psychological well-being of Hispanic elders. (However, with only one exception, coping resources did not predict well-being.) In addition, when all other factors were controlled for, national origin had a significant effect on physical and financial (but not psychological) well-being. The second hypothesis was not supported by the data, which indicated that coping resources do not moderate the effects of stress variables on the well-being of Hispanic elders.

There are limitations to this chapter. First, the interpretation of the results is limited by the cross-sectional nature of the data. Longitudinal studies are needed to determine the direction of the relationships among variables and the nature of changes in well-being over time. Second, because secondary data were utilized, it was not possible to consider the effects of qualitative variables (such as perceived adequacy of family support or familism) that were not measured in the original study. Other possible limitations center on measurement issues. Most of the coping resource variables were not significant in explaining the dependent measures. The exception was use of community-based service, which was a predictor of financial strain. All the coping resource variables were measured only quantitatively, which may account for their lack of effect on the well-being measures. The quantitative measures did not provide information concerning the elders' subjective evaluation of the quality of these coping resources.

With regard to the factors associated with the Hispanic elders' physical, financial, and psychological well-being, health-related and family stresses had the strongest predictive power in these models. Hispanic elders' perceived health was influenced by age, lower income, health-related stresses, and psychological stresses. Impairment of IADL was the strongest predictor of poorer perceived health, followed by psychological distress and ADL impairment. The association among functional impairment, psychological distress, and poorer perceived health is consistent with findings reported in the literature (Mui, 1993).

Nationality had an independent effect on perceived health. Cuban American elders, as a group, were in better health than either Puerto Rican or Mexican American elders. This finding may be explained by the difference in their immigration histories (Mui, 1993).

Cuban American elders who immigrated to the United States in the 1960s had more education and, therefore, may have been able to adjust better and enjoy better health (Angel & Angel, 1992; Bernal, 1982). Return migration affects Hispanic groups differently. Unlike their Mexican American and Puerto Rican counterparts, Cuban American elders generally do not return to their original home because of adverse political conditions there. This may be one reason that Cuban elderly constitute a higher proportion of the Hispanic subgroup than Puerto Ricans (Aguirre & Bigelow, 1983). The stability of this migration pattern may also help to explain why Cuban American elders especially benefit from close-knit ethnic enclaves that largely preserve their original culture and native language (Angel & Angel, 1992; Boswell & Curtis, 1984; Perez, 1986). The data suggest that it is important to examine subgroup differences because of differences in the social and economic contexts of their immigration experiences.

In the financial-strain model, elders' fear of depending too much on other people was the strongest predictor, followed by family conflicts, unmet service needs, and caregiving responsibility. Concern about having to depend on others too much may indicate that Hispanic elders felt they were being burdensome to others but had no alternative because of financial constraints. It is hard to tell whether this was due to deterioration of family relationships or weakening of elder care values in the family. Hispanic elders who had caregiving responsibilities and family conflicts reported more financial strain. Because the data analyzed in this chapter are cross-sectional, it is difficult to draw conclusions regarding causality. Hispanic elders who are financially strained might have to bear caregiving duties themselves because they cannot afford to hire outside help. The resulting frequent interaction may then exert tension in family relationships. Data also indicated differences among Hispanic subgroups. Mexican American elders reported higher levels of financial strain than their Cuban American counterparts.

Hispanic elders who reported higher levels of psychological distress were more likely to be women; have poorer perceived health; express more unmet service needs; be afraid of having to depend on others too much; and have family conflicts or problems. Nationality did not make any difference in explaining psychological distress. Conflicts and problems in the family were strongly positively associated with financial strain and psychological distress, a finding that is consistent with previous studies (Markides & Krause, 1985; Rook, 1984). This finding suggests that ethnic family experience is not always positive and problem free. Because family bonding and reciprocity between generations is expected within Hispanic culture (Markides & Krause, 1985, 1986), it makes sense that the absence of family conflicts plays an important role in explaining feelings of well-being. The negative impact of having an inharmonious family relationship may be much greater for Hispanic elders than for other elders.

These findings suggest several directions for improving overall well-being of elderly Hispanics. Practitioners need to be trained to understand the health-related, personal, and family stresses that are associated with the psychological, financial, and physical well-being of these elders. For service providers, it is important to recognize that the well-being of elderly Hispanics is closely tied to their gender, age, financial resources, fear of dependence, family conflicts, and caregiving responsibilities.

The findings highlight the vulnerability of Hispanic elders who are at risk of psychological distress and financial strain as well as poor health. Such Hispanic elders should be the focus of careful intervention and further research. The findings also point to the importance of considering national origin when serving Hispanic elders. Furthermore, because many Hispanic elders underutilize Medicaid (Commonwealth Fund, 1989), clinicians should encourage both poor and near-poor Hispanic elders to enroll in the Medicaid program which would provide needed assistance and remove their fear of becoming impoverished by medical bills. These steps, when incorporated into social service interventions, will maximize the long-term well-being of Hispanic elders.

## REFERENCES

Aguirre, B. E., & Bigelow, A. (1983). The aged in Hispanic groups: A review. *International Journal of Aging and Human Development, 17*, 177–201.

Aldwin, C. M. (1994). *Stress, coping, and development.* New York: Guilford.

Angel, J., & Angel, R. J. (1992). Age at migration, social connections, and well-being among elderly Hispanics. *Journal of Aging and Health, 4*, 480–499.

Arling, G. (1987). Strain, social support, and distress in old age. *Journal of Gerontology, 42*, 107–113.

Bass, D. M., Looman, W. J., & Ehrlich, P. (1992). Predicting the volume of health and social services: Integrating cognitive impairment into the modified Andersen framework. *The Gerontologist, 32*, 33–43.

Bernal, G. (1982). Cuban families. In M. McGoldrick, J. K. Pearce, & J. Giordano (Eds.), *Ethnicity and family therapy* (pp. 187–207). New York: Guilford.

Boswell, T. D., & Curits, J. R. (1984). *The Cuban experience: Culture, images, and perspective.* Totawa, NJ: Rowman and Allanheld.

Bradburn, N. M. (1969). *The structure of psychological well-being.* Chicago: Aldine.

Burnette, D., & Mui, A. C. (1995). In-home and community-based service use by three groups of elderly Hispanics: A national perspective. *Social Work Research, 19*, 197–206.

Cantor, M. H. (1979). The informal support system of New York's inner city elderly: Is ethnicity a factor? In D. E. Gelfand & A. J. Kutzik (Eds.), *Ethnicity and aging: Theory, research, and policy* (pp.153–174). New York: Springer.

Commonwealth Fund Commission on Elderly People Living Alone. (1989). *Poverty and poor health among elderly Hispanic Americans.* New York: The Commonwealth Foundation.

Davis, K. (1990). *National survey of Hispanic elderly people, 1988*. Ann Arbor, MI: In-
    teruniversity Consortium for Political and Social Research.
Escovar, L. A., & Kurtines, W. M. (1983). Psychological predictors of service utilization
    among Cuban American elders. *Journal of Community Psychology, 11*, 355–362.
Husaini, B. A., Moore, S. T., Castor, W. N., Whitten-Stovall, R., Linn, G., & Griggin,
    D. (1991). Social density, stressors, and depression: Gender differences
    among the Black elderly. *Journal of Gerontology, 46*, P236–P242.
Kemp, B. J., Staples, F., & Lopez-Aqueres, W. (1987). Epidemiology of depression
    and dysphoria in an elderly Hispanic population: Prevalence and correlates.
    *Journal of American Geriatric Society, 35*, 920–926.
Krause, N., & Goldenhar, L. M. (1992). Acculturation and psychological distress in
    three groups of elderly Hispanics. *Journal of Gerontology, 47*, S279–S288.
Lacayo, C. G. (1980). *A national chapter to assess the service needs of the Hispanic elderly*.
    Washington, DC: Library of Congress.
Lazarus, R. S., & Folkman, S. (1984). *Stress, appraisal, and coping*. New York: Springer.
Lubben, J. E., & Becerra, R. M. (1987). Social support among Black, Mexican, and
    Chinese elderly. In D. E. Gelfand & C. M. Barresi (Eds.), *Research and ethnic
    dimension of aging* (pp. 130–144). New York: Springer.
Mahard, R. E. (1988). The CES-D as a measure of depressive mood in elderly Puerto
    Rican population. *Journal of Gerontology, 43*, P24–P25.
Markides, K. S., & Krause, N. (1985). Intergenerational solidarity and psychological
    well-being among older Mexican-American: A three generations chapter.
    *Journal of Gerontology, 40*, 390–392.
Markides, K. S., & Krause, N. (1986). Older Mexican Americans: Family relationships
    and well-being. *Generations, 10*, 31–34.
Mui, A. C. (1992). Caregiver strain among Black and White daughters caregivers:
    A role theory perspective. *The Gerontologist, 32*, 203–212.
Mui, A. C. (1993). Self-reported depressive symptoms among Black and Hispanic
    frail elders: A sociocultural perspective. *Journal of Applied Gerontology, 12*,
    170–187.
Norris, F. H., & Murrell, S. A. (1984). Protective function of resources related to
    life events, global stress, and depression in older adults. *Journal of Health and
    Social Behavior, 25*, 424–437.
Perez, L. (1986). Cubans in the United States. *Annals of the American Academy of Politi-
    cal and Social Science, 487*, 126–137.
Rook, K. S. (1984). The negative side of social interaction: Impact on psychological
    well-being. *Journal of Personality and Social Psychology, 46*, 1097–1108.
Starrett, R. A., Todd, A. M., & De Leon, L. (1989). A comparison of social service
    utilization behavior of the Cuban and Puerto Rican Elderly. *Hispanic Journal
    of Behavioral Sciences, 11*, 341–353.
Starrett, R. A., Wright, R., Mindel, C. H., & Tran, T. V. (1989). The use of social ser-
    vices by Hispanic elderly: A comparison of Mexican American, Puerto Rican,
    and Cuban elderly. *Journal of Social Service Research, 13*, 1–25.

_____

# Chapter Five

# Determinants of Applications for Nursing Home Placement: A National Perspective

Nursing homes remain the most expensive long-term care reimbursement category, though public expenditure for home- and community-based long-term care has increased more rapidly than for nursing home care over the past decade. Estimates for 1993 were that 71% of all publicly funded long-term care was for institutional services, leaving only 29% for home- and community-based care (Wilson, 1995, p. 50; U.S. General Accounting Office, 1995).

Evidence from recent studies indicates that the prevalence and incidence of disability among older Americans has declined in recent years and that active life expectancy—the years expected to be lived in an active state—is increasing (Crimmins, Saito, & Reynolds, 1997; Maddox & Clark, 1992; Manton, Corder, & Stallard, 1993; Manton, Stallard, & Corder, 1995; Manton, Stallard, & Liu, 1993). Despite morbidity and disability declines, however, the rapidly increasing number of the elderly population, especially those most likely to use nursing homes (those aged 85 or older), will increase the absolute need and expenditures for nursing homes in the future. In other words, the force of mortality in those over age 85 is found to be decreasing in a pattern similar to that for those under age 85 (Rothenberg, Lentzner, & Parker, 1991). Nevertheless, the level of frailty and the probability of nursing home use increase sharply with longevity: 75% of the population survives to age 79 without a nursing home admission; about 50% of the population survives to age 85 without an admission; by age 90, only 25% of the population has survived without a nursing home admission (Freedman, 1996).

Because Medicaid funds almost half of all nursing home expenditures, the forecast of increasing nursing home use raises serious public policy issues. Moreover, despite the substantial investment of tax dollars, concerns about the quality of nursing home care persist, along with the hardships that many families face in finding suitable placement for their elderly relatives (Wilson, 1995). But the most interesting research question derives from comparisons between community-residing and institutionalized elderly persons, which often reveal that the level of frailty or disability alone is not the sole determinant of nursing home placement. In addition to physical and functional impairment, sociodemographic, economic, racial, and social-support–related factors contribute to the placement decision.

In this chapter we attempt to discover risk factors that are associated with applications for nursing home placement among frail elderly, utilizing data from the National Long-Term Care Channeling Demonstration study of 1982–1984, as a precursor to the analysis of ethnic differences that follow in Chapter 5.

## THEORETICAL FRAMEWORK AND LITERATURE REVIEW

Few studies have analyzed determinants of nursing home applications. But a number of studies that analyzed differences between frail elderly persons who remained in the community and those who were institutionalized have identified risk factors associated with nursing home admisssion. The most commonly used conceptual and analytical framework for such comparison was the Andersen–Newman model (Andersen & Newman, 1973). Another conceptual model that integrates empirical findings from epidemiological literature on risk factors with theoretical considerations and empirical findings regarding family caregiving and caregiver stress also has been used (see Aneshensel, Pearlin, Mullan, Zarit, & Whitlatch, 1995; Pearlin, Mullan, Semple, & Skaff, 1990).

### The Andersen–Newman Model

Andersen (1968) and his colleagues (Aday & Andersen, 1974; 1975; Aday, Flemming, & Andersen, 1984; Anderson & Newman, 1973) developed a widely used theoretical model that posits that the utilization of health-related services by individuals is governed by the interaction of predisposing, enabling, and need factors. *Predisposing factors* derive from the proposition that some individuals have a greater propensity for using services than others. Commonly used indicators of such a propensity include an individual's demographic background (age, gender, and marital status) and social/structural and cultural background (education, occupation, and race/ethnicity). These factors are believed to reflect individuals' relative life cycle positions and culturally determined beliefs, attitudes, and behavioral patterns that existed before a given illness episode (Andersen & Aday, 1978; Andersen & Newman, 1973; Bass & Noelker, 1987).

*Enabling factors* derive from the proposition that though the individual may be predisposed to use services, he or she may need resources or means to access and obtain the services: family income, health insurance, or Medicaid, as well as community-level institutional resources such as physician-to-population and hospital-bed-to-population ratios, nursing home bed availability, and geographic location (Bass & Noelker, 1987; McAuley & Arling, 1984; Ward, 1977; Wolinsky & Johnson, 1991). These factors are believed to represent items in individuals' socioeconomic opportunity structure that facilitate or impede service use.

The *need factors* refer to the most immediate reason the services are needed: health problems, both objective and subjective. In other words, need factors are those illness- and/or impairment-related conditions for which services are sought. Previous studies show the need factors to be the strongest predictors of health service utilization, including hospitalization and nursing home admission.

The Andersen–Newman model has since been extended to predict the use of health and social services by older persons (Wan, 1989; for a history of its application to older persons, see Wolinsky, 1990). But the major shortcoming of the original Andersen–Newman model was the absence of measures of social support from both kin and nonkin (Wolinsky & Johnson, 1991), because social support may have significant direct, buffering, and/or mediating effects on elderly's health status and their health service utilization (see Newman, Struyk, Wright, & Rice, 1990). Thus, most previous studies of nursing home admissions used an expanded Andersen–Newman model, including measures of the effect of social support, both formal and informal, as enabling factors. It is also noted that age is a reflection of need more than a predisposition (Greene & Ondrich, 1990) and that race may reflect the availablity of economic resources as well as cultural beliefs and attitudes.

### Literature Review

The findings of existing research that was conducted within the framework of the Andersen–Newman model identify advanced age, Caucasian race, living alone or living without a spouse (especially for males), physical and functional disability, and cognitive impairment as consistently significant individual risk factors for nursing home admissions (Branch & Jette, 1982; Colerick & George, 1986; Dolinsky & Rosenwaike, 1988; Greene & Ondrich, 1990; Jette, Branch, Sleeper, Feldman, & Sullivan, 1992; Kasper & Shore, 1994; Shapiro & Tate, 1988; Wan & Weissert, 1981). Advancing age and deteriorating physical, functional, and mental conditions are indicators of need. When these need factors are controlled for, Blacks and Hispanics are still less likely to enter a nursing home than are Whites. Although women constitute a large portion of nursing home residents, gender is not always a significant factor (see Branch & Jette, 1982; Greene & Ondrich, 1990).

As for income and Medicaid eligibility, findings also present mixed results; some show positive relationship, others show negative relationship, and still others show no relationship (see Freedman, 1996; Montgomery & Kosloski, 1994). The reason for the mixed results for income and Medicaid eligibility may be that while those in the upper-income strata can more easily enter a nursing home than those in the middle-income strata because of their ability to pay, those whose income is low enough to make them Medicaid eligible are also more likely than those in the middle-income range to enter a nursing home (see Montgomery & Kosloski, 1994). One resource that tends to show a consistently significant negative effect on nursing home admission is home-ownership, because it leads to the use of formal support (Freedman, 1996; Montgomery & Kosloski, 1994; Newman et al., 1990). Also, it may be easier for an owner–occupant to have a family member move in as a caregiver.

Studies that tested the nature of the relationship between social support and the risk of nursing home admission have analyzed the main effects, supplementation effects, and buffering effects of formal and informal care on the risk of institutionalization. The term *main effect* refers to the direct effects of formal or informal support on reducing or increasing the risk of institutionalization; *supplementation effect* refers to formal or informal support augmenting the need for care at institutions; and *buffering effect* refers to support moderating risk factors by mitigating the effect/risk of deteriorating health. Studies show that neither formal nor informal support, with the exception of living arrangement, is significant in the main-effects equations (Newman et al., 1990). Living alone, as mentioned, is a consistently significant risk factor for institutionalization. Those who live alone were also found to have longer nursing home and hospitalization stays (Wan & Weissert, 1981). In a similar vein, married older persons (especially males) were found to have about half the risk of nursing home admission of the unmarried counterparts, and an older person's chance of admission was reduced by about one-fourth if he or she had at least one daughter or sibling (Dolinsky & Rosenwaike, 1988; Freedman, 1996). The significance of living arrangement, marital status, and presence of children or siblings also indicates the supplementation effects of informal social support.

Unlike the effect of this informal support, the use of formal services such as paid caregiver and physician services increases the risk of nursing home admission (Greene & Ondrich, 1990; McFall & Miller, 1992; Newman et al., 1990). The explanation for this positive relationship is that those who use formal services, as compared to those who do not, are likely to have more serious health problems. That is, the use of formal service represents "the interim stage in the continuum of long-term care from primarily informal to mixed informal and formal to all formal [institutionalization] care" (Jette, Tennstedt, & Crawford, 1995, p. S10). Those who utilize formal services are also more likely to be exposed to professionals—doctors, nurses, and social workers—who may see the elderly persons' need for institutionalization and serve as a conduit to connect them to it.

Existing studies also provided only modest support for the buffering effects of formal and informal care in specific situations. Jette et al.'s study (1995) found that the number of formal care hours buffered the risk of institutionalization among cognitively impaired elderly, because formal care provided respite to caregivers.

The relationship between the caregiver burden and stress dimension of informal care and the risk of institutionalization has been extensively analyzed in studies based on a model used by Aneshensel et al. (1995). Unlike the Andersen–Newman model, which focused on the conditions that frail elderly persons face, the model used by Aneshensel et al., with their studies of demented elderly persons and their caregivers, focused on the actual demands of caregiving and caregiver stress, which are illustrated as primary and secondary stressors. The term *primary stressors* refers to objective conditions of caregiving (patient's impairment) and the caregiver's subjective reactions to these circumstances. *Secondary stressors* refers to the encroachment of care-related stress into other social roles—family, work, and finances. Aneshensel et al. found that psychological distress among caregivers did not independently contribute to the odds of nursing home admission of elderly persons with dementia once the elderly person's health status and care-related stressors, such as insufficient money, family conflict, and caregiver health, were taken into account. Other studies found that the subjective caregiver burden was significantly positively associated with nursing home admission, although the rates of such admission differed between elderly persons cared for by spouse caregivers and those cared for by child caregivers (McFall & Miller, 1992; Montgomery & Kosloski, 1994; Scott, Edwards, Davis, Cornman, & Macera, 1997).

To sum up, the majority of studies conducted to test the Andersen–Newman model as well as the Aneshensel et al. model found that informal social support may in fact play a minor role relative to that of the need factors represented by advancing age, physical and functional disability, and cognitive impairments.

The conceptual and analytical framework advanced in this chapter draws from an expanded Andersen–Newman model that includes measures of formal and informal support and measures of elderly's psychological disposition factors—perception of current living conditions and attitude toward nursing home placement. Although the Andersen–Newman model tries to capture an individual's predisposition to health service utilization by examining his or her sociocultural background, those background variables are indirect measures of the person's attitude toward a nursing home, and this attitude may be directly measured only by asking that individual the pertinent question. The National Long-Term Care Channeling Demonstration data set is unique because it includes the specific question. The answer to the question is included as a predictor variable in the analysis in this chapter.

Four sets of variables were consequently hypothesized as correlating with nursing home applications: (1) elderly sociodemographic factors, (2) elderly need factors, (3) elderly psychological disposition factors, and (4) the availability and use of formal and informal supports. The interrelationship of these clusters of variables, and the effects of these variables in explaining the difference between frail elders who applied for a nursing home and those who did not, therefore constitute the focus of this analysis.

## METHODOLOGY

### Data Source and Sample

This chapter utilizes data from the National Long-Term Care Channeling Demonstration that was initiated in 1980 by the U.S. Department of Health and Human Services. As described in Chapter 2, this demonstration encompassed a study sample of 5,626 frail older persons at high risk of institutionalization. (See Chapter 2 for detailed description of the data set.)

### Measurement of Variables

The dependent variable—nursing home placement—was dichotomously coded, with "1" indicating elderly persons who had applied for nursing home care in the preceding year or who had been wait-listed for nursing home placement (because their nursing home admission was pending). They were labeled the *preinstitutional* group. A "0" code designated those who had neither applied for nursing home placement nor been wait-listed. They were referred to as the *noninstitutional* group. The preinstitutional group totaled 375 respondents, as compared to 5,028 in the noninstitutional group, or 7 % and 93%, respectively.

As independent variables, sociodemographics of these elderly included race/ethnicity, age, gender, income, and living arrangements (alone or with others). Older persons' "need" variables were (1) cognitive impairment, (2) impairment in ADL, (3) number of medical conditions, (4) number of perceived unmet needs, and (5) number of self-reported depressive symptoms. Impairment in ADL was measured by asking elderly respondents if they had been helped during the preceding week in the following five ADL domains: eating, bathing, dressing, toileting, and getting out of bed or a chair. Cognitive impairment was measured by the Short Portable Mental Status Questionnaire (SPMSQ), a 10-item test of mental functioning. Absence of impairment or mild impairment was indicated by 9 to 10 correct answers out of a possible 10, moderate impairment by 6 to 8 correct answers, and severe impairment by 0 to 5 correct answers. Impairment in continence does not require explanation. Chronic medical problems were measured by asking respondents to report whether they suffered from the following conditions:

anemia, high blood pressure, heart disease, stroke, diabetes, arthritis, cancer, Parkinson's disease, respiratory problems, skin problems, paralysis, orthopedic problems, vision or hearing problems, and other health problems. Perceived unmet needs were measured by asking respondents if they needed more help in those ADL and IADL areas. Self-reported depressive symptoms included feeling depressed, blue, tired, or lonely; difficulty in sleeping; shortness of breath; lack of appetite; or inability to concentrate.

Psychological-disposition variables included (1) feeling of control in life and (2) attitude toward nursing home placement. Feeling of control in life was a composite score of the following five questions: (1) "In general, how satisfying do you find the way you're spending your life these days? Would you call it completely satisfying, pretty satisfying, or not very satisfying?" (2) "Day to day, how much choice do you have about what you do and when you do it? Would you say a great deal of choice, some choice, or not very much choice?" (3) "How confident are you of figuring out how to deal with your problems? Would you say you feel very confident, somewhat confident, or not very confident?" (4) "How much do you worry about not knowing who to turn to for help? Would you say you worry a lot, some, or not very much?" (5) "How confident are you of getting services when you need them? Would you say you feel very confident, somewhat confident, or not very confident?" These were rated on a three-point scale, with the high score indicating an unfavorable rating. In order to summarize the data and to avoid the problem of multicollinearity, a principal components analysis with varimax rotation was performed, yielding one component. These five items were highly correlated, with factor loadings ranging from .56 to .71. The scores of these five items were added to form the *feeling-of-control-in-life* composite measure (alpha coefficient = .74). Attitude toward nursing home placement was measured by a four-point scale, with 1 being acceptable and 4 being totally unacceptable ("would rather die than to go to a nursing home").

The use of informal and formal support variables included (1) social contacts (the degree of elder's contact with family members or friends who live apart in the preceding week, measured on a four-point scale, with 1 indicating once a day or more, 2 denoting two to six times a week, 3 once a week, and 4 not at all); (2) number of informal helpers; (3) number of formal care providers; and (4) total number of formal services used—medical care, home care, Meals on Wheels, congregate meals, health program, social center/religious participation, and/or counseling. These formal services represent both home- and community-based programs.

## Methods of Analysis

Bivariate analysis compared the noninstitutional and preinstitutional groups in the following areas: sociodemographic profiles; physical, functional, and cognitive impairments; formal and informal support use; and psychosocial disposition. Then, in an attempt to sort out the predictors of nursing home application in a multivariate framework, a maximum likelihood logistic regression analysis was conducted. Because of the dichotomous nature of the dependent variable, a logistic regression model was best suited (Maddala, 1983). Logistic regression coefficients and odds ratios indicate the direction and magnitude of association of an independent variable with a dependent variable or outcome measure. Coefficients were interpreted as in ordinary least-squares regression models, with parameter estimates indicating the change in log odds of being in a category (of the dependent variable) with a unit change in the independent variable, with the effects of all other variables in the model controlled. The parameter estimates converted to odds ratios were then tested for statistical significance.

As mentioned, as the dependent variable, the preinstitutional group was coded 1, and the noninstitutional group was coded 0. The independent variables entered in the logistic regression equation included (1) five sociodemographic variables (race [White = 1, nonwhite = 0]; gender [male = 1, female = 0]; age [80 years or older = 1, younger than 80 years = 0]; income [$1,000 or more monthly = 1, other = 0]; living arrangement [alone = 1, with others = 0]); (2) four need variables (cognitive impairment [the original SPMSQ scores entered as a continuous variable], ADL impairment [number of ADL, with difficulty entered as a continuous variable], number of medical conditions, number of perceived unmet needs, and number of depressive symptoms); (3) two psychological-disposition variables (attitude toward nursing home placement [not acceptable or totally unacceptable = 0; acceptable or minimally acceptable = 1] and sense of control in life [higher score reflecting higher sense of control]); and (4) four formal and informal supports variables (social contact, number of informal helpers, number of formal helpers, and number of formal services used).

## RESULTS

### Bivariate Analysis

A comparison of the profiles of the noninstitutional group and the preinstitutional group is presented in Table 5.1. The data show that the two groups do not significantly differ in age and gender distribution; 50.4% of the noninstitutional group and 53.6% of the preinstitutional group were 80 years of age and older, and 71.5% of the former and 68.8% of the latter were female. The two groups did not differ in marital status distribution (approximately one-third of them were married), level of education, living arrangement (approximately one-third lived alone), monthly income, and Medicaid coverage (approximately one-fourth of them were covered). The only significant difference in sociodemographic characteristics between the two

**Table 5.1**

**Comparative Profile of Noninstitutional versus Preinstitutional Frail Elderly Persons**

|  | Noninstitutional $\underline{n}$ = 5,028 (93%) | Preinstitutional $\underline{n}$ = 375 (7%) |
|---|---|---|
| **Age** | | |
| 64 to 69 | 12.2% | 8.5% |
| 70 to 74 | 16.4 | 14.7 |
| 75 to 79 | 20.9 | 23.2 |
| 80 to 84 | 23.6 | 22.4 |
| 85 to 89 | 16.7 | 18.4 |
| >=90 | 10.1 | 12.8 |
| **Race**** | | |
| Black[a] | 94.8% | 5.1% |
| White[a] | 92.4 | 7.6 |
| Hispanic | 94.6 | 5.4 |
| **Gender** | | |
| Female | 71.5% | 68.8% |
| **Marital status** | | |
| Married | 31.9% | 33.1% |
| Not married | 68.1 | 66.9 |
| **Education** | | |
| None or elementary | 58.5% | 69.6% |
| Some secondary | 15.9 | 11.2 |
| Completed high school | 13.8 | 10.3 |
| Completed college | 10.1 | 7.5 |
| Postcollege | 1.6 | 1.5 |
| **Living arrangement** | | |
| Alone | 37.2% | 32.2% |
| With spouse | 31.0 | 32.4 |
| With children | 21.0 | 23.8 |
| With others | 10.8 | 11.6 |
| **Financial condition** | | |
| Mean monthly income | $558 | $550 |
| SSI receipt | 17.9% | 15.8% |
| Medicaid receipt | 22.3% | 24.5% |

*Data Source*: National Long-Term Care Channeling Demonstration, 1982–1984.
[a]None was of Hispanic origin.
**$p < 0.01$.

groups was in racial distribution; a smaller percentage of African Americans (5.1%) and Hispanics (5.4%) than non-Hispanic Whites (7.6%) had applied for nursing home admission.

Physical and cognitive characteristics of the noninstitutional and preinstitutional groups, as observed in Table 5.2, show that a significantly higher proportion of the latter than the former had very severe and extremely severe ADL impairment as well as moderate and severe cognitive impairment. That is, 67.5% of the preinstitutional group versus 57.0% of the noninstitutional group had very severe or extremely severe ADL impairment, and 65.6% of the former versus 48.9% of the latter had moderate to severe cognitive impairment. The latter also reported that they had a higher number of perceived

**Table 5.2**
**Physical and Cognitive Functioning Characteristics of Noninstitutional versus Preinstitutional Frail Elderly Persons**

|  | Noninstitutional $\underline{n} = 5,028$ | Preinstitutional $\underline{n} = 375$ |
|---|---|---|
| **ADL impairment****** | | |
| Mild or none | 20.3% | 13.9% |
| Moderately severe | 22.8 | 18.7 |
| Very severe | 34.5 | 33.9 |
| Extremely severe | 22.5 | 33.6 |
| **Cognitive impairment[a]**** | | |
| Mild or none | 51.1% | 34.4% |
| Moderate | 33.4 | 39.6 |
| Severe | 15.5 | 26.0 |
| **Impairment in continence** | 47.4% | 48.8% |
| **Perceived health status*** | | |
| Excellent | 2.6% | 3.2% |
| Good | 14.5 | 15.1 |
| Fair | 30.9 | 22.7 |
| Poor | 52.1 | 58.9 |
| No. of medical conditions** | 4.8 | 5.1 |
| No. of depressive symptoms[b] | 3.6 | 3.7 |
| No. of perceived unmet needs (ADL and IADL)**** | 4.0 | 4.6 |

*Data Source*: National Long-Term Care Channeling Demonstration, 1982–1984.
[a]Measured by the SPMSQ, a 10-item test of mental functioning. Mild impairment was indicated by 9 to 10 correct answers out of a possible 10, moderate impairment by 6 to 8 correct answers, and severe impairment by 0 to 5 correct answers.
[b]Self-reported depressive symptoms included feeling depressed, blue, tired, or lonely; difficulty in sleeping; shortness of breath; lack of appetite, or inability to concentrate.
*$p < 0.05$; **$p < 0.01$; ****$p < 0.0001$.

unmet needs (with ADL and IADL impairment) than the former (4.6 versus 4.0, $p < 0.0001$). A slightly higher proportion of the preinstitutional group also reported their health status as "poor" (58.9% versus 52.1% of the noninstitutional group). The preinstitutional group also had statistically significantly more medical problems than the noninstitutional group, although the real difference appears to be minimal (5.1 versus 4.8 problems, $p < 0.01$). But the two groups were not different in the number of self-reported depressive symptoms (3.6 versus 3.7).

Data in Table 5.3 show that compared to the noninstitutional group, the preinstitutional group was slightly less likely to have received regular medical care in the preceding two months, but more likely to have been in the hospital and had slightly longer average hospital stays for the same period. Despite

**Table 5.3**
**Formal and Informal Support of Noninstitutional versus Preinstitutional Frail Elderly Persons**

|  | Noninstitutional $n = 5,028$ | Preinstitutional $n = 375$ |
|---|---|---|
| **Medical service use** |  |  |
| Regular medical care* | 91.9% | 88.4% |
| Hospital use in preceding 2 months** | 69.2% | 76.7% |
| No. of doctor visits | 1.8 | 1.7 |
| No. of hospital days in preceding 2 months* | 18.4 | 21.2 |
| **In-home service use** |  |  |
| Regular home care | 29.5% | 31.6% |
| Meals on Wheels | 16.3% | 13.7% |
| **Community-based service use** |  |  |
| Congregate meals** | 4.1% | 17.4% |
| Health program | 1.7% | 2.6% |
| Social center or church | 12.6% | 11.3% |
| Counseling | 4.9% | 4.5% |
| **Formal support** |  |  |
| Formal helpers (mean) | 1.1 | 1.1 |
| Formal service use[a]**** | 1.5 | 2.3 |
| **Informal support** |  |  |
| Informal helpers (mean) | 2.0 | 1.9 |
| Social contacts (mean) | 1.7 | 1.8 |

*Data Source*: National Long-Term Care Channeling Demonstration, 1982–1984.
[a]Total number of formal services used included home care, Meals on Wheels, congregate meals, health program, social center, church, and counseling.
*$p < 0.05$; **$p < 0.01$; ****$p < 0.0001$.

the slight difference, the average number of hospital stays (18.4 and 21.2 days for the noninstitutional group and the preinstitutional group, respectively), indicates that both groups were quite infirm and frail. The two groups did not differ in their reliance on home-based formal services—home care and Meals on Wheels. But those in the preinstitutional group were apparently more likely to have used at least one community-based formal service—congregate meals (17.4% versus 4.1%, $p < 0.01$). The two groups did not differ in utilization of other community-based services such as health programs, social center/church participation, and counseling services. Probably because the two groups did not differ in their use of home care services, they also did not differ in numbers of formal and informal helpers. This may well be the reason that the preinstitutional group, with its significantly more serious functional impairment, reported a significantly higher number of perceived unmet needs in terms of ADL and IADL. Although the preinstitutional group used a higher number of formal services than the noninstitutional group (2.3 versus 1.5, $p < 0.0001$), the difference is probably due to the higher proportion of the former who used congregate meals.

With respect to the sense-of-control-in-life aspect of the elderly psychological disposition variables, data in Table 5.4 show that the two groups were significantly different only in their degree of life satisfaction. The preinstitutional group was more likely than the noninstitutional group to be completely satisfied (24.7% versus 17.7%) as well as not very satisfied with life (47.2% versus 43.8%). The most striking difference between the two groups was in their attitude toward nursing home placement: 70.1% of the noninstitutional group, as opposed to 45.5% of the preinstitutional group, indicated that nursing home placement was not acceptable or was totally unacceptable.

This bivariate comparison of sociodemographic, need, and social support variables of the noninstitutional and preinstitutional groups shows the significance of race; physical, functional, and cognitive impairment; number of perceived unmet needs (ADL and IADL); and number of formal services used in elders' decision to apply for nursing home admission. Despite their more severe health problems, the preinstitutional group apparently had no more formal and informal helpers, and thus reported a higher number of perceived unmet needs. In addition, this study was able to find a significant difference in attitude toward nursing home placement, and this difference needs to be explored further in future studies.

## Multivariate Analysis

The logistic regression coefficients in Table 5.5 show that Whites and those 80 years of age or older were more likely to have applied for nursing home admission than nonwhites and those younger than age 80. Those who had $1,000 or more in monthly income and those who lived alone were less

**Table 5.4**
**Psychosocial Characteristics of Noninstitutional versus Preinstitutional Frail Elderly Persons**

|  | Noninstitutional $\underline{n} = 5,028$ (%) | Preinstitutional $\underline{n} = 375$ (%) |
|---|---|---|
| **Life satisfaction**** |  |  |
| Completely satisfied | 17.7 | 24.7 |
| Somewhat satisfied | 38.5 | 28.1 |
| Not very satisfied | 43.8 | 47.2 |
| **Sense of choice/control** |  |  |
| A great deal of choice | 31.4 | 32.7 |
| Some choice | 23.9 | 21.0 |
| Not very much choice | 44.7 | 46.3 |
| **Confident of ability to deal with problems** |  |  |
| Very confident | 35.4 | 30.5 |
| Somewhat confident | 36.5 | 36.0 |
| Not very confident | 28.1 | 33.5 |
| **Worried about not knowing whom to turn to for help** |  |  |
| Not very much | 47.0 | 41.1 |
| Some | 21.2 | 22.3 |
| A lot | 31.8 | 36.6 |
| **Confident of ability to get services when needed** |  |  |
| Very confident | 35.5 | 30.3 |
| Somewhat confident | 35.4 | 32.3 |
| Not very confident | 29.1 | 37.4 |
| **Nursing home placement attitude***** |  |  |
| Acceptable | 3.6 | 18.6 |
| Minimally acceptable | 26.3 | 35.9 |
| Not acceptable | 5.5 | 9.0 |
| Totally unacceptable (would rather die) | 64.6 | 36.5 |

*Data Source*: National Long-Term Care Channeling Demonstration, 1982–1984.
**$p < 0.01$; ****$p < 0.0001$.

likely to have applied for nursing home admission. In line with bivariate results, the likelihood of applying for or awaiting nursing home admission was also more pronounced among those who had more cognitive and ADL impairment as well as those who reported a higher number of perceived unmet needs. As expected, the unfavorable rating of nursing home placement was negatively associated with the likelihood of nursing home application. The

**Table 5.5**
**Logistic Regression Analysis of Institutional Placement of Frail Elders**

| Variables | Logit coefficients (SE) | Odds Ratio | Wald chi-square |
|---|---|---|---|
| **Sociodemographics** | | | |
| Race (White=1; nonwhite=0) | .55(.23) | 1.73** | 5.54 |
| Gender (Male=1) | .06(.20) | | |
| Age (>80=1) | .58(.18) | 1.79** | 10.65 |
| Income (>$1000=1) | -.88(.40) | .41** | 4.64 |
| Living alone (Alone=1) | -.48(.20) | .64* | 4.91 |
| **Need factors** | | | |
| Cognitive impairment | .46(.11) | 1.59*** | 16.12 |
| ADL impairment | .29(.09) | 1.30** | 8.22 |
| No. of medical conditions | -.08(.05) | | |
| No. of perceived unmet needs | .10(.03) | 1.11** | 9.33 |
| No. of depressive symptoms | -.04(.04) | | |
| **Psychological disposition factors** | | | |
| Nursing home attitude[a] | 1.07(.18) | 2.91**** | 36.13 |
| Sense of control in life | .05(.03) | | |
| **Use of informal and formal supports** | | | |
| Social Contact | .13(.08) | | |
| No. of informal helpers | -.14(.08) | | |
| No. of formal helpers | -.09(.07) | | |
| No. of formal services use | 1.29(.11) | 3.59**** | 134.93 |
| Intercept | -7.76**** | | |
| Model chi square | 250.98**** | | |

*Data Source*: National Long-Term Care Channeling Demonstration, 1982–1984.
[a]Nursing home attitude was dichotomously coded, with 1 being "Nursing home is an acceptable option" and 0 being "Nursing home is an unacceptable option."
*$p < 0.05$; **$p < 0.01$; ***$p < 0.001$; ****$p < 0.0001$.

higher the number of formal services used, the higher the likelihood of nursing home application.

## DISCUSSION

The significance of the race and age variables is no surprise, because their significance and direction of the sign of the coefficients were the same as in previous studies. The surprise is the magnitude of the odds ratio, especially in relation to the race variable; White frail elders were 73% more likely to have applied for nursing home admission than were nonwhite elders. The negative correlation between income and the likelihood of nursing home application has also been found in previous studies, although, as just discussed, the direction of the relationship between income and nursing home admission has not always been consistent in previous studies. Among the sample members of this study, those whose monthly income was $1,000 or more were significantly less likely than those whose monthly income was less than $1,000 to have applied or been wait-listed for nursing home admission.

The sign of the coefficient of the living arrangement variable contradicts the findings of previous studies in which those who lived alone were found to have a higher likelihood of nursing home admission than those who did not live alone. The findings of this study may differ from those of previous studies due to the difference between the dependent variables (application/ wait list versus actual admission). In other words, families whose elders live with them may be more primed to send in nursing home applications in preparation for the future, especially in areas where waiting lists are long. Family members often act as advocates for elders' formal service use, and are likely to seek regular outside help to relieve the excessive caregiving burden that befalls them. Another possible explanation is that, given that the numbers of informal and formal helpers do not differ between the two groups, the family members or "others" who lived with the elders were not necessarily likely to provide needed care. Especially with elders who have severe cognitive and functional impairment, caregivers often feel exhausted from excessive and escalating care-related burdens, experience inadequate or declining resources, and fall prey to their own declining health (Aneshensel et al., 1995). Thus, coresidence with relatives may not be automatically translated into having their help available. It is possible that those who lived with their family members had more serious health problems than those who lived alone. The coresidence may have been prompted by the elder's inability to live independently, but the family members had become exhausted from the daily caregiving burden. In sum, the substitution effect of informal caregivers is not proved in this study.

As for elderly need variables, three of four indicators of health problems and unmet needs were found significant, confirming especially the importance of cognitive and ADL impairment. According to the odds ratios, an increment of one point in SPMSQ increases the likelihood of nursing home application by 59%, and an increment of one more difficulty with ADL increases such likelihood by 30%. In addition, other things being equal, this study also found that the number of unmet needs with ADL and IADL was positively associated with the likelihood of nursing home application. This in fact is a logical extension of the significant association between the level of functional health problems and the likelihood of nursing home application. The number of medical conditions or physical illnesses and the number of depressive symptoms were not found to be significantly associated with the likelihood of nursing home application. The absence of association between the number of medical conditions and the decision to apply for nursing home admission may be due to the limitations of the numeric variable, which gave equal weight to both life-threatening, debilitating conditions such as cancer, stroke, and paralysis and non-life-threatening conditions such as hearing and vision problems. Further analysis is needed to discover how different kinds of physical illnesses affect the likelihood of nursing home application. Depressive symptoms alone may not be a sufficient reason for an elder to apply for nursing home admission.

As mentioned, elders' attitudes toward nursing home placement had not been entered as a predictor variable in previous studies of nursing home admission. This study found that, when sociodemographic, need, and social support variables are controlled for, an elder's attitude is significantly correlated with the likelihood of his or her application for nursing home admission. Those who opposed nursing home placement as an acceptable option for themselves were significantly less likely than those who did not strongly object to such placement to have applied for nursing home admission. The odds ratio indicates that those with a positive attitude toward nursing home placement were almost three times more likely than those with negative attitude to have applied for nursing home admission.

But because of the fuzzy time frame, a caveat is needed in interpreting the direction of the relationship between the attitude variable and the nursing home application. That is, the data are not clear as to whether the positive attitude of some preinstitutional elderly was the reason for or the result of their nursing home application. If the attitude question were asked ipso facto, the answer might reflect some preinstitutional elders' rationalization of the inevitable. Such a rationalization may in fact be beneficial for elders whose institutionalization is pending, because those with a positive attitude are likely to experience a lower level of stress at the transition from community to institution. If the attitude were really an antecedent variable, we may indeed state that it affected the application decision. Thus, although decisions regarding applications for a nursing home bed and subsequent admission to a nursing home are most likely to be conjointly made among an elderly individual, his or her family members, and/or health care professionals (especially for a nursing home stay following an episode of hospitalization), our finding indicates that the elder's attitude toward institutionalization may in reality influence such decisions to a significant degree.

The significant positive relationship between the number of formal services used and the likelihood of nursing home application is also in line with the findings of previous studies of nursing home admissions. As discussed, formal services tend to be utilized by elders and their families as the elder's health problems deteriorate and the informal support system alone becomes no longer able to cope with the care-related demand. Elders connected to formal services are more likely to apply and be admitted to a nursing home than those not yet linked to formal services, because they are already in the system.

Unlike formal service use, informal support as measured by the level of elders' social contact and number of informal helpers was not a significant predictor of nursing home application. As shown in previous studies, informal support may indeed play a minor or insignificant role when it comes to main, buffering, or substituting effects on elders' institutionalization. Again, however, the lack of significance of informal support in this study may be due to limitations in measurement of the informal support variables. The type of informal helpers (i.e., spouse, child, other relative, or friend) was not differentiated. Given the findings that spouses provide longer and more caregiving than children (Montgomery & Kosloski, 1994), the source of informal support may need to be differentiated, together with other important dimensions of informal support networks, namely, caregiver's gender and employment status.

## SUMMARY

Overall, the findings in this chapter are largely similar to those of previous studies of nursing home admissions, in the sense that the risk factors identified under the conceptual framework of the expanded Andersen–Newman model were also found to be significant determinants of nursing home applications among frail elders. In addition, the findings add a significant new dimension of psychological disposition to the Andersen–Newman model.

This chapter also found that, as suggested by the odds ratio, the explanatory power of each variable that was found to be a significant predictor was quite strong, and thus the additive effects of multiple risk factors would be even stronger. In reality, a decision regarding an elder's institutionalization is made based on multiple factors or on the combined effects of his or her circumstances. Elders who applied for nursing home admission are likely to have multiple problems related to old age, poor health, and inadequate support, and they may not be receiving proper care in the community if informal and formal support is inadequate. In those circumstances, the elder's placement in a high-quality nursing home through prompt processing of the application is a desired outcome in the continuum of long-term care.

## REFERENCES

Aday, L., & Andersen, R. M. (1974). A framework for access to medical care. *Health Services Research, 9*, 208–220.

Aday, L., & Andersen, R. M. (1975). *Access to medical care.* Ann Arbor, MI: Health Administration Press.

Aday, L., Flemming, G. V., & Andersen, R. M. (1984). *Access to medical care in the U.S.: Who has it, who doesn't?* Chicago: Pluribus Press.

Andersen, R. M. (1968). *A behavioral model of families' use of health services.* Chicago: Center for Health Administration Studies.

Andersen, R. M., & Aday, L. (1978). Access to medical care in the U.S.: Realized and potential. *Medical Care, 16*, 533–546.

Andersen, R. M., & Newman, J. F. (1973). Societal and individual determinants of medical care utilization in the U.S. *Milbank Memorial Fund Quarterly, 51*, 95–124.

Aneshensel, C. S., Pearlin, L. I., Mullan, J. T., Zarit, S. H., & Whitlatch, C. J. (1995). *Profiles in caregiving: The unexpected career.* San Diego: Academic Press.

Bass, D. M., & Noelker, L. S. (1987). The influence of family caregivers on elders' use of in-home services: An expanded conceptual framework. *Journal of Health and Social Behavior, 28*, 184–196.

Branch, L. G., & Jette, A. M. (1982). A prospective study of long-term care institutionalization among the aged. *American Journal of Public Health, 72*, 1373–1379.

Colerick, E. J., & George, L. K. (1986). Predictors of institutionalization among caregivers of patients with Alzheimer's disease. *Journal of American Geriatric Society, 34*, 493–498.

Crimmins, E. M., Saito, Y., & Reynolds, S. L. (1997). Further evidence on recent trends in the prevalence and incidence of disability among older Americans from two sources: The Longitudinal Survey of Aging and the National Health Interview Survey. *Journal of Gerontology, 52B*, S59–S71.

Dolinsky, A. L., & Rosenwaike, J. (1988). The role of demographic factors in the institutionalization of the elderly. *Research on Aging, 10*, 235–257.

Freedman, V. A. (1996). Family structure and the risk of nursing home admission. *Journal of Gerontology, 51B*, S61–S69.

Greene, V. L., & Ondrich, J. I. (1990). Risk factors for nursing home admissions and exits: A discrete-time hazard function approach. *Journal of Gerontology, 45*, S250–S258.

Jette, A. M., Branch, L. G., Sleeper, L. A., Feldman, H., & Sullivan, L. M. (1992). High-risk profiles for nursing home admission. *The Gerontologist, 32*, 634–640.

Jette, A. M., Tennstedt, S., & Crawford, S. (1995). How does formal and informal community care affect nursing home use? *Journal of Gerontology, 50B*, S4–S12.

Kasper, J. D., & Shore, A. D. (1994). Cognitive impairment and problem behaviors as risk factors for institutionalization. *Journal of Applied Gerontology, 13*, 371–385.

Maddala, G. S. (1983). *Limited dependent and qualitative variables in econometrics.* Cambridge, UK: Cambridge University Press.

Maddox, G. L., & Clark, D. O. (1992). Trajectories of functional impairment in later life. *Journal of Health and Social Behavior, 33*, 114–125.

Manton, K. G., Corder, L. S., & Stallard, E. (1993). Estimates of changes in chronic disability and institutional incidence and prevalence rates in the U.S. elderly population from the 1982, 1984, and 1989 National Long-Term Care Surveys. *Journal of Gerontology, 48*, S153–S166.

Manton, K. G., Stallard, E., & Corder, L. (1995). Changes in morbidity and chronic disability in the U.S. elderly population: Evidence from the 1982, 1984, and 1989 National Long-Term Care Surveys. *Journal of Gerontology, 50B*, S194–S204.

Manton, K. G., Stallard, E., & Liu, K. (1993). Forecast of active life expectancy: Policy and fiscal implications. *Journal of Gerontology, 48*, 11–26.

McAuley, W. J., & Arling, G. (1984). Use of in-home care by very old people. *Journal of Health and Social Behavior, 25*, 54–64.

McFall, S., & Miller, B. H. (1992). Caregiver burden and nursing home admission of frail elderly persons. *Journal of Gerontology, 47*, S73–S79.

Montgomery, R. J. V., & Kosloski, K. (1994). A longitudinal analysis of nursing home placement for dependent elders cared for by spouse versus adult children. *Journal of Gerontology, 49,* S62–S74.

Newman, S. J., Struyk, R., Wright, P., & Rice, M. (1990). Overwhelming odds: Caregiving and the risk of institutionalization. *Journal of Gerontology, 45,* S173–S183.

Pearlin, L. I., Mullan, J. T., Semple, S. J., & Skaff, M. M. (1990). Caregiving and the stress process: An overview of concepts and their measures. *The Gerontologist, 30,* 583–594.

Rothenberg, R., Lentzner, H. R., & Parker, R. A. (1991). Population aging patterns: The expansion of mortality. *Journal of Gerontology, 46,* S66–S70.

Scott, W. K., Edwards, K. B., Davis, D. R., Cornman, C. B., & Macera, C. A. (1997). Risk of institutionalization among community-long-term care clients with dementia. *The Gerontologist, 37,* 46–51.

Shapiro, E., & Tate, R. (1988). Who is really at risk of institutionalization? *The Gerontologist 28,* 237–245.

U.S. General Accounting Office (GAO). (1995). Long-term care: Current issues and future directions. GAO/HEHS-95-109. Washington, DC: U.S. Government Printing Office.

Wan, T. T. H. (1989). The behavioral model of health care utilization and older people. In M. Ory & K. Bond (Eds.), *Aging and health care* (pp. 52–77). New York: Routledge.

Wan, T. T. H., & Weissert, W. G. (1981). Social support networks, patient status, and institutionalization. *Research on Aging, 3,* 240–256.

Ward, R. A. (1977). Services for older people: An integrated framework for research. *Journal of Health and Social Behavior, 18,* 61–78.

Wilson, N. L. (1995). Long-term care in the United States: An overview of the current system. In L. B. McCullough & N. L. Wilson (Eds.), *Long-term care decisions: Ethical and conceptual dimensions* (pp. 35–59). Baltimore: Johns Hopkins University Press.

Wolinsky, F. D. (1990). *Health and health behavior among elderly Americans: An age-stratification perspective.* New York: Springer.

Wolinsky, F. D., & Johnson, R. J. (1991). The use of health services by older adults. *Journal of Gerontology, 46,* S345–S357.

# Chapter Six

# Determinants of Applications for Nursing Home Placement among Frail African American and White Elders

Although racial disparities in the rates of utilization of nursing homes have been closing over the past 30 years, it is still estimated that African American elders are admitted to nursing homes at between one-half and three-fourths of the rate of White elders (Belgrave, Wykle, & Choi, 1993; Hing, 1987). The previous chapter also found that the rate of applications for nursing home admission among African American elders is much lower than that among their White peers.

The realization that Whites, like the very old, have an increased chance of being institutionalized was already apparent during the 1950s and 1960s (Riley, 1968). Palmore (1976) corroborated those conclusions when analyzing the data of the First Duke Longitudinal Study of Aging, adding that a lower level of educational attainment plus lack of income similarly reduced access to nursing home care. However, Palmore also found that the lower rates of institutionalization among African Americans held constant even after income and educational differentials were controlled for, and thus surmised that race itself had to be the explanation for what appeared to be limited access to nursing home care. A majority of studies that ensued found time and again the lower rate of nursing home placements among African American elders, despite their generally lower physical and functional health status and even after instrumental support from informal support networks was controlled for (Belgrave & Bradsher, 1994; see the literature review section of Chapter 5 for other relevant studies).

In continuation of the analysis in Chapter 5, this chapter, utilizing data from the National Long-Term Care Channeling Demonstration study of 1982–1984, examines factors associated with the differential rates of applications for institutional services between the two ethnic groups in reference.

We begin with a summary of findings of previous studies of racial differences in health status and institutionalization. The analytical framework for analysis is again the expanded Andersen–Newman (Andersen & Newman, 1973) behavioral model of health services utilization.

## RACIAL DIFFERENCES IN THE ELDERLY'S HEALTH STATUS

Studies of racial differences in health status present unanimous findings, namely, that older African Americans suffer from higher levels of physical and functional impairment and higher rates of mortality than older Whites. Clark and Maddox (1992), utilizing 10-year data from the longitudinal Retirement History Survey for those aged 58 to 63 in 1969, found that African Americans had mean levels of impairment one-and-a-half times higher than the levels of nonblacks. Other studies documented higher mortality and morbidity rates among African American adults for conditions such as arthritis, cancer, hypertension, diabetes, diseases of the circulatory system, nervous and mental disorders, and functional impairment (Bernard, 1993; Manton, Patrick, & Johnson, 1987). Research by Schoenbaum and Waidmann (1997), based on the more recent Asset and Health Dynamics Among the Oldest Old (AHEAD) study, shows that the self-rated health of African Americans is significantly worse than that of their White counterparts. African American men and women also reported significantly higher prevalence of hypertension, diabetes, stroke, and arthritis, although they reported lower prevalence of lung disease, heart problems, and, for women only, cancer. African Americans had significantly higher functional impairments—walking several blocks, lifting 10 pounds, going up stairs, walking across a room, and showering/bathing.

Differences in health status between African Americans and Whites have often been attributed to socially determined factors, including differences in lifestyle and health behavior, differences in access to medical care resulting from differences in the socioeconomic statuses (SES) of the two groups, different knowledge of health practice, different occupational and environmental exposure to risk factors, and racism (Schoenbaum & Waidman, 1997, p. 61). Especially in regard to the effect lower economic status has on African Americans' health vis-à-vis Whites, previous studies found that SES explained a substantial portion, but not all, of the racial difference in mortality, morbidity, and self-reported health status. Mutchler and Burr (1991) found that when they controlled for differences in wealth, income, education, and access to private health insurance, the African American disadvantage was narrowed or eliminated in an index of functional limitation and an index of mobility, but not in self-rated general health, among those aged 55 and over in 1984. Clark and Maddox (1992) also found that controlling for income and education attenuated but did not eliminate the racial differences in chronic illness, functional limitation, and self-rated health status. Schoenbaum and Waidman

(1997) report that the differences in SES accounted for three-fourths or more of African American/White differences in most measures of health status—physical function, functional ability, and self-rated health status—for both men and women. Schoenbaum and Waidman also found, through their simulations of the effects of improved SES, that marginal increases in SES generally had larger positive effects on the health of African Americans than on the health of Whites, particularly in measures of physical function. The authors' interpretation of this finding was that, because of the existence of discrimination, declines in SES may diminish the health of African Americans more than a similar decline would diminish the health of Whites (p. 71).

In conjunction with the findings of African American adults' general health disadvantage compared to White adults, many previous studies also attempted to answer the question of whether such health differentials between Whites and African Americans increase with age. Two hypotheses that have been forwarded to test this question are (1) the *double jeopardy hypothesis* and (2) the *age-as-a-leveler hypothesis*. The double jeopardy hypothesis posits that being both old and a member of a minority group creates a double disadvantage to the health of people in this subpopulation (Dowd & Bengtson, 1978; Ferraro, 1987). Racial discrimination throughout one's life and age discrimination in later life may have a combined negative impact on health and mortality of minorities (Hummer, 1996). Thus, age is likely to amplify the racial differences in health status. The age-as-a-leveler hypothesis, in contrast to the double jeopardy hypothesis, posits that aging is likely to level or attenuate the racial differences in health status for the following reasons: (1) public income-maintenance programs that serve the older population (e.g., SSI) in effect help improve the economic status of African Americans in old age and thus reduce the racial gap in SES in old age; (2) aging brings such basic challenges to health and functional ability that racial inequality is not as important; and/or (3) minority persons adopt coping strategies throughout their life course to deal with racial discrimination, and this helps them deal with age discrimination (Ferraro & Farmer, 1996).

Recent empirical studies that tested these hypotheses generally show some evidence supporting the double jeopardy hypothesis, indicating that health inequalities that are present early in life continue in later life. Based on 15-year longitudinal data from the National Health and Nutrition Examination Survey—I Epidemiological Follow-up Study, Ferraro and Farmer (1996) found that lower education, less income, having a regular physician, and being on Medicaid (characteristics that are more prevalent among African Americans than among Whites) were associated with more rapid declines in selected measures of health. In terms of chronic illness and disability, older African Americans were worse off than their White peers, and the racial gap was wider among older than younger people. But Ferraro and Farmer (1996) also found that, in terms of mortality, the African American disadvantage leveled off in later years (after the 1970s or 1980s) and that greater age changes in impairment among African Americans who survived were not present, lending some evidence to selective survival as a leveler (Clark & Maddox, 1992; Ferraro & Farmer, 1996; Gibson, 1994).

## THEORETICAL PERSPECTIVES ON RACIAL DIFFERENCES IN NURSING HOME UTILIZATION

The double jeopardy and the age-as-a-leveler hypotheses also serve as major theoretical perspectives for the explanation of racial disparities in the rates of nursing home placement (Belgrave et al., 1993). Within the framework of the double jeopardy hypothesis, the lower utilization rate of nursing homes by African Americans than by White elders is conceptualized as deriving from interaction between the racism throughout life and the age discrimination in later life that block procurement of adequate health resources.

Do lower rates of institutionalization constitute ipso facto evidence of discrimination? Jackson (1988) cautions that allegations of possible bias are often based on the unverified assumption that the lower rates of African American placement in nursing homes, as compared to Whites, confirm the presence of such discriminatory practices in admissions. Race per se may not be a cause of discriminatory practice in the admissions process, but lower socioeconomic conditions that are closely associated with the African American race are likely to cause both discrimination by nursing homes as well the shunning of nursing homes by minority elders and their families. Petchers and Milligan (1988) found that affordability was a major barrier to medical care for a sample of poor minority elderly, despite high enrollment rates in Medicare and Medicaid. Given that public insurance programs do not provide 100% coverage of health care expenses, these elderly had difficulty in meeting the uncovered portions and were less likely to buy supplemental private health insurance. Out-of-pocket charges are a burden even when public insurance coverage is available, and hence poor people tend to avoid formal service use.

Under the age-as-a-leveler hypothesis, the lower rate of institutionalization among African Americans is conceptualized as the result of the mortality crossover and the selective survival of healthier older African American persons who have relatively less need for institutionalization. As discussed earlier, however, empirical data show that African American elders suffer from poorer health than White elders, and despite their poorer health, African American elders are less likely to be institutionalized. Thus, the age-as-a-leveler hypothesis is not supported at all. But the true test of this hypothesis may need to be conducted by comparing the utilization rates of health care services other than nursing homes with the utilization rate of nursing homes by different age groups of African American elders vis-à-vis those of White elders.

In addition to these two perspectives, a third theoretical perspective has been advanced to explain the lower rate of nursing home placement among African Americans. This perspective interprets race as a sociocultural modality, which may preclude the option of institutional placement because it is viewed as antithetical to the dominant values in the African American community. This *cultural aversion hypothesis* (Morrison, 1983) postulates that minority families—and African Americans especially—prefer to take care of their own elders because placing them in institutions might be experienced as a stigma. The African American cultural values emphasizing strong family ties and their preference for caring for the aged at home may be reflected in the higher rate of coresidence of African American elderly parents and adult children than is found among their White counterparts (Belgrave et al., 1993).

A recent review and analysis of the empirical research on the impact of race, culture, and/or ethnicity on the dementia caregiving experience indicates that the majority of the studies confirmed cultural differences in the following aspects: Compared to White caregivers, (1) African American (and Hispanic) caregivers were more likely to be extended families—adult children, other family members, and friends; (2) African American caregivers reported lower levels of caregiver stress, burden, and strain, and higher levels of caregiving mastery and satisfaction, even though they expressed a greater need for services and reported more unmet service needs; (3) African American caregivers reported more traditional caregiving ideology and more strongly held attitudes of filial support, and they were more likely to use prayer, faith, or religion as a coping mechanism (Connell & Gibson, 1997).

Gibson (1988) also underscored the importance of what she describes as "special help-seeking paradigms" in the life of African American elders. As compared to White elders, African American elders draw from a more varied pool of informal helpers and are more flexible and versatile in the manipulation, substitution, and complementation of all these sources of help. Johnson and Barer (1990) similarly found that inner-city older African Americans compensate for the lack of stable family supports with extensive friendship and associational networks. These older persons have a unique ability to create extensions of their biological kinship systems that result in "dense and often emotionally supportive networks" (p. 732) of distant relatives and friends. These fictive kin are thus assigned the roles of more immediate relatives and take on the rights and obligations of real kin. In the same vein, African American churches also create "spiritual families" and assign kinship terms to their members, consequently forging effective support systems.

Morrison (1983), though confirming the validity of the cultural hypothesis in her own study, warned against its unqualified acceptance. The hypothesis may work only up to a point, and may be conditioned by each family's stamina, endurance, and access to the material resources needed to sustain the informal care. Morrison also mentioned the danger of "overselling" the hypothesis, that is, using it as a rationalization for justifying the unavailability or even the denial of services. There is also the possibility of a self-fulfilling prophecy, when hospital staff, guided by the assumptions of such a "cultural aversion" hypothesis, do not refer African American patients to nursing homes.

In fact, a recent study that analyzed posthospital home care of elders found that African American elders used more informal and less formal care but rated the quality and quantity of care lower than White elders (Chadiha, Proctor, Morrow-Howell, Darkwa, & Dore, 1995). Another recent study, based on data on 3,793 functionally impaired persons age 65 and over from the 1989 National Long-Term Care Survey, found no differences by race in the size of caregiving networks that assist older disabled people (Burton, Kasper, Shore, Cagney, LaVeist, Cubbin, & German, 1995). The racial difference was found in the composition of the unpaid caregiving network: Older disabled African Americans had a greater likelihood of having at least one caregiver who was not part of the immediate family. Thus, this finding parallels those of Gibson (1988) and Johnson and Barer (1990), which showed a more varied source of informal support among African American elders; it also shows, however, that the size of the informal support network of African American elders is not bigger than that of White elders.

The empirical test of these theoretical perspectives on racial differences in nursing home utilization has not yet been conducted. Because of the limitations of the data set, we are not able to successfully test the hypotheses either. But in this chapter we use the three perspectives as a backdrop in our analysis of factors associated with the disparate rates of nursing home applications among African American and White frail elders. As in the previous chapter, the main conceptual and analytical framework advanced here draws from the expanded Andersen–Newman (Andersen & Newman, 1973) behavioral model. Four sets of variables were consequently hypothesized as correlating with nursing home applications: (1) elderly sociodemographic factors, (2) elderly need factors, (3) elderly psychological-disposition factors, and (4) the availability and use of informal and formal supports. We also hope that the interrelationship of these clusters of variables in explaining the racial differences in nursing home applications will provide additional insight on the three theoretical perspectives. We think that the psychological-disposition and social-support variables are especially likely to shed light on the cultural perspective.

## METHODOLOGY

### Data Source and Sample

This chapter utilizes data from the National Long-Term Care Channeling Demonstration that was initiated in 1980 by the U.S. Department of Health and Human Services. For a detailed description of the data set, refer to Chapter 2.

## Measurement of Variables

The dependent variable—nursing home placement—was dichotomously coded, with 1 indicating elderly persons who had applied for nursing home care in the preceding year, or had been wait-listed for nursing home placement. They were labeled the preinstitutional group (because their nursing home admission was pending). A 0 code designated those who had neither applied for nursing home placement nor been wait-listed. They were referred to as the noninstitutional group. The preinstitutional group totaled 375 respondents, as compared to 5,028 in the noninstitutional group, or 7% and 93%, respectively.

The elderly sociodemographic variables included race/ethnicity, age, gender, income, and living arrangement (alone or with others). Older persons' "need" variables were (1) cognitive impairment, (2) ADL impairment, (3) number of medical problems, and (4) perceived unmet needs (ADL and IADL). Cognitive impairment was measured by the SPMSQ, a 10-item test of mental functioning. No impairment or mild impairment was indicated by 9 to 10 correct answers out of a possible 10, moderate impairment by 6 to 8 correct answers, and severe impairment by 0 to 5 correct answers. Impairment in ADL was measured by asking respondents if they had been helped during the preceding week in the following five ADL domains: eating, bathing, dressing, toileting, and getting out of bed or a chair. Chronic medical problems were measured by asking the respondents to report whether they had suffered from the following conditions: anemia, high blood pressure, heart disease, stroke, diabetes, arthritis, cancer, Parkinson's disease, respiratory problems, skin problems, paralysis, orthopedic problems, vision or hearing problems, and other health problems. Perceived unmet needs were measured by asking the respondents if they needed more help in those ADL and IADL areas.

Psychological-disposition variable included (1) feeling of control in life and (2) attitude toward nursing home placement. Feeling of control in life was a composite score of the following five questions: (1) "In general, how satisfying do you find the way you're spending your life these days? Would you call it completely satisfying, pretty satisfying, or not very satisfying?" (2) "Day to day, how much choice do you have about what you do and when you do it? Would you say a great deal of choice, some choice, or not very much choice?" (3) "How confident are you of figuring out how to deal with your problems? Would you say you feel very confident, somewhat confident, or not very confident?" (4) "How much do you worry about not knowing whom to turn to for help? Would you say you worry a lot, some, or not very much?" (5) "How confident are you of getting services when you need them? Would you say you feel very confident, somewhat confident, or not very confident?" These were rated on a three-point scale, with the high score indicating an unfavorable rating. In order to summarize the data and to avoid the problem of multicollinearity, a principal components analysis with varimax rotation was performed and yielded one component. These five items were highly correlated, with factor loadings ranging from .56 to .71. The scores of these five items were added to form the feeling-of-control-in-life composite measure (alpha coefficient = .74). Attitude toward nursing home placement was measured by a four-point scale, with 1 being acceptable and 4 being totally unacceptable ("would rather die than to go to nursing home").

The use of informal and formal supports variables included (1) frequency of social contacts (in the preceding week with family members and/or friends who lived apart), (2) number of informal helpers, (3) number of formal care providers, and (4) total number of formal services used.

## Methods of Analysis

First, bivariate analysis compared all African American and White sample members with respect to their sociodemographic characteristics, physical, functional, and cognitive impairments, formal and informal support, and psychosocial dispositions. Then, preinstitutional African American frail elders were compared with preinstitutional White frail elders on their sociodemographic characteristics, health status, formal and informal support, and nursing home placement attitudes. Finally, two separate parallel logistic regression models were used to analyze the determinants of nursing home applications within the African American and White samples. For dependent variables, African American and White frail elders in the preinstitutional group were given a value of 1, and those in the noninstitutional group were given a value of 0. In line with the Andersen–Newman model, the logistic regression models included the following cluster of independent variables: four sociodemographic variables—age (80 years and older = 1, other = 0), gender (male = 1, female = 0), Medicaid (receiving = 1, not receiving = 0; Medicaid, instead of income, was chosen, because it is believed to be more appropriate as an enabling factor within each group), and living arrangement (alone = 1, with others = 0)—as predisposing and/or enabling variables; four need and condition variables—cognitive impairment (SPSQM score), number of ADL impairments, number of perceived unmet needs in terms of ADL and IADL impairments, and number of items of depressive symptomatology; and three informal and formal support variables—frequency of social contact, number of informal helpers, and number of formal services utilized. In addition, the model included two psychological-disposition variables—attitude toward nursing home placement (not acceptable or totally unacceptable = 1; acceptable or minimally acceptable = 0) and sense of control in life (higher score reflecting higher sense of control).

## RESULTS

### Bivariate Analysis of African American and White Frail Elders

A comparison of the profiles of the African American and White study participants is presented in Table 6.1. As observed, African Americans numbered 1,272, or 23.5% of the total national sample of frail elderly. There were several significant sociodemographic differences between the two ethnic groups: Whites tended to be an older (51.7% were aged 80 years or older as compared to 46.4% of the African Americans), better-educated, and higher-income group, and more of them either were married or lived alone. Conversely, fewer African Americans lived alone, as more resided with children and "others" (relatives, friends, or neighbors; 20.1% of African Americans versus only 7.9% of Whites in this category), and they were more dependent on Medicaid to cover health expenses.

Table 6.2 points to significant differences in the health status of the two groups. African Americans had an obvious disadvantage in the areas of functional capacities (ADL), incontinence, and cognitive ability, and they reported significantly higher numbers of perceived unmet needs with respect to their difficulties with ADL and IADL. African Americans also reported slightly more medical conditions than Whites. (Further analysis showed that African Americans had higher rates of anemia, high blood pressure, stroke, diabetes, arthritis, paralysis, and vision impairment. Whites, in turn, had more pronounced rates of cancer and neurological, respiratory, orthopedic, dermatologic, and hearing problems.) But Whites showed significantly more depressive symptoms. In terms of self-assessment of health, the two groups appear to be on a par in practical sense, although the statistical test indicated a marginal difference.

Table 6.3 shows Whites also tending to be more frequent consumers of formal health services, such as regular medical care, outpatient visits to doctors' offices, home-delivered meals, and counseling. Although the two groups had practically the same rates of hospitalization in the preceding two months, the temporary use of nursing home care in either of the preceding two- or six-month intervals—possibly for posthospital convalescence and/or rehabilitation—appears to be far higher among Whites. African Americans, on the other hand, relied more heavily on their less-formal community-based supports, including their social, recreational, and religious membership organizations. African Americans also had statistically significantly more informal helpers than did Whites, although the real numerical difference (2.2 for African Americans versus 1.9 for Whites) does not appear to be substantial.

When it came to applying for nursing home care, the differences between the two groups became more pronounced: 5.2% of the Whites were already accepted and wait-listed for admission, as compared to only half as many, or

Table 6.1
Sociodemographic Characteristics of African American and White Frail Elders

|  | African American[a] n = 1,272 | White[a] n = 4,133 |
|---|---|---|
| **Age ****** | | |
| 65 to 69 | 14.5% | 10.7% |
| 70 to 74 | 18.5 | 15.4 |
| 75 to 79 | 20.6 | 22.1 |
| 80 to 84 | 22.6 | 23.3 |
| 85 to 89 | 13.7 | 18.2 |
| >=90 | 10.1 | 10.2 |
| **Gender** | | |
| Female | 70.7% | 71.9% |
| Male | 29.3 | 28.1 |
| **Marital status******** | | |
| Married | 26.4% | 33.0% |
| Not married | 73.6 | 67.0 |
| **Education******** | | |
| None or elementary | 71.3% | 57.5% |
| Some secondary | 14.0 | 13.9 |
| Completed high school | 8.0 | 16.8 |
| Completed college | 5.7 | 9.5 |
| Post college | 0.9 | 2.2 |
| **Living arrangement******** | | |
| Alone | 31.2% | 39.7% |
| With spouses | 25.2 | 32.3 |
| With children | 23.5 | 20.1 |
| With others | 20.1 | 7.9 |
| **Financial condition** | | |
| Monthly income | | |
| Mean ($)******** | $464.0 | $594.0 |
| <$500 | 75.4% | 38.6% |
| $500 to $999 | 16.9% | 42.0% |
| >=$1,000 | 7.7% | 19.4% |
| SSI receipt******** | 29.3% | 12.0% |
| Medicaid receipt******** | 35.1% | 16.7% |

*Data Source*: National Long-Term Care Channeling Demonstration, 1982–1984.
[a]None was of Hispanic origin.
****$p < 0.0001$.

2.6%, of the African Americans ($p$ = < 0.0001). The gap was slightly narrower among those who had applied in the preceding two months but had not yet been formally accepted (6.3% and 4.2%, respectively; $p < 0.01$). By combining those already wait-listed and those who had applied in the preceding two months, a subsample of preinstitutional respondents was created, with 7.6%

**Table 6.2**
**Medical and Functional Status of African American and White Frail Elders**

|  | African American $\underline{n} = 1,272$ | White $\underline{n} = 4,133$ |
|---|---|---|
| **Medical conditions** | | |
| Anemia**** | 24.0% | 17.3% |
| High blood pressure**** | 51.6 | 40.0 |
| Heart disease | 46.2 | 49.4 |
| Stroke**** | 36.1 | 28.2 |
| Diabetes**** | 24.9 | 19.7 |
| Arthritis* | 73.8 | 69.6 |
| Cancer* | 11.0 | 11.3 |
| Parkinson's disease**** | 21.8 | 22.8 |
| Respiratory problems**** | 18.5 | 27.9 |
| Skin problems**** | 20.8 | 24.9 |
| Orthopedic disease**** | 9.6 | 16.5 |
| Paralysis**** | 18.0 | 13.1 |
| Vision problem**** | 40.2 | 35.9 |
| Hearing problem**** | 13.4 | 19.1 |
| Smoking**** | 13.8 | 12.5 |
| **Perceived health status*** | | |
| Excellent | 2.6% | 2.8% |
| Good | 15.3 | 15.1 |
| Fair | 31.0 | 29.7 |
| Poor | 51.1 | 52.5 |
| **ADL impairment**** | | |
| Mild or none | 15.4% | 20.9% |
| Moderately severe | 23.3 | 22.7 |
| Very severe | 33.7 | 35.2 |
| Extremely severe | 27.7 | 21.2 |
| **Impairment in continence**** | 54.2% | 45.1% |
| **Cognitive impairment**** | | |
| None or mild | 47.2% | 51.0% |
| Moderate | 38.4 | 32.4 |
| Severe | 14.4 | 16.6 |
| **No. of medical conditions*** | 4.9 | 4.7 |
| **No. of depressive symptoms**** | 3.0 | 3.7 |
| **No. of unmet perceived needs (ADL & IADL)**** | 4.6 | 3.8 |

*Data Source*: National Long-Term Care Channeling Demonstration, 1982–1984.
*p < 0.05; **p < 0.01; ***p < 0.001; ****p < 0.0001.

**Table 6.3**
**Formal and Informal Supports of African American and White Frail Elders**

|  | African American $\underline{n}$ = 1,272 | White $\underline{n}$ = 4,133 |
|---|---|---|
| **Medical service use** | | |
| Regular medical care* | 89.9% | 92.0% |
| Used hospital in preceding 2 months | 69.3% | 69.5% |
| No. of doctor visits* | 1.7 | 1.8 |
| No. of hospital days in preceding 2 months | 19.1 | 18.7 |
| **In-home service use** | | |
| Regular home care | 28.0% | 30.3% |
| Meals on Wheels**** | 11.8% | 17.5% |
| **Community-based service use** | | |
| Congregate meals | 3.4% | 4.5% |
| Health program | 0.8% | 2.1% |
| Social center or church**** | 15.8% | 12.0% |
| Counseling* | 3.6% | 5.1% |
| No. of formal helpers (mean)**** | 0.9 | 1.1 |
| No. of formal services used (mean)[a]*** | 1.5 | 1.6 |
| **Institutional service use** | | |
| Used nursing home in preceding 6 months* | 4.0% | 10.1% |
| Used nursing home in preceding 2 months* | 42.4% | 53.5% |
| Had applied for nursing home admission [b]**** | 2.6% | 5.2% |
| **Informal support** | | |
| No. of informal helpers (mean)**** | 2.2 | 1.9 |
| No. of social contacts (mean) | 1.7 | 1.7 |

*Data Source*: National Long-Term Care Channeling Demonstration, 1982–1984.
[a]Total number of formal services used included home care, Meals on Wheels, congregate meals, health program, social center, church, and counseling.
[b]Includes those who had applied but were not yet accepted and those who had been accepted and wait-listed.
*$p < 0.05$; **$p < 0.01$; ***$p < 0.001$; ****$p < 0.0001$.

of the Whites and 5.1% of the African Americans falling into this category. The difference remained statistically significant, at the $p < 0.01$ level.

Despite their higher level of disability, more African American than White elders reported that they felt their life was completely satisfying or somewhat satisfying and that they were confident of their ability to deal with problems. In terms of sense of choice/control, a slightly higher proportion of White elders believed that they had a great deal of choice. Nevertheless, African American elders were again less likely to worry about where they would turn for help and more likely to feel confident that they would get services when needed. Probably because of their confidence in getting necessary services in the community, African American elders were more likely to indicate that nursing home placement would be either not acceptable or totally unacceptable (72.7% of African Americans versus 65.9% of Whites).

Separate from racial comparison, overall assessment of data in Table 6.4 reveals a stark picture of the psychosocial well-being of both African American and White frail elders. That is, close to one-third of African American elders

Table 6.4
**Psychosocial Characteristics of African American and White Frail Elders**

|  | African American<br>n = 1,272<br>(%) | White<br>n = 4,133<br>(%) |
|---|---|---|
| **Life satisfaction****** | | |
| Completely satisfying | 23.9 | 16.2 |
| Somewhat satisfying | 44.3 | 35.8 |
| Not very satisfying | 31.8 | 48.0 |
| **Sense of choice/control*** | | |
| A great deal of choice | 28.2 | 32.5 |
| Some choice | 26.3 | 22.3 |
| Not very much choice | 45.5 | 45.2 |
| **Confident of ability to deal<br>with problems****** | | |
| Very confident | 44.0 | 32.5 |
| Somewhat confident | 34.3 | 37.4 |
| Not very confident | 21.7 | 30.1 |
| **Worried about not knowing to<br>whom to turn for help****** | | |
| Not very much | 57.1 | 44.5 |
| Some | 17.8 | 21.6 |
| A lot | 25.1 | 33.9 |
| **Confident of ability to get<br>services when needed**** | | |
| Very confident | 40.7 | 33.9 |
| Somewhat confident | 33.0 | 35.8 |
| Not very confident | 26.3 | 30.3 |
| **Nursing home placement<br>attitude***** | | |
| Acceptable | 4.3 | 4.8 |
| Minimally acceptable | 23.0 | 29.2 |
| Not acceptable | 6.4 | 5.6 |
| Totally unacceptable (would rather die) | 66.3 | 60.3 |

*Data Source*: National Long-Term Care Channeling Demonstration, 1982–1984.
$*p < 0.05$; $**p < 0.01$; $***p < 0.001$; $****p < 0.0001$.

and one-half of White elders indicated that their life was "not very" satisfying, and one-fourth of African Americans and one-third of Whites worried "a lot" about whom they would turn to for help. In the same vein, more than 26% to 30% of them felt "not very" confident of their ability to get services when needed. Not knowing where and how needed assistance would be obtained must be a real source of anxiety and frustration for these frail elders. Moreover, a majority of them considered a nursing home bed to be an unacceptable choice. In short, it appears that a large proportion of these elders suffered from poor psychosocial health as much as from poor physical and functional health. It would not be inaccurate to project that, with deteriorating health and limited sources of assistance, the rest of the elders were also at risk for experiencing deteriorating psychosocial well-being in the near future.

## Bivariate Analysis of Preinstitutional African American and White Frail Elders

The second procedural step consisted of focusing the analysis specifically on both the African American and White frail elders that fell in the newly identified preinstitutional category. The objectives were (1) to establish whether the differences and similarities noted in the previous bivariate analysis of characteristics of the two racial groups still held when contrasting the preinstitutional African American and White subsamples; (2) to capture within-group differences by conducting parallel logistic regression analysis separately for Whites and African Americans (the aim of this procedure was to determine the extent to which the preinstitutional group of each ethnic sample resembled its noninstitutional counterparts); and (3) to find out whether the same predictor variables hold for the two ethnic groups.

As shown in data in Table 6.5, many of the differences noted in the total population of African American and White respondents (as reported in Tables 6.1, 6.2, and 6.3) have been narrowed or no longer reach statistical significance in the preinstitutional subgroups. The only sociodemographic variables that retain such significance are, first, income, with African Americans' average income falling 33% below Whites', and, second and consistent with the preceding difference, Medicaid, with more than twice as many African Americans as Whites (42.2% versus 19.3%, respectively) reported utilizing Medicaid or public assistance coverage for their medical care.

On the whole, both preinstitutional subsamples retained the same profile noted in the parent samples of African American and White frail elders. There are, however, some exceptions, as both African American and White preinstitutional subsamples contained higher proportions of males and those living with someone than did the total samples.

As shown in Table 6.6, in physical and functional health statuses the medical profile of the two preinstitutional subsamples become more similar, but African

**Table 6.5**
**Sociodemographic Characteristics of African American and White Frail Elders Who Were Pending for Nursing Home Admission**

| | African American[a] $\underline{n} = 64^b$ | White[a] $\underline{n} = 300^b$ |
|---|---|---|
| **Age** | | |
| 65 to 69 | 12.5% | 8.0% |
| 70 to 74 | 17.2 | 13.7 |
| 75 to 79 | 20.3 | 24.0 |
| 80 to 84 | 14.1 | 24.0 |
| 85 to 89 | 17.2 | 18.7 |
| >=90 | 18.8 | 11.6 |
| **Gender** | | |
| Female | 65.5% | 71.0% |
| Male | 37.5 | 29.0 |
| **Marital status** | | |
| Married | 25.0% | 33.3% |
| Not married | 75.0 | 66.7 |
| **Education** | | |
| None or elementary | 78.1% | 62.0% |
| Some secondary | 10.9 | 10.0 |
| Completed high school | 6.3 | 17.3 |
| Completed college | 4.7 | 9.7 |
| Postcollege | 0.0 | 1.0 |
| **Living arrangement** | | |
| Alone | 25.0% | 34.8% |
| With others | 75.0 | 65.2 |
| **Medicaid receipt****** | 42.2% | 19.3% |
| **Monthly income (mean)*****| $394.0 | $588.0 |

*Data Source*: National Long-Term Care Channeling Demonstration, 1982–1984.
*Note*: Chi-square and *t* statistics were used.
[a]None was of Hispanic origin.
[b]The nursing home pending subsample for African Americans was 5.1% and 7.6% for Whites. Chi-square test indicated that these proportions were significant ($p = 0.003$).
****$p < 0.0001$.

Americans appear to be much more severely impaired than White elders in terms of their ADL and cognitive functional levels. Whites, although objectively in better functional shape, subjectively assessed their health condition more negatively, as "poor."

The greater similarities between the two preinstitutional subsamples are also manifested in their patterns of utilization of formal health services, both

Table 6.6
**Medical and Functional Status of African American and White Frail Elders Who Were Pending for Nursing Home Admission**

|  | African American<br>$\underline{n} = 64$<br>(%) | White<br>$\underline{n} = 300$<br>(%) |
|---|---|---|
| **Medical conditions** |  |  |
| Anemia | 23.7 | 15.7 |
| High blood pressure | 49.2 | 40.6 |
| Heart disease | 51.7 | 46.5 |
| Stroke | 41.9 | 34.8 |
| Diabetes[a] | 27.4 | 17.1 |
| Arthritis | 66.1 | 67.0 |
| Cancer | 14.3 | 13.2 |
| Neurological problems | 26.6 | 23.3 |
| Respiratory problems | 15.6 | 24.8 |
| Skin problems | 28.1 | 30.1 |
| Orthopedic problems | 10.9 | 19.2 |
| Paralysis | 22.2 | 14.2 |
| Vision problem | 49.2 | 41.8 |
| Hearing problem | 20.6 | 23.5 |
| **Perceived health status** |  |  |
| Excellent | 3.2 | 3.0 |
| Good | 17.5 | 14.9 |
| Fair | 23.8 | 22.0 |
| Poor | 55.6 | 60.1 |
| **ADL impairment*** |  |  |
| Mild or none | 10.9 | 14.7 |
| Moderately severe | 9.4 | 21.0 |
| Very severe | 32.8 | 34.7 |
| Extremely severe | 46.9 | 29.7 |
| **Impairment in continence** | 56.3 | 47.0 |
| **Cognitive impairment**** |  |  |
| None or mild | 17.0 | 38.7 |
| Moderate | 57.6 | 35.9 |
| Severe | 25.4 | 25.3 |

*Data Source*: National Long-Term Care Channeling Demonstration, 1982–1984.
*Note*: Chi-square statistics were used.
[a]$p = 0.059$; *$p < 0.05$; **$p < 0.01$.

inpatient and outpatient, as shown in Table 6.7. But African Americans had slightly more informal helpers and significantly more unmet needs, and at the same levels previously observed in their parent sample (2.2 versus 1.9 for Whites, $p < 0.05$ for informal helpers, and 4.6 versus 3.9 for Whites, $p < 0.001$ for unmet needs). Finally, as compared to their parent samples, both African

**Table 6.7**
**Formal and Informal Supports of African American and White Frail Elders Who Were Pending for Nursing Home Admission**

|  | African American $\underline{n} = 64$ | White $\underline{n} = 300$ |
|---|---|---|
| **Medical service use** | | |
| Regular medical care | 84.1% | 89.3% |
| Used hospital in preceding 2 months | 77.8% | 76.6% |
| No of doctor visits[a] | 2.2 | 1.5 |
| No. of hospital days in preceding 2 months | 21.5 | 21.1 |
| **In-home service use** | | |
| Regular home care | 23.4% | 33.9% |
| Meals on Wheels | 12.7% | 13.8% |
| **Community-based service use** | | |
| Congregate meals* | 0.0% | 9.2% |
| Health program | 4.0% | 2.4% |
| Social center or church | 7.9% | 12.1% |
| Counseling | 6.2% | 3.5% |
| **Institutional service use** | | |
| Used nursing home in preceding 6 months | 7.8% | 15.1% |
| Used nursing home in preceding 2 months | 50.0% | 70.0% |
| **No. of informal helpers*** | 2.2 | 1.9 |
| **Nursing home placement attitude** | | |
| Acceptable | 26.9% | 17.0% |
| Minimally acceptable | 34.6 | 36.4 |
| Not acceptable | 0.0 | 11.0 |
| Totally unacceptable (would rather die) | 38.5 | 35.6 |

*Data Source*: National Long-Term Care Channeling Demonstration, 1982–1984.
*Note*: Chi-square and *t* statistics were used.
[a]$p = 0.056$; *$p < 0.05$; **$p < 0.001$.

American and White preinstitutional groups revealed a much higher rate of previous use of long-term institutional services, but this pattern accelerated far more rapidly among Whites than among African Americans.

It is noteworthy to find a relatively high level of rejection of institutional placement in a population—both African American and White—that had already applied for and/or was expecting receipt of precisely such services. As observed in Table 6.7, there was no statistically significant difference between the two preinstitutional groups as far as their psychological/attitudinal disposition toward nursing home living. But more than one-third (38.5%) of the African Americans and nearly one-half of the Whites (46.5%) who had

applied or been wait-listed for nursing home admission still vehemently re-
jected the thought of such placement, a fact suggesting that their application
may have been done against their will, by their caregivers or surrogates. They
may also have abhorred the thought and even "preferred to die" rather than
move into a nursing home, but may have realized that they had exhausted all
other options. They may also have decided that they would not be able to
continue imposing and requiring sacrifices from their informal caregivers. In
any event, the rate of nursing home acceptability (the "acceptable" or "minimally acceptable" categories) barely exceeded the 50% level (51.5% for African Americans and 53.4% for Whites). Ambivalence, resentment, and
possible resignation may characterize the emotional disposition of the other
half lined up for imminent placement or review of their applications.

## Multivariate Analysis

As detailed in Table 6.8, the logistic regression coefficients show that the two
racial groups share the same three main predictors of institutional application:
(1) a higher prevalence of cognitive impairments (odds ratios = 2.55 for African Americans and 1.45 for Whites); (2) a more positive attitude toward institutionalization (odds ratios = 4.42 for African Americans and 2.56 for Whites);
and (3) a higher previous frequency and experience of formal services utilization (odds ratios = 3.21 for African Americans and 3.59 for Whites). The
positive association between the likelihood of nursing home applications
and the higher degree of cognitive impairment and the higher number of
formal services used confirms the findings of previous studies of nursing
home admissions. Caution is required, however, in interpreting the positive
relationship between the likelihood of nursing home application and the
attitude toward nursing home placement. The comparatively more positive
attitude among the preinstitutional groups than among the noninstitutional
groups may be a reflection of learned psychological disposition, rather than
a predisposition resulting from a sense of resignation or acquiescence in the
face of the inevitability of the prospective nursing home placement.

The logistic regression coefficients show that these three variables are the
only significant predictors of nursing home application among African
Americans. For Whites, in addition to these three predictors, older age
(those aged 80 years and older), higher number of functional impairments
(ADL), and higher number of unmet needs (in regard to ADL and IADL)
were found to be significant predictors of nursing home applications.

Thus, the findings of multivariate analysis indicate that the determinants
of nursing home application (and, subsequently, admission) among African
American frail elders are not quite the same as those among White frail elders. Especially given the insignificance among African Americans of age,
level of functional impairments, and unmet needs, the sweeping application

Table 6.8
Logistic Regression Analysis of Nursing Home Pending Frail Elders

| Variables | African American Coefficients (SE) | Odds Ratio | White Coefficients (SE) | Odds Ratio |
|---|---|---|---|---|
| **Predisposing variables** | | | | |
| Sex (male=1; female=0) | 0.32(0.40) | | 0.08(0.22) | |
| Age ( age > 80=1) | 0.64(0.44) | | 0.60(0.19)** | 1.82 |
| Medicaid (yes=1) | 0.39(0.47) | | -0.18(0.25) | |
| Living arrangements (alone=1) | -0.29(0.55) | | 0.40(0.21) | |
| **Need variables** | | | | |
| Cognitive impairments | 0.93(0.29)*** | 2.55 | 0.37(0.12)** | 1.45 |
| ADL impairments | 0.38(0.23) | | 0.23(0.10)* | 1.26 |
| No. of medical conditions | -0.04(0.11) | | 0.08(0.05) | |
| No. of perceived unmet needs | 0.09(0.07) | | 0.09(0.04)* | 1.10 |
| No. of depressive symptoms | 0.05(0.11) | | 0.05(0.05) | |
| **Psychological disposition variables** | | | | |
| Nursing home attitude | 1.48(0.45)** | 4.42 | 0.94(0.19)**** | 2.56 |
| Sense of control in life | 0.03(0.08) | | -0.02(0.03) | |
| **Use of informal and formal support** | | | | |
| Social contacts | 0.19(0.19) | | -0.12(0.09) | |
| No. of informal helpers | 0.03(0.15) | | 0.14(0.09) | |
| Formal service use | 0.46(0.13)**** | 3.21 | 1.28(0.12)**** | 3.59 |
| Intercept | -9.53**** | | -7.02**** | |
| Model chi square | 97.11**** | | 187.67**** | |

Data Source: National Long-Term Care Channeling Demonstration, 1982–1984.
aOdds ratios were calculated for the significant regression coefficients.
*p < 0.05; **p < 0.01; ***p < 0.001; ****p < 0.0001.

to minority elders of the findings of previous studies that consistently identified these three variables as significant determinants of nursing home placement needs to be reconsidered.

## DISCUSSION

The findings of this chapter confirmed that African American frail elders, though younger, had significantly more physical, functional, and cognitive impairments than their White peers. Nevertheless, they were less likely to use formal services (e.g., Meals on Wheels, counseling, and nursing homes) than were Whites. This may be due to a higher proportion of African American elders who coresided with someone and relied on services provided by social centers, churches, and informal helpers. The racial difference in these matters was not substantial, however, although it was statistically significant.

Among the nursing-home pending or preinstitutional elders, African Americans again had more functional and cognitive, if not physical (with the exception of diabetes), impairments than Whites, but their formal service use was not more frequent. Again, it may be because they had more informal helpers and more positive perceptions of their own health, although their health was in fact poorer than that of Whites. This weaker connection to formal service systems may be a reason for African American's significantly lower rate of nursing home application, especially given the magnitude of the significance of formal service use as a predictor of their nursing home applications.

Unlike the number of formal services used, the number of informal helpers was not a significant predictor of nursing home application for African Americans and Whites when they were analyzed separately. Thus, African American as well as White elders who had a smaller number of informal helpers were not more likely to apply for nursing home admission, nor were those who had a larger number of informal helpers less likely to apply. In Chapter 5 (and in previous studies), the number of informal helpers was not found to be a significant factor either.

But the lack of significant difference between the preinstitutional and the noninstitutional groups of African Americans with respect to age, functional impairment, and perception of unmet needs may suggest the following: African American study participants had support systems that were not deterred by their chronic functional impairments (see Connell & Gibson, 1997). Also African American disabled elders either accepted their own frailty with more fortitude and did not make service demands (despite functional impairments that were more severe than those of their White peers) or felt better supported by their informal networks (see data in Table 6.4 regarding their higher confidence and lower level of worry about getting services). In other words, they did not seem as troubled as their White counterparts by presumed deficits in the provision of formal and informal services. This was so despite the fact that the average numbers of informal and formal helpers and the number of formal services used, relative to the degree of their physical and functional disabilities, indicate a clear deficit in service provision.

Informal supports for whites do not appear to be substantially numerically smaller, but they seem to be less available or able to handle both the functional and cognitive disabilities of their dependents. It is therefore not only a question of measuring the size and density of the informal networks, but also of assessing their coping readiness. This racial difference seems to rest with the more effective coping resources found among the African American respondents. Also, White elders may be accustomed to receiving more formal services and, given their better economic status, could invariably afford to pay for such services. Social class considerations may therefore be intervening to explain a higher threshold of demand. Also, given their more pronounced negative self-assessment of their own health, Whites are more apprehensive and feel a greater sense of urgency about receiving intensive care. African Americans, in turn, even when assisted by Medicaid and Medicare, have known throughout their lives the limits to affordability, and they may have consequently internalized a greater sense of self-sufficiency and restraint in the use of formal services. Further, they may have succeeded better than Whites in reaching a viable balance between formal and informal supports.

In short, it is apparent from Table 6.8 that there is greater tolerance for frailties and disabilities among African Americans, both elders and their caregivers. Such tolerance may be a learned adaptation to constraints in available resources and a result of diversified and effective coping strategies. But it may also be a product of such cultural heritage as strong extended familism and respect for elders. As Gibson (1988) observed, even when disabled African American elderly still may constitute a psychological resource and play a vital socialization role in their communities. "Older Blacks [in Gibson's words] maintain control over some valued resources that are associated with the economic and psychological survival of younger family members" (p. 125). Thus, an elderly person at home in the community, even when disabled, may not necessarily be viewed as a burden to his or her relatives and friends.

## SUMMARY

Regrettably, given the content limitations of the original data set, there was no way to ascertain whether real or anticipated discrimination, aging process as a leveler, or a sense of cultural aversion contribute to explaining the lower rates of African American applications for nursing home care. Considering the much worse objective measures of health status among African American elders, however, the age-as-a-leveler hypothesis does not appear to have any basis for support. There is, in turn, more support for the interpretation that African American elders draw assistance from more committed and flexible informal networks, and may consequently experience a less pressing need for institutional placement. If this interpretation is valid, the initial question of "what accounts for the much lower rates of nursing home applications" would have to be reversed. We need not ponder why African Americans have lower rates of nursing home applications than Whites, but why do Whites exceed the African American rates? The original question presupposes a normative bias: that the rates exhibited by Whites constitute the benchmark that other ethnic groups ought to equal or approximate. Reversing the question makes it possible to recognize the inner strengths of the African American community and establishes a paradigm for building more effective informal networks in White society than now exist.

But, as Morrison (1983) warned, we must also be careful not to oversell the cultural-strength aspects in explaining the lower rates of nursing home placement among African American elders at the expense of their informal support system. Nor must we use cultural heritage as a rationalization for justifying the unavailability or even the denial of institutional services for African American elders who need them.

There is also the possibility that the greater attitudinal rejection of nursing homes expressed by African Americans reflects their dislike or fear of the idea of being placed in institutions dominated by a White majority of residents. Had the interviewees been asked how they would feel about moving into a nursing home exclusively or largely populated by people of their same ethnic group, the results of this study might have been appreciably different.

## REFERENCES

Andersen, R. M., & Newman, J. F. (1973). Societal and individual determinants of medical care utilization in the U.S. *Milbank Memorial Fund Quarterly, 51*, 95–124.

Belgrave, L. L., & Bradsher, J. E. (1994). Health as a factor in institutionalization: Disparities between African Americans and Whites. *Research on Aging, 16*, 115–141.

Belgrave, L. L., Wykle, M. L., & Choi, J. M. (1993). Health, double jeopardy, and culture: The use of institutionalization by African-Americans. *The Gerontologist, 33*, 379–385.

Bernard, M. A. (1993). The health status of African-American elderly. *Journal of National Medical Association, 85*, 521–528.

Burton, L., Kasper, J., Shore, A., Cagney, K., LaVeist, T., Cubbin, C., & German, P. (1995). The structure of informal care: Are there differences by race? *The Gerontologist, 35*, 744–752.

Chadiha, L. A., Proctor, E. K., Morrow-Howell, N., Darkwa, O. K., & Dore, P. (1995). Post-hospital homecare for African-American and White elderly. *The Gerontologist, 35*, 233–239.

Clark, D. O., & Maddox, G. L. (1992). Racial and social correlates of age-related changes in functioning. *Journal of Gerontology, 47*, S222–S232.

Connell, C. M., & Gibson, G. D. (1997). Racial, ethnic, and cultural differences in dementia caregiving: Review and analysis. *The Gerontologist, 37*, 355–364.

Dowd, J. J., & Bengtson, V. L. (1978). Aging in minority populations: An examination of the double jeopardy hypothesis. *Journal of Gerontology, 33*, 427–436.

Ferraro, K. F. (1987). Double jeopardy to health for Black older adults? *Journal of Gerontology, 42*, 528–533.

Ferraro, K. F., & Farmer, M. M. (1996). Double jeopardy, aging as leveler, or persistent health inequality? A longitudinal analysis of White and Black Americans. *Journal of Gerontology, 51B*, S319–S328.

Gibson, R. (1988). Aging in Black America: The effects of an aging society. In E. Gore (Ed.), *Aging in cross cultural perspective* (pp. 105–129). New York: Phelps-Stokes Institute.

Gibson, R. C. (1994). The age-by-race gap in health and mortality in the older population: A social science research agenda. *The Gerontologist, 34*, 454–462.

Hing, E. (1987). Use of nursing homes by the elderly: preliminary data from the 1985 National Nursing Home Survey. Advance Data No.135, National Center for Health Statistics, May 14.

Hummer, R. A. (1996). Black–White differences in health and mortality: A review and conceptual model. *Sociological Quarterly, 37*, 105–125.

Jackson, J. J. (1988). The applicability of the modernization theory of the status of the Blacks in the United States and attitudes and behaviors associated with their aging. In E. Gore (Ed.), *Aging in cross cultural perspective* (pp. 69–103). New York: Phelps-Stokes Institute.

Johnson, C. L., & Barer, B. M. (1990). Families and networks among older inner-city Blacks. *The Gerontologist, 30*, 726–733.

Manton, K. G., Patrick, C. H., & Johnson, K. W. (1987). Health differentials between Blacks and Whites: Recent trends in mortality and morbidity. *Milbank Quarterly, 65*, 129–199.

Morrison, B. J. (1983). Sociocultural dimensions: Nursing homes and the minority aged. *Journal of Gerontological Social Work, 5*, 127–148.

Mutchler, J. E., & Burr, J. A. (1991). Racial differences in health and health care service utilization in later life: The effect of socioeconomic status. *Journal of Health and Social Behavior, 32*, 342–356.

Palmore, E. (1976). Total chance of institutionalization, *The Gerontologist, 16*, 504–507.

Petchers, M. K., & Milligan, S. E. (1988). Access to health care in a Black urban elderly population, *The Gerontologist, 28*, 213–217.

Riley, M. (1968). *Aging and society: An inventory of research findings* (Vol. 1). New York: Russell Sage.

Schoenbaum, M., & Waidman, T. (1997). Race, socioeconomic status, and health: Accounting for race differences in health. *Journal of Gerontology, 52B*, 61–73.

# Chapter Seven

# Utilization of In-Home and Community-Based Services among White, African American, and Hispanic Elders

A growing awareness of and sensitivity to the ethnic and cultural diversity of older Americans, as well as pressing fiscal constraints on the provision of services, have confirmed the imperative to revise current models of health and social service delivery to better target specific populations' needs. Overall trends toward healthier lifestyles and improvements in morbidity and mortality rates for older persons over the past decade have not held for racial/ethnic minority elders, who continue to fare comparatively worse than their White counterparts on both objective and subjective measures of health and well-being (U.S. Department of Health and Human Services, 1990).

Despite their generally poor health status compared to White elders, ethnic minority elders tend to underutilize the services that could enhance their health status and quality of life (Eribes & Bradley-Rawls, 1978; Hu, Snowden, Jerrell, & Nguyen, 1991; Kart, 1991; Mindel & Wright, 1982). These elders are much poorer than same-age Whites, but even in programs designated for the poor and marginally poor, they are represented far less than their reported objective needs would warrant. According to 1989 U.S. Census data, the poverty rate among African American elders (30.8%, or 766,000 persons) was more than triple the poverty rate among White elders (9.6%, or 2,542,000 persons), and among Hispanic elders (20.6%, or 211,000 persons) it was more than double (U.S. Senate Special Committee on Aging, 1991). Yet ethnic minority elders comprise less than 3% of participants in all poverty programs for the elderly. They are even more consistently underserved by U.S. Administration on Aging programs, which are not means tested but are largely geared to and staffed by White middle-class workers (Kamikawa, 1991). And although 35.2% of Medicaid expenditures go to poor elders (Health Care Financing Administration, 1990), 69% of these outlays are for institutional care (Reilly, Clauser, & Baugh, 1990), which ethnic elders barely use (Belgrave, Wykle, & Choi, 1993; Morycz, Malloy, Bozich, & Martz, 1987; Nelson, 1980).

Empirical data on formal service use by minority elders are scarce, and reasons for their persistent underutilization are not well known or understood (Kulys, 1990). Systematic investigations are needed to look at within- and between-group differences of older racial and ethnic subgroups. These studies should consider economic well-being, health status and health care, and family structure, and they should be conducted with the goal of further understanding how decisions about the use of long-term care service are reached (Belgrave et al., 1993; Jackson, 1989; Lockery, 1991; Mindel & Wright, 1982; Mitchell & Register, 1984; Taeuber, 1990). This chapter applies the Andersen–Newman behavioral model of health services utilization (Andersen & Newman, 1973) to understand the needs and in-home and community-based service-use patterns of a large national sample of frail African American and Hispanic elders. It also compares them with their White counterparts.

## THE STATUS OF IN-HOME AND COMMUNITY-BASED CARE

The institutional emphasis of our long-term care system is still firmly in place. Most Medicaid long-term-care spending for the elderly goes for care in nursing homes; in 1994 the costs for 69% of residents in 1994 were at least partly financed by Medicaid (Wiener, 1996). In the past decade or two, however, in-home and community-based care for frail elders has been rapidly emerging as a key component of the nation's long-term care system (Applebaum & Phillips, 1990). Driven by demographic and economic factors, there is growing pressure for expansion and improvement of these services. With the aging of the population, especially the dramatic increase in the 85-and-over age group, changes in family structure, long waiting lists for institutions, and the increasing cost of institutionalization, the demand for home- and community-based care has been increasing.

In-home and community-based services have appealed to policymakers mainly because they have been viewed as having a potential to cut long-term-care cost by reducing institutionalization and the length of stays. That is, in-home and community-based care has been seen primarily as a potentially cost-saving substitute for hospitalization and nursing home care and not as a means of meeting needs and improving disabled elders' quality of life (Spector & Kemper, 1994). With the promise of cost savings from prevention of institutionalization, a spate of community-based demonstration programs has been implemented under Medicaid Section 1115 and Medicaid Section 2176 waiver programs. Unfortunately, however, extensive research findings are almost unanimous in suggesting that expanding home care is more likely to increase rather than decrease total long-term care costs (Spector & Kemper,

1994; Wiener, 1996). This lack of cost effectiveness of in-home and community-based programs is often attributed to problems of loose eligibility criteria and inefficient targeting (Green, Lovely, & Ondrich, 1993; Leutz, Abrahams, & Capitman, 1993). But the truth is that long hours of home care for nursing-home-level persons who lack extensive informal support may marginally reduce hospital and nursing home use but cost more than nursing home care. With the increase in the number of frail elders who need extensive care for disabilities, the dream of cost saving from in-home and community-based care is not likely to be realized.

Cost effectiveness aside, however, the real goal and benefit of home care needs to be understood in the context of meeting unmet needs and improving the quality of life of frail elders (Spector & Kemper, 1994). Most frail elders strongly prefer to stay at home rather than enter an institution. This aversion to nursing homes is such that, given a choice between nursing home care and no formal services at home, many elders choose to stay at home with no services (Wiener, 1996). A large percentage of elders, often home owners, have spent a significant proportion of their adult life in the same house, and they are often reluctant to leave it for an institution. More important, "home provides dignity, freedom, and choice, in contrast to the well-known dangers of institutions, such as iatrogenic illness and acceleration of dependence" (Leutz, Capitman, MacAdam, & Abrahams, 1992, p. 3). Thus, health and social services that are delivered to elders' homes or that can be utilized by elderly residents in the community to meet their health needs would not only prolong their independence but also contribute to maintaining their quality of life.

The studies of client outcomes of the National Long-Term Care Channeling Demonstration indeed found that participation in the demonstration improved access to formal in-home care, reduced unmet needs, and enhanced life satisfaction for frail elders and their informal caregivers (Kemper, 1988; Rabiner, 1992; Rabiner, Mutran, & Stearns, 1995). Community-based programs such as senior centers also contribute to elders' quality of life by providing them a wide range of health screening, illness prevention, meal, education, and recreation programs, and social interaction opportunities (Krout, 1989).

These real and potential benefits of in-home and community-based services notwithstanding, their utilization by frail elders is very low. The 1987 National Medical Expenditure Survey showed the following percentges of persons aged 65 or older who had any functional difficulty and were using selected in-home and community-based services: home care, 19.7% (homemakers, 8.1%; home health aides, 4.9%; visiting nurses, 4.5%; physicians, 1.6%; and other medical services, 0.5%); home meals, 6.1%; senior centers, 7.3%; congregate meals, 6.1%; transportation, 5.3%; and telephone checks, 4.2%. More than 50% of those who had difficulty in three or more ADL did not receive any formal services (Short & Leon, 1990, cited in Callahan, 1996, and in Miller et al., 1996).

The reality is that for every elderly nursing home resident, there are at least two or three community-residing elders with a similar level of chronic illness and disability. Given the significantly lower rate of institutionalization among minority elders and their poorer health status, it is likely that there are at least three or four community-residing frail minority elders for each nursing home resident (Leutz et al., 1992). Apparently, a majority of these community-residing frail elders are not connected to in-home and community-based services.

Many frail elders, especially minorities, rely on informal support networks as their sole and/or primary support system, and they and their caregivers have not sought formal sources of care for various reasons. Barriers to their utilization of formal services include limited availability or unavailability of services in certain geographic areas, lack of knowledge about or awareness of services, limited access to services due to lack of transportation and/or language problems, negative attitudes toward services, negative prior experience with services due to insensitive and/or unsupportive environments, and cultural differences (Krout, 1983; Mindel & Wright, 1982; Ralston, 1991; Spence & Atherton, 1991; Yeatts, Crow, & Folts, 1992). Wallace (1990) summarized these barriers as availability, accessibility (and affordability), and acceptability in community-based long-term care. To reiterate, availability refers to whether a service is available and, even if available, whether it is adequately provided; accessibility encompasses personal finances (hence affordability), consumers' knowledge of availability and function of a service, limited funding and agency–management deficiencies, transportation problems of both workers and consumers, and lack of adequate linking mechanisms; and acceptability problems often arise from consumers' dissatisfaction with the quality of care, fear of and stigma related to dependency, cultural inappropriateness of services, and racial tensions between service providers and consumers (Wallace, 1990).

## RACIAL DIFFERENCES IN SERVICE UTILIZATION

With respect to racial differences in in-home and community-based service use, previous studies report mixed findings. Based on a national data set collected in 1968, Mindel and Wright (1982) found that Blacks tended to perceive that fewer services were available, which in turn was related to the number of services used—home-delivered meals, housekeeping, home repairs, counseling, visiting nurse, employment guidance, someone to drive the elder to places, and someone to call or visit the elder regularly. Based on data from the Longitudinal Study of Aging, however, Wolinsky and Johnson (1991) did not find race to be a significant factor for use of any type of health services (including home health care). But the interaction effects between race and health needs suggested that Blacks who need assistance with advanced ADL and upper-body limitations use more home health services.

Based on three different data sets (Supplement on Aging, National Long-Term Care, and National Medical Expenditure), Miller et al. (1996) also found no bivariate or multivariate differences between African American, Hispanic, or White frail elders aged 70 or older in the use of community long-term care services (home health aide, visiting nurse, and senior center). Significant predictors were living arrangements, Medicaid use, and overall health and functional status. Krout, Cutler and Coward's analysis (1990) of correlates of senior center participation, also based on the 1984 Supplement on Aging, confirmed that living alone, having fewer ADL/IADL difficulties, being female, having decreasing income, and living in suburbs and rural nonfarm areas, but not race (White versus all the other races), were significant factors. But Miller et al. (1996) qualified their findings of no racial difference by stating that they might have been due to possible methodological limitations of national sample surveys: Recruitment of minorities into national samples is more likely to occur in high-density, urban, predominantly minority areas where services may be more available than in low-density, rural areas. Norgard and Rodgers's analysis (1997) of racial differences, based on yet another national data set, Asset and Health Dynamics among the Oldest Old (AHEAD), also did not find race effect on any formal service use, but it did find that age, living arrangements, and health needs were significant predictors.

Besides the possible minority sampling biases, the cross-sectional nature of these analyses may have something to do with the findings of lack of racial difference. That is, using the longitudinal component of the national Long-Term Care Survey, Miller, McFall, and Campbell (1994) found that race was not a major influence on changes in sources (informal or formal) of community long-term care when other variables were held constant. But, although equally likely to use mixed sources of help at baseline, African Americans were less likely to do so two years later and more likely to shift to strictly informal help.

Although the baseline Channeling data set that is the basis of analysis in this chapter is also cross-sectional, it may contain fewer of the minority sampling biases because of the wide geographic distribution of the demonstration sites among both metropolitan and nonmetropolitan areas. Moreover, unlike the sample members of other national surveys, those of the Channeling data set were all frail elders who were at risk of institutionalization, and thus had obvious need for in-home and community-based services, either informal, formal, or both. We tested the effect of race on the likelihood of in-home and community-based service use among these frail elders.

## CONCEPTUAL AND ANALYTICAL FRAMEWORK

See Chapter 5 for a discussion of the Andersen–Newman (Andersen & Newman, 1973) model. In this chapter, we elaborate on the strengths and limitations of the model that apply to older persons' social service use. Ward (1977), for example, suggested that age, sex, race, education, health beliefs, and patterns of service use established earlier in life may predispose an elder to becoming an effective service user. Family income, social supports, and other resources have also been reported to contribute to successful service use by elders (Bass & Noelker, 1987; Coulton & Frost, 1982; McAuley & Arling, 1984; Nelson, 1993; Starrett, Mindel, & Wright, 1983). Wolinsky (1994) also pointed out that the model's eclectic approach, combining a diversity of discipline-oriented perspectives, was a strength and considered it to be the most amenable conceptualization for framing secondary data analyses of health services utilization among older persons.

But Kart (1991) discusses several critical limitations inherent in the Andersen–Newman (1973) model that are relevant to this chapter. First, the framework does not adequately attend to the bureaucratic characteristics of service settings, most specifically, the organizational features that are potential barriers to service utilization (Wolinsky & Arnold, 1989). The model also ignores the potentially powerful influence of "lay referral structures," which can impede or promote the use of professional services by ethnic elders (House, Landis, & Umberson, 1988). Furthermore, it does not clarify how enabling measures relate to predisposing or need variables (Mutran & Ferraro, 1988). A final concern is that enabling and predisposing factors contribute little to the explanatory power of the model. Rather, in the end, illness or disability (hence need) explains most of the variance in service use found in the statistical multivariate analysis (Coulton & Frost, 1982; Wan, 1982; Wolinsky, 1978; Wolinsky & Johnson, 1991).

Aware of these limitations, this chapter applies the Andersen–Newman model to address the following questions: (1) What are the distinctive demographic characteristics of African American, Hispanic, and White frail elders? (2) What proportion of these older persons use in-home and community-based services? (3) What predisposing, enabling, and need factors are associated with the use of in-home and community-based services by each ethnic group? The data analysis proceeds to ascertaining the odds of each group's using each type of long-term care services. The chapter hypothesizes that the odds of frail elders using each of these types of services will differ by ethnicity.

## METHODOLOGY

### Data Source and Sample

As presented in Chapter 2, the 1982–1984 Long-Term Care Channeling Demonstration study was used to examine the patterns of in-home and community-based service use among White, African American, and Hispanic elders.

## Measurement of Variables

The utilization status of each in-home (home health care and Meals on Wheels) and community-based (congregate meal program, social center/church, and counseling) service, as a dependent variable, was measured on the same scale. The self-reported use of each of these services in the preceding six months was coded dichotomously, with 1 indicating users of each type of service and 0 denoting nonusers. These dichotomous outcome measures represent contact rather than volume (metrics of the amount of services) or episodes (measuring the stream of services) of care (see Wolinsky, 1994). The limitations of the data set do not allow measurement of volume or frequency, which would have been a more useful measure, given the frailty of the sample population.

Unlike all the other services considered, social center or church activities may not be considered formal services. However, because social centers/churches are outside the immediate family circle, and especially because Black churches have often functioned as alternative support systems and provided a range of formal and informal services for elders in need of care, they are considered community-based resources similar to senior centers (for a review of church support for Black elders, see Walls & Zarit, 1991; Wilson & Netting, 1988).

Independent variables were as follows: Predisposing factors are gender, age, and race/ethnicity; enabling factors are income, living arrangement, attitude toward nursing home use, sense of control in life, contact with family and friends, informal support network, and use of other long-term care services; and need factors include cognitive impairment, ADL impairment, number of physical illnesses, and perceived unmet ADL and IADL needs.

The predisposing variables were measured as follows: gender and age groupings were coded dichotomously, with male gender and age 80 or more coded 1, and female gender and age less than 80 coded 0. Two dummy variables, African American and Hispanic, permitted examination of differences among the three racial/ethnic groups, with Whites as the reference. As for the enabling factors, income and living arrangements were dichotomized, with an income of $1,000 monthly or more and living alone coded 1, and income under $1,000 monthly and living with others 0. Attitude toward nursing home placement, as it had been expressed by the elders, was also dichotomized, with 1 indicating positive attitude and 0 denoting negative attitude.

The sense-of-control-in-life variable was a composite score based on five questions with three Likert-type responses ranging from (1) "very much" to (2) "somewhat" to (3) "not at all": (1) "In general, how satisfying do you find the way you're spending your life these days?" (2) "Day to day, how much choice do you have about what you do and when you do it?" (3) "How confident are you of figuring out how to deal with your problems?" (4) "How much do you worry about not knowing whom to turn to for help?" (5) "How confident are you of getting services when you need them?" To summarize the data and to avoid problems of multicollinearity, a principal-components analysis with varimax rotation was performed that yielded one component. The five items were highly correlated, with factor loadings ranging from .56 to .71. Their summed scores thus yielded a composite measure of sense of control in life (alpha coefficient = .74).

Social contacts were measured as the self-reported frequency of both face-to-face and telephone contacts with relatives and friends during the preceding week. Responses were categorized as (1) once or more daily, (2) two to six times, (3) once, and (4) none. Number of informal caregivers was a self-report of all family and friends who provided unpaid help. Use of the other types of long-term care services was included in the regression model to control for the role of other contacts within the service-delivery system when examining use of a particular type of service. Thus, in assessing the likelihood that the respondents would use each type of in-home (home health care and Meals on Wheels) service, use of both community-based (congregate meal program, social center/church, and counseling services) and nursing home services were included; in examining use of community-based services, use of both in-home and nursing home services was included.

Need factors included cognitive impairment, which was assessed with the SPMSQ, a 10-item test of mental functioning (Pfeiffer, 1975). Mild or no impairment was indicated by 9 to 10 correct answers, moderate impairment by 6 to 8, and severe impairment by 5 or fewer. Test–retest reliability was greater than .80 (Kane & Kane, 1981). The number of ADL impairments was determined by asking respondents if they had been helped during the preceding week with eating, bathing, dressing, toileting, and/or getting out of bed or chair (alpha coefficient for entire sample = .79; Whites = .79, African Americans = .76, Hispanics = .82).

Physical illnesses included self-reported anemia, high blood pressure, heart disease, stroke, diabetes, arthritis, cancer, Parkinson's disease, respiratory problems, skin problems, paralysis, orthopedic conditions, vision or hearing problems, and other health conditions. Finally, the number of unmet needs was determined by asking respondents if they needed additional help with ADL and IADL.

## Methods of Analysis

The first analytic step consisted of obtaining the descriptive statistics of the amount and pattern of service use by the frail elderly respondents. Sixteen variables were then entered into a hierarchical logistic regression model, with the predisposing factors entered first, the enabling factors second, the need factors third, and race/ethnicity dummy coded variables entered last (Bass, Looman, & Ehrlich, 1992; Bass & Noelker, 1987). The effects of race/

ethnicity on service use was thus assessed after the effects of other variables in the model were controlled for. This strategy is the analytic procedure best suited for examining prediction equations with dichotomous outcomes (Cox, 1978; Hosmer & Lemeshow, 1989).

The probability of a respondent's using each type of service was thus estimated by calculating the odds ratio through the antilogs of the parameter estimate of each independent variable. For example, an odds ratio of 1.48 for in-home services means that a respondent is 48% more likely to use these services than not, while an odds ratio of .30 indicates a 70% less likelihood. Zero-order correlations of the 16 variables in the model ranged from .001 to .39, with no evidence of problems with multicollinearity. To measure and compare the relative impact of each independent variable on each type of service use, corresponding Wald chi-square statistics were also presented (Selvin, 1991).

## RESULTS

Table 7.1 presents data on use of the three types of long-term care services and informal supports. Whites had the highest percentage of regular home health care use (30.3%), Hispanics used home-delivered meal services more than African Americans, and the latter had the highest church and social center participation (15.8%). Whites reported significantly more nursing home use during the preceding six (10.1%) and two (61.6%) months and more nursing home applications (5.2%), while African Americans and Hispanics reported significantly more (but not numerically substantially more) informal helpers.

Overall, the percentages of in-home and community-based service users indicate that a relatively small proportion of these frail elders are consumers of these services. Although the sample members all were at risk of institutionalization and as many as 40% to 62% of them had used nursing home services as recently as in the preceding two months, only one-fourth (Hispanics) to less than one-third (Whites) used home health care, and less than one-sixth (Whites) to a little over one-tenth (African Americans) used Meals on Wheels. Only a tiny fraction used congregate meals and counseling services. As discussed earlier, the low rate of in-home service use may be due to problems of service availability, accessibility, affordability, and acceptability. Community-based services may also not be available in the neighborhood or may be in a location where access to them is difficult. Thus, many elders' needs may have been unmet, or been met primarily by informal support networks. Such informal support networks, particularly when made up of family members, have been found to be primary caregiving resources (Stone, Cafferata, & Sangl, 1987). Informal support networks of racial/ethnic minority groups, inclusive of immediate and extended families and friends, are especially central to the process of social integration and become a primary caregiving resource in late life (Lockery, 1991). These complex familial patterns are likely

**Table 7.1**
**Formal and Informal Support of Frail Elders by Ethnicity**

|  | African American n = 1,272 | White n = 4,133 | Hispanic n = 211 |
|---|---|---|---|
| **In-home service use** | | | |
| Home health care | 28.0% | 30.3% | 25.2% |
| Meals on wheels**** | 11.8 | 17.5 | 17.1 |
| **Community-based service use** | | | |
| Congregate meals | 3.4% | 4.5% | 5.3% |
| Health program | 0.8 | 2.1 | 1.6 |
| Social center/church*** | 15.8 | 12.0 | 10.1 |
| Counseling* | 3.6 | 5.1 | 8.6 |
| **Nursing home use** | | | |
| Nursing home use in preceding 6 months* | 4.0% | 10.1% | 3.8% |
| Nursing home use in preceding 2 months* | 42.4 | 61.6 | 40.0 |
| Nursing home application**** | 2.6 | 5.2 | 3.4 |
| **Informal support** | | | |
| Informal helpers (mean)[a]**** | 2.2 | 1.9 | 2.0 |

*Data Source*: National Long-Term Care Channeling Demonstration, 1982–1984.
*Note*: Chi-square and *t* statistics were used.
[a]ANOVA statistics were used to test the differences between means.
*$p < 0.05$; **$p < 0.01$; ***$p < 0.001$; ****$p < 0.0001$.

due to a combination of cultural and economic factors (Chatters, Taylor, & Jackson, 1986; Gibson, 1986; Johnson & Barer, 1990; Mitchell & Register, 1984; Mutran, 1985; Weeks & Cuellar, 1981).

Tables 7.2, 7.3, 7.4, 7.5, and 7.6 present logistic regression coefficients of home health care service, Meals on Wheels, congregate meals, social centers, churches, and counseling services, respectively. Service use was significantly influenced by all three categories of independent variables—predisposing, enabling, and need factors. Race/ethnicity was entered last in each case in order to test for its effects after other variables in the model were controlled for.

### Factors Associated with Home Health Care and Meals on Wheels

Significant predictors of home health care service use included being younger than age 80, greater utilization of institutional nursing home care,

**Table 7.2**
**Logistic Regression Analysis of Use of Home Health Care Service by Frail Elders**

| Variables | Home health care service | | |
|---|---|---|---|
| | Unstandardized logit coefficients (SE)[a] | Odds Ratio[b] | Wald chi-square |
| **Predisposing factors** | | | |
| Sex (male=1) | 0.07(0.25) | | |
| Age (> 80=1) | -0.59(0.08) | 0.55**** | 50.27 |
| **Enabling factors** | | | |
| Income (>$1000=1) | 0.22(0.15) | | |
| Living alone (alone=1) | -0.06(0.09) | | |
| Nursing home attitude (positive=1) | -0.16(0.08) | | |
| Sense of control in life | 0.00(0.01) | | |
| Social contact | -0.09(0.04) | | |
| Informal helpers | 0.03(0.03) | | |
| Community-based service use | -0.02(0.06) | | |
| Nursing home service use | 0.16(0.08) | 1.18* | 3.73 |
| **Need factors** | | | |
| Cognitive impairment | -0.27(0.06) | 0.77**** | 17.83 |
| ADL impairment | 0.28(0.04) | 1.33**** | 41.99 |
| No. of illnesses | 0.17(0.02) | 1.18**** | 66.96 |
| Unmet needs | -0.00(0.01) | | |
| **Race/ethnicity** | | | |
| African American (vs. White=0) | 0.16(0.10) | | |
| Hispanic (vs. White=0) | -0.69(0.26) | 0.50** | 6.96 |
| Intercept | -.1.52(0.26)**** | | |
| Model chi square | 235.77**** | | |

*Data Source*: National Long-Term Care Channeling Demonstration, 1982–1984.
[a]Standard error.
[b]Odds ratios were calculated for the significant coefficients.
*$p < 0.05$; **$p < 0.01$; ***$p < 0.001$; ****$p < 0.0001$.

less cognitive impairment, more ADL impairment, more physical illnesses, and being White (as opposed to Hispanic). Among these predictors, number of physical illnesses was the strongest predictor of home health care service use, followed by age and ADL impairment. Persons aged 80 or older were 45% less likely than those under 80 to use the services, and White elders were 50% more likely than Hispanic elders to use the services.

Need factors, as a set, had the highest predictive power, followed by predisposing factors. Three need-related variables, more ADL impairment, more physical illnesses, and less cognitive impairment were associated with higher

**Table 7.3**
**Logistic Regression Analysis of Use of Meals on Wheels Service by Frail Elders**

| Variables | Meals on Wheels service | | |
| | Unstandardized logit coefficients (SE)[a] | Odds ratio[b] | Wald chi-square |
|---|---|---|---|
| **Predisposing factors** | | | |
| Sex (male=1) | 0.05(0.11) | | |
| Age (> 80=1) | -0.11(0.09) | | |
| | | | |
| **Enabling factors** | | | |
| Income (>$1000=1) | -0.41(0.22) | | |
| Living alone (Alone=1) | 0.88(0.11) | 2.42**** | 68.81 |
| Nursing home attitude | | | |
| (positive=1) | 0.17(0.09) | 1.18* | 3.13 |
| Sense of control in life | 0.05(0.02) | | |
| Social contact | 0.04(0.05) | | |
| Informal helpers | -0.03(0.04) | | |
| Community-based service use | -0.35(0.07) | 0.71**** | 23.60 |
| Nursing home service use | 0.19(0.09) | 1.21* | 3.92 |
| | | | |
| **Need factors** | | | |
| Cognitive impairment | -0.00(0.07) | | |
| ADL impairment | 0.23(0.05) | 1.26**** | 22.45 |
| No. of illnesses | 0.06(0.02) | 1.06** | 6.94 |
| Unmet needs | -0.03(0.02) | | |
| | | | |
| **Race/ethnicity** | | | |
| African American (vs. White=0) | -0.18(0.12) | | |
| Hispanic (vs. White=0) | 0.47(0.24) | 1.60* | 3.75 |
| | | | |
| Intercept | -.1.81(0.29)**** | | |
| Model chi square | 191.48**** | | |

*Data Source*: National Long-Term Care Channeling Demonstration, 1982–1984.
[a]Standard error.
[b]Odds ratios were calculated for the significant coefficients.
*$p < 0.05$; **$p < 0.01$; ***$p < 0.001$; ****$p < 0.0001$.

probabilities of using home health care services. Nursing home use was a significant enabling factor, with elders who had used such services being more likely to also use home health care services. However, the number of informal helpers did not predict the extent of home health care service use.

Significant predictors of Meals on Wheels service use were living alone, having a positive attitude toward nursing home placement, using more community-based as well as nursing home services, more ADL impairment, more physical illnesses, and being Hispanic. Living alone was the strongest predictor of utilization of Meals on Wheels services, followed by less community-based

**Table 7.4**
**Logistic Regression Analysis of Use of Congregate Meal Service by Frail Elders**

| Variables | Use of social centers/churches | | |
| --- | --- | --- | --- |
| | Unstandardized logit coefficients (SE)[a] | Odds ratio[b] | Wald chi-square |
| **Predisposing factors** | | | |
| Sex (male=1) | -0.12(0.12) | | |
| Age (≥80=1) | -0.12(0.10) | | |
| **Enabling factors** | | | |
| Income (>$1000=1) | 0.03(0.21) | | |
| Living alone (alone=1) | 0.43(0.11) | 1.54*** | 14.25 |
| Nursing home attitude | | | |
| (positive=1) | 0.48(0.10) | 1.62**** | 21.70 |
| Sense of control in life | 0.05(0.02) | 1.05** | 8.23 |
| Social contact | -0.26(0.06) | 0.77**** | 16.65 |
| Informal helpers | -0.08(0.05) | | |
| In-home service use | -0.42(0.09) | 0.66**** | 19.62 |
| Nursing home service use | -0.01(0.12) | | |
| **Need factors** | | | |
| Cognitive impairment | 0.12(0.07) | | |
| ADL impairment | -0.22(0.05) | 0.80**** | 17.02 |
| No. of illnesses | -0.07(0.03) | 0.93** | 6.80 |
| Unmet needs | -0.00(0.02) | | |
| **Race/ethnicity** | | | |
| African American (vs. White=0) | 0.39(0.12) | 1.48** | 9.96 |
| Hispanic (vs. White=0) | 0.21(0.29) | | |
| Intercept | -0.29(0.32) | | |
| Model chi square | 160.20**** | | |

*Data Source*: National Long-Term Care Channeling Demonstration, 1982–1984.
[a]Standard error.
[b]Odds ratios were calculated for the significant coefficients.
*$p < 0.05$; **$p < 0.01$; ***$p < 0.001$; ****$p < 0.0001$.

service use and more ADL impairment. Enabling factors, as a set, had the highest predictive power, followed by need factors. Two need-related variables—more ADL impairment and more physical illnesses—were associated with higher probabilities of using Meals on Wheels services. Nursing home use was a significant enabling factor, with elders who had used nursing home services being more likely to have also used Meals on Wheels services. Controlling for other variables, Hispanic elders were 60% more likely than White elders to use Meals on Wheels services. As in the case of home health care service use, number of informal helpers did not predict Meals on Wheels

**Table 7.5**
**Logistic Regression Analysis of Use of Social Centers/Churches by Frail Elders**

| Variables | Use of social centers/churches | | |
| --- | --- | --- | --- |
| | Unstandardized logit coefficients (SE)[a] | Odds Ratio[b] | Wald chi-square |
| **Predisposing factors** | | | |
| Sex (male=1) | -0.12(0.12) | | |
| Age (> 80=1) | -0.12(0.10) | | |
| **Enabling factors** | | | |
| Income (>$1000=1) | 0.03(0.21) | | |
| Living alone (alone=1) | 0.43(0.11) | 1.54*** | 14.25 |
| Nursing home attitude (positive=1) | 0.48(0.10) | 1.62**** | 21.70 |
| Sense of control in life | 0.05(0.02) | 1.05** | 8.23 |
| Social contact | -0.26(0.06) | 0.77**** | 16.65 |
| Informal helpers | -0.08(0.05) | | |
| In-home service use | -0.42(0.09) | 0.66**** | 19.62 |
| Nursing home service use | -0.01(0.12) | | |
| **Need factors** | | | |
| Cognitive impairment | 0.12(0.07) | | |
| ADL impairment | -0.22(0.05) | 0.80**** | 17.02 |
| No. of illnesses | -0.07(0.03) | 0.93** | 6.80 |
| Unmet needs | -0.00(0.02) | | |
| **Race/ethnicity** | | | |
| African American (vs. White=0) | 0.39(0.12) | 1.48** | 9.96 |
| Hispanic (vs. White=0) | 0.21(0.29) | | |
| Intercept | -0.29(0.32) | | |
| Model chi square | 160.20**** | | |

*Data Source*: National Long-Term Care Channeling Demonstration, 1982–1984.
[a]Standard error.
[b]Odds ratios were calculated for the significant coefficients.
*$p < 0.05$; **$p < 0.01$; ***$p < 0.001$; ****$p < 0.0001$.

use, but this finding may be due to the inadequacy of this single-item indicator to capture critical qualitative aspects of informal support systems.

## Factors Associated with Congregate Meals, Senior Center, and Counseling Service Use

Six predictor variables were significantly associated with the likelihood of congregate meal service use. Respondents with lower income and those who lived alone were more likely to use these services. Also, a positive attitude toward nursing home placement, having fewer informal helpers, and

**Table 7.6**
**Logistic Regression Analysis of Use of Counseling Service by Frail Elders**

| Variables | Use of counseling service | | |
| | Unstandardized logit coefficients (SE)[a] | Odds ratio[b] | Wald chi-square |
| --- | --- | --- | --- |
| **Predisposing factors** | | | |
| Sex (male=1) | -0.40(0.21) | | |
| Age (> 80=1) | -0.59(0.18) | 0.55** | 10.69 |
| **Enabling factors** | | | |
| Income (>$1000=1) | 0.52(0.28) | | |
| Living alone (alone=1) | -0.08(0.19) | | |
| Nursing home attitude (positive=1) | 0.28(0.17) | | |
| Sense of control in life | -0.16(0.03) | 0.83**** | 24.20 |
| Social contact | 0.09(0.09) | | |
| Informal helpers | -0.07(0.07) | | |
| In-home service use | -0.22(0.15) | | |
| Nursing home service use | 0.14(0.20) | | |
| **Need factors** | | | |
| Cognitive impairment | 0.34(0.11) | 1.41** | 9.15 |
| ADL impairment | -0.33(0.09) | 0.72*** | 12.74 |
| No. of illnesses | 0.04(0.04) | | |
| Unmet needs | 0.10(0.03) | 1.11** | 9.63 |
| **Race/ethnicity** | | | |
| African American (vs. White=0) | -0.22(0.23) | | |
| Hispanic (vs. White=0) | 0.80(0.38) | 2.22* | 4.43 |
| Intercept | -4.73(0.56)**** | | |
| Model chi square | 107.29**** | | |

*Data Source*: National Long-Term Care Channeling Demonstration, 1982–1984.
[a]Standard error.
[b]Odds ratios were calculated for the significant coefficients.
*$p < 0.05$; **$p < 0.01$; ***$p < 0.001$; ****$p < 0.0001$.

less in-home service use enabled use of congregate meals. Finally, less ADL impairment was associated with increased odds of congregate meal service use. Race was not a significant factor.

Significant predictors for senior or social center/church participation included living alone, positive attitude toward nursing home placement, higher sense of control in life, fewer family contacts, less in-home service use, fewer functional impairments, and better health condition. Enabling factors made the greatest contribution in explaining the extent of social center/church participation. Race/ethnicity also had a significant independent effect on use of these services, as African American elders were 48%

more likely than White elders to participate in social or senior center services, once other variables in the model were controlled for.

Predictors of counseling service use included being younger than age 80; feeling less sense of control in life; experiencing more mental impairment, less functional impairment, and more unmet needs; and being Hispanic. The sense of loss of control in life was the strongest predictor of counseling service use in the model. Moreover, after other factors in the model were controlled for, Hispanic elders were found to be 122% more likely than White elders to obtain counseling services.

## DISCUSSION

This chapter examined the use of in-home and community-based services by African American, Hispanic, and White elders. Consistent with previous studies, only a small proportion of frail elders used these services, indicating possible problems with availability and accessibility, among other things. Also consistent with the findings of most previous studies, multivariate results show that African American elders were not significantly different from White elders in their likelihood of utilizing home health care, Meals on Wheels, congregate meal services, and counseling services, when other predisposing, enabling, and need factors were controlled for. But, as expected, African American elders were far more likely to participate in social centers and churches. This greater participation is consistent with Watson's (1990) observation of the important role of African American churches in assisting the members of their congregations.

Compared to White elders, Hispanic elders were significantly less likely to utilize home health care services, but more likely to use Meals on Wheels and counseling services, a finding that was unexpected but that may be due to more extensive provision of these services to their ethnic community. Hispanics' far greater likelihood of using counseling services is especially interesting. Most Hispanics in the sample were Cuban immigrants, and their choice of this type of service may be due to a combination of inadequate informal supports in the United States and cultural preference. Further research is needed to explain this finding and to determine the adequacy of these services, given Hispanics' economic disadvantage and reports of their higher levels of cognitive and functional impairment and depressive symptoms. Given their higher likelihood of using Meals on Wheels and counseling services, it is unclear why Hispanics were less likely to use home health care services, in spite of their higher level of functional and cognitive impairment. More research is needed to understand the service utilization patterns of all the different nationality groups. (In Chapter 8, the 1988 data set of the National Survey of Hispanic Elderly People was used to answer some of these questions.)

In addition to race/ethnicity (which had the lowest relative impact among the significant predictors), all three types of factors (predisposing, enabling, and need) in the Andersen–Newman (1973) model of health service use contributed significantly to explaining use of each type of in-home and community-based service by this frail elderly population. However, consistent with previously cited empirical studies that used the Andersen–Newman model, need factors had the highest predictive power for home health care service use, followed by a predisposing factor, age. The increased likelihood that younger elders and Whites will use home health care services may be due to greater awareness and financial accessibility and/or cultural acceptance of these services.

Higher levels of cognitive and functional impairment and more physical illnesses also contributed significantly to an explanation of the use of Meals on Wheels and other community-based services. In terms of relative impact, however, enabling factors had the strongest effect on the use of congregate meal and social center services. That is, informal social support indicators such as living alone, fewer contacts with friends and families, and fewer informal helpers were associated with increased odds of congregate meal and social center/church use, and a psychological factor, sense of control in life, was strongly positively associated with the likelihood of counseling service use. It stands to reason that living alone and having less informal support increased the odds of an elder's using congregate meal services and participating in social centers and churches, both of which also frequently provide outlets and opportunities for social interaction among similarly situated elders as well as with younger generations. Regardless of their race/ethnicity background, elders who had fewer family or friend contacts and lived by themselves were at risk for social isolation. The decision to use congregate meal services may thus meet both their nutritional and psychosocial needs. Likewise, participation in social centers and churches may contribute to improving their psychological well-being, as well as improving their access to other tangible benefits.

Elders who had already used in-home services were less likely to use community-based services—congregate meals and social centers/churches. Also, elders who had already used community-based services were less likely to use home health care services, while those who had used nursing home services were more likely to use such services. This finding and the negative association between community-based service use and functional and physical impairments suggest a hierarchy of need and a continuum of long-term care services whereby frail elders who use community-based services have the least intensive needs, followed by those who use home health care services, and then those who needed nursing home services. This trajectory is, of course, influenced by factors such as eligibility and affordability of services, availability of caregivers, and cultural preferences. The significant association between positive attitude toward nursing home placement and the likelihood of using home health care and Meals on Wheels services may also reflect more generalized access and greater receptivity to formal services.

In summary, utilization of different services depends very much on the availability, accessibility, affordability, and acceptability issues. Variations observed in service use also raise important questions about availability, accessibility, and acceptability of different services for frail elders with different needs, including different racial/ethnic groups. For example, what does African American elders' higher rate of participation in social centers and churches suggest? Do they feel more comfortable in those settings than in formal service settings? If they do (and most likely they do), should we develop social centers/churches as a focal point for delivering formal services for African American frail elders? Why are Hispanics, but not African Americans, more likely than Whites to use Meals on Wheels? It is our hope that this chapter provides directions for future research and stimulates some thoughts for improving service delivery systems for frail minority elders.

## REFERENCES

Andersen, R. M., & Newman, J. F. (1973). Societal and individual determinants of medical care utilization in the U.S. *Milbank Memorial Fund Quarterly, 51*, 95–124.

Applebaum, R., & Phillips, P. (1990). Assuring the quality of in-home care: The other challenge for long-term care. *The Gerontologist, 30*, 444–450.

Bass, D. M., Looman, W. J., & Ehrlich, P. (1992). Predicting the volume of health and social services: Integrating cognitive impairment into the modified Andersen framework. *The Gerontologist, 32*, 33–43.

Bass, D. M., & Noelker, L. S. (1987). The influence of family caregivers on elders' use of in-home services: An expanded conceptual framework. *Journal of Health and Social Behavior, 28*, 184–196.

Belgrave, L. L., Wykle, M. L., & Choi, J. M. (1993). Health, double jeopardy, and culture: The use of institutionalization by African-Americans. *The Gerontologist, 33*, 379–385.

Callahan, J. J. (1996). Care in the home and other community settings: Present and future. In R. H. Binstock, L. E. Cluff, & O. Von Mering (Eds.), *The future of long-term care: Social and policy issues* (pp. 169–188). Baltimore: Johns Hopkins University Press.

Chatters, L. M., Taylor, R. J., & Jackson, J. S. (1986). Aged Blacks' choices for an informal helper network. *Journal of Gerontology, 41*, 94–100.

Coulton, C., & Frost, A. K. (1982). Use of social and health services by the elderly. *Journal of Health and Social Behavior, 23*, 330–339.

Cox, D. (1978). *Analysis of binary data.* London: Chapman and Hall.

Eribes, R. A., & Bradley-Rawls, M. (1978). The underutilization of nursing home facilities by Mexican-American elderly in the Southwest. *The Gerontologist, 18*, 363–371.

Gibson, R. (1986). Outlook for the Black family. In A. Pifer & L. Bronte (Eds.), *Our aging society.* New York: Norton.

Greene, V. L., Lovely, M. E., & Ondrich, J. I. (1993). The cost-effectiveness of community services in a frail elderly population. *The Gerontologist, 33*, 177–189.

Greene, V. L., & Ondrich, J. I. (1990). Risk factors for nursing home admissions and exits: A discrete-time hazard function approach. *Journal of Gerontology, 45*, S250–S258.

Health Care Financing Administration. (1990). *1990 HCFA Statistics.* Bureau of Data Management and Strategy: HCFA Pub. No. 03313, September, 1990.

Hosmer, D. W., & Lemeshow, S. (1989). *Applied logistic regression.* New York: John Wiley & Sons.

House, J. S., Landis, K. R., & Umberson, D. (1988, June). Social relationships and health. *Science,* 540–545.

Hu, T., Snowden, L. R., Jerrell, J. M., & Nguyen, T. D. (1991). Ethnic populations in public mental health: Services choices and level of use. *American Journal of Public Health, 81*, 1429–1434.

Jackson, J. S. (1989). Methodological issues in survey research on older minority adults. In M. P. Lawton & A. R. Herzog (Eds.), *Special research methods for gerontology* (pp. 137–161). Amityville, NY: Baywood.

Johnson, C. L., & Barer, B. M. (1990). Families and networks among older inner-city Blacks. *The Gerontologist, 30*, 726–733.

Kamikawa, L. (1991, Fall/Winter). Public entitlements: Exclusionary beneficence. *Generations,* 21–24.

Kane, R. A., & Kane, R. L. (1981). *Assessing the elderly: A practical guide to measurement.* Lexington, MA: Lexington Books.

Kart, C. S. (1991). Variation in long-term care service use by aged Blacks. *Journal of Aging and Health, 3*, 511–526.

Kemper, P. (1988). Overview of findings. *Health Services Research, 23*, 161–174.

Krout, J. (1989). *Senior centers in America.* Westport, CT: Greenwood.

Krout, J. A. (1983). Knowledge and use of services by the elderly: A critical review of the literature. *International Journal of Aging and Human Development, 17*, 153–167.

Krout, J. A., Cutler, S. J., & Coward, R. J. (1990). Correlates of senior center participation: A national analysis. *The Gerontologist, 30*, 72–79.

Kulys, R. (1990). The ethnic factor in the delivery of social services. In A. Monk (Ed.), *Handbook of gerontological services* (2d ed., pp. 629–661). New York: Columbia University Press.

Leutz, W., Abrahams, R., & Capitman, J. (1993). The administration of eligibility for community long-term care. *The Gerontologist, 33*, 92–104.

Leutz, W. N., Capitman, J. A., MacAdam, M., & Abrahams, R. (1992). *Care for frail elders: Developing community solutions.* Westport, CT: Auburn House.

Lockery, S. A. (1991, Fall/Winter). Caregiving among racial and ethnic minority elders. *Generations,* 58–62.

McAuley, W. J., & Arling, G. (1984). Use of in-home care by very old people. *Journal of Health and Social Behavior, 25*, 54–64.

Miller, B., Campbell, R. T., Davis, L., Furner, S., Giachello, A., Prohasks, T., Kaufman, J., Li, M., & Perez, C. (1996). Minority use of community long-term care services: A compartive analysis. *Journal of Gerontology, 51B*, S70–S81.

Miller, B., McFall, S., & Campbell, R. T. (1994). Changes in sources of community long-term care among African American and White frail older persons. *Journal of Gerontology, 49*, S14–S24.

Mindel, C. H., & Wright, R., Jr. (1982). The use of social services by Black and White elderly: The role of social support systems. *Journal of Gerontological Social Work, 4,* 107–125.

Mitchell, J., & Register, J. C. (1984). An exploration of family interaction with the elderly by race, socioeconomic status, and residence. *The Gerontologist, 24,* 48–54.

Morycz, R. K., Malloy, J., Bozich, M. A., & Martz, D. (1987). Racial differences in family burden: Clinical implications for social work. *Journal of Gerontological Social Work, 10,* 133–154.

Mutran, E. (1985). Intergenerational family support among Blacks and Whites: Response to culture or to socioeconomic differences. *Journal of Gerontology, 40,* 382–389.

Mutran, E., & Ferraro, K. F. (1988). Medical need and use of services among older men and women. *Journal of Gerontology, 43,* S162–S171.

Nelson, G. (1980). Contrasting services to the aged. *Social Service Review, 54,* 376–389.

Nelson, M. A. (1993). Race, gender, and the effect of social supports on the use of health services by elderly individuals. *International Journal of Aging and Human Development, 37,* 227–246.

Norgard, T. M., & Rodgers, W. L. (1997). Patterns of in-home care among elderly Black and White Americans. *Journal of Gerontology, 52B,* 93–101.

Pfeiffer, E. (1975). A short portable mental status questionnaire for the assessment of organic brain deficit in elderly patients. *Journal of the American Geriatric Society, 23,* 433–441.

Rabiner, D. J. (1992). The relationship between program participation, use of formal in-home care, and satisfaction with care in an elderly population. *The Gerontologist, 32,* 805–812.

Rabiner, D. J., Mutran, E., & Stearns, S. C. (1995). The effect of channeling on home care utilization and satisfaction with care. *The Gerontologist, 35,* 186–195.

Ralston, P. A. (1991). Senior centers and minority elders: A critical review. *The Gerontologist, 31,* 325–331.

Reilly, T. W., Clauser, S. B., & Baugh, D. K. (1990, December). Trends in Medicaid payments and utilization, 1975–1989. *Health Care Financing Review,* 15–33.

Selvin, S. (1991). *Statistical analysis of epidemiologic data.* New York: Oxford.

Short, P. F., & Leon, J. (1990, cited in Callahan, 1996). Use of home and community services by persons age 65 and older with functional difficulties. *National Medical Expenditures Survey. Research Findings 5,* U.S. Department of Health and Human Services, Washington, DC: U.S. Government Printing Office.

Spector, W. D., & Kemper, P. (1994). Disability and cognitive impairment criteria: Targeting those who need the most home care. *The Gerontologist, 34,* 640–651.

Spence, S. A., & Atherton, C. R. (1991). The Black elderly and the social service delivery system: A study of factors influencing the use of community-based services. *Journal of Gerontological Social Work, 16,* 19–35.

Starrett, R. A., Mindel, C. H., & Wright, R. (1983). Influence of support systems on the use of social services by the Hispanic elderly. *Social Work Research and Abstracts, 19,* 35–45.

Stone, R., Cafferata, G. L., & Sangl, J. (1987). Caregivers of the frail elderly: A national profile. *The Gerontologist, 27,* 616–626.

Taeuber, C. (1990). Diversity: The dramatic reality. In S. A. Bass, E. A. Kutza, & F. M. Torres-Gil (Eds.), *Diversity in aging* (pp. 1–45). Glenview, IL: Scott, Foresman.

U.S. Department of Health and Human Services. (1990). *Healthy People 2000: National Health Promotion and Disease Prevention Objectives.* Summary Report No. (PHS) 91-50213. Washington, DC: U.S. Department of Health and Human Services. Public Health Service.

U.S. Senate Special Committee on Aging, American Association of Retired Persons, Federal Council on the Aging, and U.S. Administration on Aging. *Aging America: Trends and Projections* (1991 edition). U.S. Department of Health and Human Services Pub. No. (FCoA) 91-28001, Washington, D.C.

Wallace, S. P. (1990). The no-care zone: Availability, accessibility, and acceptability in community-based long-term care. *The Gerontologist, 30,* 254–261.

Walls, C. T., & Zarit, S. H. (1991). Informal support from Black churches and the well-being of elderly Blacks. *The Gerontologist, 31,* 490–495.

Wan, T. T. H. (1982). Use of health services by the elderly in low-income communities. *Milbank Memorial Fund Quarterly, 60,* 82–107.

Wan, T. T. H. (1989). The behavioral model of health care utilization and older people. In M. Ory & K. Bond (Eds.), *Aging and health care* (pp. 52–77). New York: Routledge.

Ward, R. A. (1977). Services for older people: An integrated framework for research. *Journal of Health and Social Behavior, 18,* 61–78.

Watson, W. H. (1990). Family care, economics, and health. In Z. Harel, E. A. McKinney, & M. Williams (Eds.), *Black aged: Understanding diversity and service needs* (pp. 50–68). Newbury Park, CA: Sage.

Weeks, J., & Cuellar, J. (1981). The role of family members in the helping networks of older people. *The Gerontologist, 21,* 388–394.

Wiener, J. M. (1996). Can Medicaid long-term care expenditures for the elderly be reduced? *The Gerontologist, 36,* 800–811.

Wilson, V., & Netting, F. E. (1988). Exploring the interface of local churches with the aging network: A comparison of Anglo and Black congregations. *Journal of Religion and Aging, 5,* 5–16.

Wolinsky, F. D. (1978). Assessing the effects of predisposing, enabling, and illness-morbidity characteristics on health service utilization. *Journal of Health and Social Behavior, 19,* 394–396.

Wolinsky, F. D. (1994). Health services utilization among older adults: Conceptual, measurement, and modeling issues in secondary analysis. *The Gerontologist, 34,* 470–475.

Wolinsky, F. D., & Arnold, C. L. (1989). *Health and illness behavior among elderly Americans.* Detroit, MI: Wayne State University Press.

Wolinsky, F. D., & Johnson, R. J. (1991). The use of health services by older adults. *Journal of Gerontology, 46,* S345–S357.

Yeatts, D. E., Crow, T., & Folts, E. (1992). Service use among low-income minority elderly: Strategies for overcoming barriers. *The Gerontologist, 32,* 24–32.

_____

# Chapter Eight

# Use of In-Home and Community-Based Services among Mexican American, Cuban American, and Puerto Rican Elders

At present, about 5% of all persons living in the United States who are aged 65 and over are Hispanic (U.S. Bureau of the Census, 1996). Between 1990 and 2030, however, although the older White population is expected to grow by 92%, the projected increase for Hispanics of the same age is 395% (U.S. Bureau of the Census, 1996). The complex needs and considerable diversity within this burgeoning population present challenges for social work practice and public policy that are only beginning to be appreciated.

This study uses data from the 1988 National Survey of Hispanic Elderly People to examine (1) the status and needs of Mexican American, Cuban American, and Puerto Rican elders, and (2) the determinants of in-home and community-based health and social service use for these subnationality groups. Implications for social work practice and public policies aimed at improving access to services for different groups of Hispanic elders are discussed.

## PREVIOUS STUDIES

Recent analyses of data from the U.S. Census Bureau and several national data sets have begun to document the very serious financial, health, and social problems that Hispanic elderly persons face in the United States (Andrews, Lyons, & Rowland, 1992; Angel & Angel, 1992; Bastida, 1984; Krause & Goldenhar, 1992; Maldonado, 1989; Moscicki, Rae, Regier, & Locke, 1987). These studies confirm that Hispanic elders experience both the absolute and relative disadvantages suffered by most older ethnic minorities. For example, in comparing a national random sample of all American elders (Commonwealth Fund Commission on Elderly People Living Alone, 1989) with Hispanic elders in a companion data set (Westat, Inc., 1989),

Andrews et al. (1992) found that Hispanic elders fare worse on most major dimensions of health and well-being, particularly in terms of income, health status, facility with English, educational attainment, and functional status. Persons with low incomes and/or those in poor health were determined to be especially vulnerable.

Despite these needs, Hispanic elders tend not to use long-term care services (Eribes & Bradley-Rawls, 1978; Greene & Monahan, 1984; Starrett, Wright, Mindel, & Tran, 1989). This pattern is consistent with that of other groups of ethnic minority elders, who tend to underutilize all types of formal services (Hu, Snowden, Jerrell, & Nguyen, 1991; Kart, 1991; Mui & Burnette, 1994), including those designated for the poor and marginally poor. Starrett, Wright, Mindel, and Tran (1989) point out that research on formal service utilization by Hispanic elders has been stymied by inadequate funding and various methodological problems (see also Becerra & Zambrana, 1985; Estrada, 1985). For example, they note that most studies have been purely descriptive. Further, most researchers have ignored the diverse cultural, historical, demographic, and ecological conditions of Hispanic subnational groups in the United States (Aguirre & Bigelow, 1983), merging Mexican Americans, Cuban Americans, and Puerto Ricans into one "Hispanic" category.

Recent studies that use inferential statistical models to examine among- and within-group differences in large national samples of Hispanic elders reveal substantial group variations that exert both direct and indirect effects on socioeconomic status (Biafora & Longino, 1990; Guarnaccia, Good, & Kleinman, 1990; Lacayo & Crawford, 1980) and on physical, social, and psychological well-being (Angel & Angel, 1992; Bean & Tienda, 1987; Krause & Goldenhar, 1992). Group variations are also expected to create differential patterns of need and service use (Starrett, Todd, & De Leon, 1989; Starrett, Wright, Mindel, & Tran, 1989). A recent analysis of the likelihood of Hispanic elders' formal in-home service use—home health nurse, home health aide, and/or homemaker—based on the same data set we used shows, in fact, no significant differences among nationality groups: Puerto Ricans are mostly likely to use the services, followed by Cuban Americans, Mexican Americans, and then other Hispanics (Wallace, Campbell, & Lew-Ting, 1994). Wallace et al.'s study also found that need factors (hospitalization, physician use, and ADL/IADL), poverty status, Medicaid coverage, and living arrangements, but not level of acculturation (measured by language ability and age at which the respondent arrived in the United States), are significant predictors.

This chapter applies the Andersen–Newman behavioral model to examine among-group as well as within-group needs and patterns of in-home and community-based service use by Mexican American, Cuban American, and Puerto Rican elders.

## CONCEPTUAL FRAMEWORK

See Chapter 5 for comprehensive discussion of the Andersen–Newman (1973) model. Using that model, Starrett and his colleagues confirmed the importance of need and income variables for Hispanic elders and identified other predictors of service use for this population. Their studies indicate that overall social service use is low (Starrett, Wright, Mindel, & Tran, 1989); that environmental awareness is the strongest direct predictor of use (see also Starrett & Decker, 1984), followed by need, family income, and ethnicity (Starrett, Bresler, Decker, Walters, & Rogers, 1990); and that predictors of use differ among Mexican American, Cuban American, and Puerto Rican elders (Starrett, Todd, & De Leon, 1989; Starrett, Wright, Mindel, & Tran, 1989).

The following data analyses begin with a sociodemographic profile of these three subgroups of Hispanic elders and then compare their health and functional status, support from adult children, and in-home and community-based service use. Logistic regression models are then used to determine the predisposing, enabling, and need factors associated with use of each type of service. Not all respondents used both types of services, and the analysis examines the odds of each group's using each type of service.

## METHODOLOGY

### Data Source and Sample

Data are from the 1988 National Survey of Hispanic Elderly People. A part of the Commonwealth Fund Commission's project on elderly people living alone (Commonwealth Fund Commission on Elderly People Living Alone, 1989), the study surveyed a sample by telephone to obtain a profile of the health, economic, and social circumstances of all Hispanic persons aged 65 and over. Between August and October 1988, trained bilingual interviewers gathered information on living arrangements, dates of immigration to the United States, economic resources, health and functional status, social networks, family support, and psychological well-being (Davis, 1990).

The survey provides a nationally representative sample of Hispanics who were aged 65 and over and living within telephone exchanges that had at least 30% concentrations of Hispanic residents in three subuniverses in the United States. Using random-digit dialing, 48,183 households were screened for Hispanics aged 65 and over, resulting in completed interviews of 2,299 older Hispanics. The overall response rate was 80%, and 87% of these interviewees chose to be interviewed in Spanish. Details of sample selection and survey procedures are described elsewhere (Westat, Inc., 1989).

Several caveats are needed regarding the sampling and procedures. First, persons unable to participate in telephone interviews due to severe physical or cognitive impairments are underrepresented. Telephone surveys also underestimate low-income individuals, who are less likely to have a telephone in the home. However, Census data indicate that about 92% of elderly Hispanics live in households with telephones. Finally, all data are self-reported, and survey constraints prohibited independent verifications of responses. The data analyses that follow are based on a subsample of Mexican Americans ($n = 773$), Cuban Americans ($n = 714$), and Puerto Ricans ($n = 368$). Other Hispanic groups are not included because their numbers were limited.

## Measurement of Variables

The dependent variables are the types of long-term care service used: home health care, Meals on Wheels, congregate meals, and senior centers/churches. As outcome measures, service use is coded 1 for users of each of these services during the year prior to the interview and 0 for nonusers.

Independent variables include predisposing, enabling, and need factors, and their coding schemes are presented in Table 8.1.

With regard to predisposing factors, missing data on income were excessive, so level of education was used as a measure of social class standing (Krause & Goldenhar, 1992). Receipt of public assistance provides a rough measure of income but is unreliable because the proportion of eligible persons who do receive these services is unknown. Two dummy variables, Mexican American and Puerto Rican, were created in order to examine subgroup differences, with Cuban Americans designated as the reference group.

Psychological distress, a measure of need, was assessed by self-reported experience in the preceding few weeks of feeling restless, lonely, bored, depressed, and/or upset (each coded dichotomously). A principal components analysis with varimax rotation was performed, and the five items were summed to create a composite score of psychological distress (alpha coefficient = .71).

Use of the type of service not being examined was included as an independent variable in each regression model to control for the role of other contacts with the service-delivery system. Thus, the number of community-based services used appears in the model for assessing likelihood of in-home service use and vice versa.

## Methods of Analysis

Descriptive statistics were used to generate a profile of the three groups of Hispanic elders and their patterns of use of different types of in-home and community-based services. Twenty-one variables were then entered into a hierarchical logistic regression model with predisposing factors entered first, followed by enabling, then need factors, and finally national-origin group variables (Bass, Looman, & Ehrlich, 1992). This strategy represents a rigorous analytic procedure for examining prediction equations with dichotomous outcomes (Cox, 1978; Hosmer & Lemeshow, 1989).

The probability of a respondent using each type of service was thus estimated by calculating the odds ratio through the antilogs of the parameter estimate of each independent variable. For example, an odds ratio of 1.58 for in-home service use means that a respondent is 58% more likely to use the service than not, whereas an odds ratio of .30 indicates 70% less likelihood. Zero-order correlations of the 21 variables in the model ranged from .07 to .42, and there was no evidence of problems with multicollinearity. The relative impact of each independent variable on each type of service use was determined by comparing corresponding Wald chi-square statistics (Selvin, 1991).

## RESULTS

Table 8.2 shows that Cuban American elders are in better physical and functional health than their Mexican American and Puerto Rican counterparts. A larger percentage of Cuban Americans reported being in either excellent or good health, and they were the least impaired on every ADL and IADL.

Table 8.3 presents sources of social support, including the two types of formal service use (in home and community based) and informal network variables for the three subgroups. Puerto Rican elders reported much higher use of homemaker services (16.0%) and regular visiting nurses (17.9%) than the other two groups, and they also used more transportation and senior center services during the preceding year. Mexican Americans, on the other hand, reported greater use of mobile meals and church programs. This group also reported having more living children and more frequent contact with children each week.

Tables 8.4, 8.5, 8.6, and 8.7 present logistic regression models of home health care, Meals on Wheels, congregate meals, and senior center/church participation, respectively. The national-origin group item was entered last in both models to test for its effects after controlling for other variables.

### Factors Associated with Home Health Care and Meals on Wheels Service Use

All significant independent variables that were associated with the two types of in-home service use are presented in Tables 8.4 and 8.5.

Significant predictors of home health care service use included being older, living alone, having more children, being on public assistance, using more community-based service, suffering high levels of both ADL and IADL impairment, and a higher level of hospital use. A comparison of Wald chi-square statistics shows that hospital use was the strongest predictor of home health care service, followed by community-based service use, number of children, and

**Table 8.1**
**Variables and Measures**

| Variables | Code |
|---|---|
| **Predisposing factors** | |
| Age | < 80=0; ≥ 80 =1 |
| Gender | Female=0; male=1 |
| Length of stay in the United States | Actual years |
| Puerto Rican, Mexican American, or Cuban American | Binary variable with Cuban American as the reference group |
| **Enabling factors** | |
| Education | Categorical with higher score denoting more education/training |
| Living arrangements | Living alone=1; living with others=0 |
| English-language ability | Able to speak English=1; able to read English=1; able to write English=1 |
| No. of children | Actual no. |
| Frequency of children contact | No. of times each week |
| Recipient of public assistance | Recipient of food stamps, SSI, and/or Medicaid |

**Need for care factors**

ADL impairments (Cronbach alpha=.86)[a]
: No. of impairments (including bathing, dressing, eating, getting into & out of bed, walking, getting outside, using toilet)

IADL impairments (Cronbach alpha=.82)[a]
: No. of impairments (including preparing meals, managing money, using telephone, grocery shopping, doing heavy or light work)

Perceived health
: 1=excellent to 4=poor

Doctor visits (proxy of medical needs)
: No. of visits during the preceding 12 months

Hospital use (proxy of severity of illness)
: In the hospital during preceding 12 months; 1=yes; 0=no

Psychological distress (Cronbach alpha=.76)[a]
: Actual no. of symptoms (including feeling restless, remote, bored, depressed, upset, lonely, and anxious)

Unmet service needs (Cronbach alpha=.86)[a]
: Total no. of in-home and community-based services needed

**Utilization of Services**

In-home service use
: No. of services used (including Meals on Wheels, homemaker, home health aide, visiting nurse)

Community-based service use
: No. of services (including senior center, congregate meals, transportation, church, telephone assurance program)

---

*Data Source:* 1988 National Survey of Hispanic Elderly People.
[a]Measures were validated with factor analyses, and Cronbach alphas were calculated using the source data.

131

**Table 8.2**
**Physical and Psychological Well-Being of Hispanic Elders**

|  | Mexican American $\underline{n} = 773^a$ (%) | Cuban American $\underline{n} = 714^a$ (%) | Puerto Rican $\underline{n} = 368^a$ (%) |
|---|---|---|---|
| **Perceived health status****** |  |  |  |
| Excellent | 12.4 | 16.6 | 10.4 |
| Good | 30.3 | 37.4 | 24.3 |
| Fair | 44.8 | 37.1 | 51.1 |
| Poor | 12.5 | 8.9 | 14.2 |
| **Psychological distress variable** |  |  |  |
| Feeling restless**** | 23.7 | 22.3 | 36.9 |
| Feeling lonely*** | 25.2 | 22.6 | 33.2 |
| Feeling bored**** | 26.8 | 23.9 | 37.5 |
| Feeling depressed* | 29.1 | 27.7 | 35.9 |
| Feeling upset* | 11.8 | 8.1 | 11.7 |
| **ADL impairment** |  |  |  |
| Bathing* | 16.2 | 11.9 | 17.9 |
| Dressing* | 11.3 | 10.4 | 16.3 |
| Eating | 4.9 | 4.6 | 7.3 |
| Transfer**** | 22.8 | 15.6 | 28.0 |
| Walk**** | 30.3 | 18.1 | 35.6 |
| Going outside**** | 20.3 | 15.6 | 25.8 |
| Using toilet | 8.4 | 5.7 | 8.4 |
| **IADL impairment** |  |  |  |
| Preparing meals** | 17.9 | 11.9 | 19.8 |
| Managing money**** | 13.8 | 7.3 | 14.7 |
| Using the phone**** | 16.3 | 7.4 | 10.6 |
| Grocery shopping* | 22.1 | 17.4 | 22.8 |
| Doing heavy work**** | 39.3 | 31.8 | 44.8 |
| Doing light work** | 15.0 | 13.0 | 20.7 |

*Data Source*: 1988 National Survey of Hispanic Elderly People.
*Note*: Chi-square statistics were used.
[a]Unweighted Ns.
*$p < 0.05$; **$p < 0.01$; ***$p < 0.001$; ****$p < 0.0001$.

then IADL and ADL impairment. Persons who had used hospital and community-based services were more likely to have used home health service during the preceding 12 months.

Need factors, as a set, had the highest predictive power for home health care service use, followed by enabling conditions. Three need variables, higher ADL and IADL impairment and more hospital use were associated with increased odds of using home health care services. Hispanic group membership had no independent effect on in-home service use, when other variables in the model were controlled for.

**Table 8.3**
**Social Support of Hispanic Elders**

| | Mexican American n = 773 | Cuban American n = 714 | Puerto Rican n = 368 |
|---|---|---|---|
| **In-home service use (%)[a]** | | | |
| Home maker service**** | 6.7 | 4.8 | 16.0 |
| Visiting nurse**** | 8.9 | 9.5 | 17.9 |
| Home health aide | 4.1 | 5.7 | 6.8 |
| Meals on Wheels**** | 8.5 | 3.4 | 3.5 |
| **Community-based service use (%)[a]** | | | |
| Transportation**** | 8.9 | 18.1 | 22.6 |
| Senior center**** | 12.0 | 9.4 | 19.8 |
| Congregate meals** | 14.9 | 10.2 | 15.8 |
| Telephone checks | 4.7 | 3.5 | 4.1 |
| Church programs**** | 8.4 | 2.7 | 5.4 |
| **Informal support network[b]** | | | |
| No. of children (mean)* | 4.6 | 2.0 | 3.8 |
| Frequency of children contact per week (mean)* | 2.5 | 1.6 | 1.3 |

*Data Source*: 1988 National Survey of Hispanic Elderly People.
[a]Chi-square statistics were used.
[b]ANOVA statistics were used to test the differences between means.
*$p < 0.05$; **$p < 0.01$; ***$p < 0.001$; ****$p < 0.0001$.

Significant predictors of Meals on Wheels use were having the ability to read English, more community-based service use, and being Mexican American. Elders who used community-based service were 18 times more likely to use Meals on Wheels service, while need factors did not predict Meals on Wheels service use. Hispanic group membership had an independent effect on Meals on Wheels service use, with Mexican Americans more likely to use Meals on Wheels services than Cuban Americans, when other variables in the model were controlled for.

### Factors Associated with Congregate Meal and Senior Center/Church Programs

Significant predictor variables associated with the likelihood of use of congregate meals and services provided by senior centers/churches are presented in Tables 8.6 and 8.7.

Congregate meal service use was associated with a longer length of stay in the United States, living alone, having the ability to read English, using more in-home services, and a lower level of hospital use. Being a user of in-home

**Table 8.4**
**Logistic Regression Analysis of Home Health Care Service Use by Hispanic Elders**

| Variables | Home care service use | | |
| | Unstandardized logit coefficients ($\underline{SE}$)[a] | Odds ratio[b] | Wald chi-square |
|---|---|---|---|
| **Predisposing factors** | | | |
| Age (≥80=1) | 0.67(0.21) | 1.96** | 10.33 |
| Gender (Male=1) | -0.14(0.19) | | |
| Length of stay in the United States | -0.01(0.01) | | |
| | | | |
| **Enabling factors** | | | |
| Education | -0.03(0.02) | | |
| Living alone (alone=1) | 0.56(0.21) | 1.74** | 7.14 |
| Able to speak English | 0.03(0.13) | | |
| Able to read English | -0.14(0.30) | | |
| Able to write English | 0.13(0.31) | | |
| No. of children | -0.48(0.24) | 0.62* | 3.81 |
| Frequency of children contact | 0.07(0.06) | | |
| On public assistance[c] | 0.25(0.10) | 1.28* | 6.47 |
| Community-based service use | 0.36(0.09) | 1.43**** | 15.66 |
| | | | |
| **Need for care factors** | | | |
| ADL impairment | 0.18(0.07) | 1.20** | 8.00 |
| IADL impairment | 0.16(0.08) | 1.20* | 4.54 |
| Self-rated health | 0.01(0.04) | | |
| Doctor visits | 0.01(0.01) | | |
| Hospital use | 1.19(0.18) | 3.30**** | 40.83 |
| Psychological distress | 0.04(0.07) | | |
| Unmet service needs | 0.04(0.04) | | |
| | | | |
| **Hispanic subgroup** | | | |
| Mexican American (vs. Cuban=0) | -0.14(0.29) | | |
| Puerto Rican (vs. Cuban=0) | -0.10(0.24) | | |
| | | | |
| Intercept | -2.51**** | | |
| Model chi square | 249.74**** | | |

*Data Source*: 1988 National Survey of Hispanic Elderly People.
[a]Standard error.
[b]Odds ratios were calculated for the significant coefficients.
[c]Recipients of food stamps, SSI, and/or Medicaid.
*$p < 0.05$; **$p < 0.01$; ***$p < 0.001$; ****$p < 0.0001$.

services was also associated with increased odds of using congregate meal service. Hispanic group membership had no independent effect on congregate meal service use. The use of senior center or church programs was associated with use of in-home services and lower levels of ADL impairments. Using other in-home services was associated with increased odds of using senior center and church programs.

**Table 8.5**
**Logistic Regression Analysis of Meals on Wheels Service Use by Hispanic Elders**

| Variables | Meals on Wheels service use | | |
| --- | --- | --- | --- |
| | Unstandardized logit coefficients (SE)[a] | Odds ratio[b] | Wald chi-square |
| **Predisposing factors** | | | |
| Age (≥80=1) | 0.35(0.36) | | |
| Gender (Male=1) | 0.02(0.19) | | |
| Length of stay in the United States | 0.20(0.02) | | |
| **Enabling factors** | | | |
| Education | 0.14(0.26) | | |
| Living alone (alone=1) | 0.10(0.20) | | |
| Able to speak English | -0.37(0.36) | | |
| Able to read English | 0.14(0.30) | 3.86*** | 8.87 |
| Able to write English | 0.58(0.46) | | |
| No. of children | 0.01(0.05) | | |
| Frequency of children contact | 0.08(0.08) | | |
| On public assistance[c] | 0.03(0.16) | | |
| Community-based service use | 0.36(0.09) | 18.35**** | 184.15 |
| **Need for care factors** | | | |
| ADL impairment | 0.06(0.12) | | |
| IADL impairment | 0.05(0.08) | | |
| Self-rated health | -0.13(0.12) | | |
| Doctor visits | 0.00(0.01) | | |
| Hospital use | -0.34(0.18) | | |
| Psychological distress | -0.04(0.07) | | |
| Unmet service needs | 0.14(0.10) | | |
| **Hispanic subgroups** | | | |
| Mexican American (vs. Cuban=0) | 1.22(0.49) | 3.40** | 6.90 |
| Puerto Rican (vs. Cuban=0) | 0.41(0.40) | | |
| Intercept | -5.54**** | | |
| Model chi square | 677.28**** | | |

*Data Source*: 1988 National Survey of Hispanic Elderly People.
[a]Standard error.
[b]Odds ratios were calculated for the significant coefficients.
[c]Recipients of food stamps, SSI, and/or Medicaid.
*$p < 0.05$; **$p < 0.01$; ***$p < 0.001$; ****$p < 0.0001$.

## DISCUSSION AND SUMMARY

Using a national-area probability sample of Hispanic elders, this study extends current knowledge about addressing gaps in service delivery by examining among- and within-group differences for Mexican Americans, Cuban Americans, and Puerto Ricans and by examining the predictors of different in-home and community-based services.

**Table 8.6**
**Logistic Regression Analysis of Congregate Meal Service Use by Hispanic Elders**

| Variables | Unstandardized logit coefficients (SE)[a] | Odds ratio[b] | Wald chi-square |
|---|---|---|---|
| | Congregate meal service use | | |
| **Predisposing factors** | | | |
| Age (≥80=1) | 0.59(0.47) | | |
| Gender (Male=1) | -0.08(0.19) | | |
| Length of stay in the United States | 0.03(0.01) | 1.10** | 5.48 |
| **Enabling factors** | | | |
| Education | -0.71(0.51) | | |
| Living alone (alone=1) | 1.33(0.46) | 3.78*** | 8.07 |
| Able to speak English | -0.67(0.30) | | |
| Able to read English | 1.75(0.62) | 5.76*** | 7.82 |
| Able to write English | -1.32(0.35) | | |
| No. of children | 0.00(0.00) | | |
| Frequency of children contact | -0.06(0.15) | | |
| On public assistance[c] | 0.25(0.22) | | |
| In-home service use | 0.36(0.09) | 35.84**** | 100.84 |
| **Need for care factors** | | | |
| ADL impairment | -0.14(0.07) | | |
| IADL impairment | 0.23(0.16) | | |
| Self-rated health | -0.23(0.12) | | |
| Doctor visits | 0.01(0.01) | | |
| Hospital use | -1.72(0.52) | 0.18** | 10.78 |
| Psychological distress | 0.00(0.01) | | |
| Unmet service needs | 0.02(0.04) | | |
| **Hispanic subgroups** | | | |
| Mexican American (vs. Cuban=0) | -0.13(0.29) | | |
| Puerto Rican (vs. Cuban=0) | 0.32(0.30) | | |
| Intercept | -6.68** | | |
| Model Chi Square | 678.65*** | | |

*Data Source*: 1988 National Survey of Hispanic Elderly People.
[a]Standard error.
[b]Odds ratios were calculated for the significant coefficients.
[c]Recipients of food stamps, SSI, and/or Medicaid.
*$p < 0.05$; **$p < 0.01$; ***$p < 0.001$; ****$p < 0.0001$.

Knowledge of the availability of services is a powerful determinant of use (Chapleski, 1989; Snider, 1980; Starrett et al., 1990), and several studies suggest that knowledge may depend in part on ethnic density. High concentrations of ethnic groups may facilitate the dissemination of knowledge and may increase the availability and accessibility of services (D. Holmes, M. Holmes, Steinbach, Hausner, & Rocheleau, 1979). The dispersal of Mexican

**Table 8.7**
**Logistic Regression Analysis of Senior Center/Church Use by Hispanic Elders**

| Variables | Senior center/church service use | | |
|---|---|---|---|
| | Unstandardized logit coefficients ($\underline{SE}$)[a] | Odds ratio[b] | Wald chi-square |
| **Predisposing factors** | | | |
| Age ($\geq$80=1) | 0.18(0.13) | | |
| Gender (Male=1) | 0.02(0.14) | | |
| Length of stay in the United States | 0.35(0.23) | | |
| **Enabling factors** | | | |
| Education | 0.18(0.13) | | |
| Living alone (alone=1) | 0.00(0.00) | | |
| Able to speak English | 0.51(0.36) | | |
| Able to read English | 0.54(0.30) | | |
| Able to write English | 0.20(0.16) | | |
| No. of children | -0.08(0.05) | | |
| Frequency of children contact | -0.08(0.12) | | |
| On public assistance[c] | 0.08(0.10) | | |
| In-home service use | 0.89(0.32) | 2.40** | 7.44 |
| **Need for care factors** | | | |
| ADL impairment | -0.93(0.40) | 0.39** | 5.43 |
| IADL impairment | 0.23(0.14) | | |
| Self-rated health | 0.08(0.12) | | |
| Doctor visits | 0.01(0.01) | | |
| Hospital use | 0.28(0.18) | | |
| Psychological distress | 0.04(0.07) | | |
| Unmet service needs | 0.06(0.06) | | |
| **Hispanic subgroups** | | | |
| Mexican American (vs. Cuban=0) | 0.56(0.49) | | |
| Puerto Rican (vs. Cuban=0) | 0.98(0.39) | | |
| Intercept | -5.32*** | | |
| Model chi square | 127.48*** | | |

*Data Source*: 1988 National Survey of Hispanic Elderly People.
[a]Standard error.
[b]Odds ratios were calculated for the significant coefficients.
[c]Recipients of food stamps, SSI, and/or Medicaid.
*$p < 0.05$; **$p < 0.01$; ***$p < 0.001$; ****$p < 0.0001$.

Americans, particularly in rural areas, may contribute to a lack of awareness of and hence to lower use of services.

Return migration also affects Hispanic groups differently. Unlike immigrant Mexican American and Puerto Rican elders, Cuban American counterparts do not return to their original homes because of political conditions there. This may be one reason that Cuban American elders constitute a higher proportion of their Hispanic subgroup than Puerto Rican or Mexican American elders (Aguirre & Bigelow, 1983). The stability of this migration pattern may also help explain why Cuban American elders benefit from close-knit ethnic enclaves that largely preserve their original culture and native language (Angel & Angel, 1992; Perez, 1986).

With regard to multivariate findings, the Andersen–Newman model was useful in explaining each type of long-term care service use. The greater likelihood of older elders using home health care services is likely due to increased frailty. Previous studies using the Andersen–Newman model to explain service use by older adults consistently reported that illness or disability, hence need, explains most of the variance in service utilization in multivariate analysis (Coulton & Frost, 1982; Wan, 1982; Wolinsky & Johnson, 1991). Need factors, as a set, had the strongest effect on home health care use, a finding that is consistent with previous research (Burnette & Mui, 1995). However, enabling factors played a more significant role in predicting utilization of Meals on Wheels, congregate meals, and senior center/church programs.

Living alone was also a predictor of using congregate meal services. Older persons who live alone are less likely to have reliable informal support systems and may be more likely to enjoy congregate meals and socialization with other elders in meal sites.

The other enabling factor that predicted use of home health service was the use of other community-based services. For congregate meal and senior center/church program use, the strongest predictor was the use of in-home services. These findings are likely attributable to the benefits derived from already being in the service-delivery system. Having more children was associated with use of home health service. Family members of these Hispanic elderly may be serving as mediators for the elderly relative, negotiating with the system to get the home health service. Ethnic minority elders often depend on family for this more intensive, hands-on type of care. Unique predictors for home health care service use were need-related factors of ADL and IADL impairment and hospital use. Mexican American and Puerto Rican elders were neither more nor less likely than their Cuban American counterparts to use home health care, congregate meals, and senior centers. The findings seem to suggest that these three groups of Hispanic elders were not different in their experience of using long-term care services except that Mexican Americans were more likely than Cuban Americans to use Meals on Wheels services. The dispersal of Mexican Americans, particularly in rural areas, may contribute to a need for Meals on Wheels services.

In summary, these data support and extend the findings of previous studies that have used the Andersen–Newman model to evaluate service utilization by Hispanic elders. Needs were the strongest predictor of home health care service use, followed by enabling, then predisposing factors. Enabling factors, on the other hand, make the greatest contribution to use of Meals on Wheels, congregate meals, and senior center/church services. Social workers are crucial to making the current service-delivery system more responsive to an increasingly racially and ethnically diverse population of older Americans. Knowledge is the single most mutable variable necessary to increase the use of social services; focusing outreach efforts on those with the greatest needs and at same time increasing the general level of knowledge about services can compensate for some of the common structural barriers (Starrett & Decker, 1984).

Social workers can improve access to needed services by decreasing barriers such as inadequate income and insurance and by promoting individual and programmatic sensitivity to cultural norms, customs, and beliefs (Parra & Espino, 1992; Rivera, 1990). They should also seek to maximize the powerful influence of "lay referral structures," which can impede or promote use of professional services by ethnic elders (Birkel & Reppucci, 1983; House, Landis, & Umberson, 1988). Finally, Sotomayor (1989) points out that empowerment, or the process of self-help and mutual help to gain mastery, is a cultural tool traditionally used by Hispanics to ameliorate stress from adverse socioeconomic and political conditions. Community human services networks can be used effectively to assess community resources, encourage intra-agency cooperation, and target appropriate services to their most vulnerable constituents.

## REFERENCES

Aguirre, B. E., & Bigelow, A. (1983). The aged in Hispanic groups: A review. *International Journal of Aging and Human Development, 17*, 177–201.

Andersen, R., & Newman, J. F. (1973). Societal and individual determinants of medical care utilization in the U.S. *Milbank Memorial Fund Quarterly, 51*, 95–124.

Andrews, J. W., Lyons, B., & Rowland, D. (1992). Life satisfaction and peace of mind: A comparative analysis of elderly Hispanic and other elderly Americans. *Clinical Gerontologist, 11*, 21–42.

Angel, J., & Angel, R. J. (1992). Age at migration, social connections, and well-being among elderly Hispanics. *Journal of Aging and Health, 4*, 480–499.

Bass, D. M., Looman, W. J., & Ehrlich, P. (1992). Predicting the volume of health and social services: Integrating cognitive impairment into the modified Andersen framework. *The Gerontologist, 32*, 33–43.

Bastida, E. (1984). The elderly of Hispanic origin: Population characteristics for 1980. *Mid-American Review of Sociology, 9*, 41–47.

Bean, F. D., & Tienda, M. (1987). *The Hispanic population of the United States.* New York: Russell Sage.

Becerra, R. M., & Zambrana, R. E. (1985). Methodological approaches to research on Hispanics. *Social Work Research and Abstracts, 21*, 42–49.

Biafora, F. A, & Longino, C. F. (1990). Elderly Hispanic migration in the United States. *Journal of Gerontology, 45*, S212–S219.

Birkel, R. C., & Reppucci, N. D. (1983). Social networks, information-seeking, and the utilization of services. *American Journal of Community Psychology, 11*, 185–205.

Burnette, D., & Mui, A. C. (1995). In-home and community-based service use by three groups of elderly Hispanics: A national perspective. *Social Work Research, 19,* 197–206.

Chapleski, E. E. (1989). Determinants of knowledge of services to the elderly: Are strong ties enabling or inhibiting? *The Gerontologist, 29,* 539–545.

Commonwealth Fund Commission on Elderly People Living Alone. (1989). *Poverty and poor health among elderly Hispanic Americans.* New York: The Commonwealth Foundation.

Coulton, C., & Frost, A. K. (1982). Use of social and health services by the elderly. *Journal of Health and Social Behavior, 23,* 330–339.

Cox, D. (1978). *Analysis of binary data.* London: Chapman and Hall.

Davis, K. (1990). *National survey of Hispanic elderly people, 1988.* Ann Arbor, MI: Interuniversity Consortium for Political and Social Research.

Eribes, R. A., & Bradley-Rawls, M. (1978). The underutilization of nursing home facilities by Mexican-American elderly in the Southwest. *The Gerontologist, 18,* 363–371.

Estrada, L. F. (1985). The dynamics of Hispanic populations: A description and comparison. *Social Thought, 11,* 23–39.

Greene, V. L., & Monahan, D. J. (1984). Comparative utilization of community-based long-term care services by Hispanic and Anglo elderly in a case management system. *Journal of Gerontology, 39,* 730–735.

Guarnaccia, P. J., Good, B. J., & Kleinman, A. (1990). A critical review of epidemiological studies of Puerto Rican mental health. *American Journal of Psychiatry, 147,* 1449–1456.

Holmes, D., Holmes, M., Steinbach, L., Hausner, T., & Rocheleau, B. (1979). The use of community-based services in long-term care of older minority persons. *The Gerontologist, 19,* 389–397.

Hosmer, D. W., and Lemeshow, S. (1989). *Applied logistic regression.* New York: John Wiley & Sons.

House, J. S., Landis, K. R., & Umberson, D. (1988, June 28). Social relationships and health. *Science,* 540–545.

Hu, T., Snowden, L. R., Jerrell, J. M., & Nguyen, T. D. (1991). Ethnic populations in public mental health: Services choices and level of use. *American Journal of Public Health, 81,* 1429–1434.

Kart, C. S. (1991). Variation in long-term care service use by aged Blacks. *Journal of Aging and Health, 3,* 511–526.

Krause, N., & Goldenhar, L. M. (1992). Acculturation and psychological distress in three groups of elderly Hispanics. *Journal of Gerontology, 47,* S279–S288.

Lacayo, C. G., & Crawford, J. K. (1980). *A national study to assess the service needs of the Hispanic elderly.* Los Angeles, CA: Association National Pro Personas Mayores.

Maldonado, D. (1989). The Latino elderly living alone: The invisible poor. *California Sociologist, 12,* 8–21.

Moscicki, E. K., Rae, D. S., Regier, D. A., & Locke, B. Z. (1987). The Hispanic health and nutrition survey: Depression among Mexican American, Cuban Americans, and Puerto Ricans. In M. Gaviria & J. D. Arana (Eds.), *Health and behavior: Research agenda for Hispanics.* Chicago: University of Chicago Press.

Mui, A. C., & Burnette, D. (1994). Long-term care service use by frail elders: Is ethnicity a factor? *The Gerontologist, 34,* 190–198.

Parra, E. O., & Espino, D. V. (1992). Barriers to health care access faced by elderly Mexican Americans. (Special Issue: Hispanic aged mental health). *Clinical Gerontologist, 11*, 171–177.

Perez, L. (1986). Cubans in the United States. *Annals of the American Academy of Political and Social Science, 487*, 126–137.

Rivera, R. (1990). *The effects of social class on health care utilization of Puerto Ricans in the United States.* Unpublished doctoral dissertation, Brandeis University, Waltham, Massachusetts.

Selvin, S. (1991). *Monographs in epidemiology and biostatistics.* New York: Oxford University Press.

Snider, E. (1980). Factors influencing health services knowledge among the elderly. *Journal of Health and Social Behavior, 21*, 371–377.

Sotomayor, M. (1989). Empowerment and the Latino elderly. *California Sociologist, 12*, 65–83.

Starrett, R. A., & Decker, J. T. (1984). The utilization of discretionary services by the Hispanic elderly: A causal analysis. *California Sociologist, 7*, 159–180.

Starrett, R. A., Bresler, C., Decker, J. T., Walters, G. T., & Rogers, D. (1990). The role of environmental awareness and support networks in Hispanic elderly persons' use of formal social services. *Journal of Community Psychology, 18*, 218–227.

Starrett, R. A., Todd, A. M., & De Leon, L. (1989). A comparison of social service utilization behavior of the Cuban and Puerto Rican elderly. *Hispanic Journal of Behavioral Sciences, 11*, 341–353.

Starrett, R. A., Wright, R., Mindel, C. H., & Tran, T. V. (1989). The use of social services by Hispanic elderly: A comparison of Mexican American, Puerto Rican, and Cuban elderly. *Journal of Social Service Research, 13*, 1–25.

U.S. Bureau of the Census. (1996). *Population projections of the United States by age, sex, race, and Hispanic origin: 1995–2050.* Current Population Reports, P24-1130. Washington, DC: U.S. Government Printing Office.

Wallace, S. P., Campbell, K., & Lew-Ting, C. (1994). Structural barriers to the use of formal in-home services by elderly Latinos. *Journal of Gerontology, 49*, S253–S263.

Wan, T. T. H. (1982). Use of health services by the elderly in low-income communities. *Milbank Memorial Fund Quarterly, 60*, 82–107.

Westat, Inc. (1989). *A survey of elderly Hispanics.* Report of the Commonwealth Fund Commission on Elderly People Living Alone. Rockville, MD: Author.

Wolinski, F. D., & Johnson, R. J. (1991). The use of health services by older adults. *Journal of Gerontology, 46*, S345–S357.

_____

# Chapter Nine

# Living Arrangements and
# Utilization of Formal Services

Minority elders have significantly different living arrangements than White elders: They are much less likely to live alone or with only their spouse and are more likely to live with other family members. The analysis of the 1990 Census data (Himes, Hogan, & Eggebeen, 1996) shows that almost half of White elders aged 60 or older lived with their spouse only, but fewer than one-third of African American and Hispanic elders lived with their spouse only. A little more than one-fourth of White elders, as compared to fewer than one-fifth of African American and one-sixth of Hispanic elders, lived alone. But both African Americans and Hispanics were more than twice as likely to live with kin with or without a spouse.

Because living arrangements constitute an important predictor for receiving assistance and utilizing informal and formal services for frail elders, we analyze in this chapter (1) the differences in sociodemographic and health characteristics of White, African American, and Hispanic elders by living arrangements, (2) the association between living arrangements and informal support, and (3) the association between living arrangements and the likelihood of using in-home and community-based services among White, African American, and Hispanic elders.

## RACIAL DIFFERENCE IN LIVING ARRANGEMENTS

Married older persons almost always live with their spouse, with or without other kin in the household, and the spouse usually serves as the primary caregiver when their health deteriorates. Unmarried older persons have the choice of living alone or with others—children, grandchildren, other relatives, or nonrelatives. But one of the most notable demographic shifts that has occurred among unmarried older persons since the middle part of this century has been a significant increase in the proportion of those who live alone. The increasing propensities of unmarried older persons to live alone has been attributed to the availability of retirement income from public and private sources and the resulting improvement in economic status of the elderly (Michael, Fuchs, & Scott, 1980; Mutchler, 1992; Mutchler & Burr, 1991; Worobey & Angel, 1990a). In addition to economic affordability, the increasing tendency to live alone has been attributed to general demographic shifts such as the increase in divorce and single parenthood, the decrease in fertility, and the increase in single-person households among the younger generation and the subsequent aging of this population (Santi, 1988).

With respect to determinants of elderly's living arrangements, studies have also shown that the availability of kin, especially children, and health status were closely associated with the living arrangements of unmarried older persons (Macunovich, Easterlin, Schaeffer, & Crimmins, 1995; Spitze, Logan, & Robinson, 1992; Wolf, 1990; Worobey & Angel, 1990b). Kasper (1988) found that older persons who live alone are less likely to have living children than those who live with others. Mutchler (1992) reported that the number of children ever born to a person was the only significant variable in the transition from living alone to living with others among nonmarried individuals aged 55 and over during a two-and-a-half-year period. But Soldo, Wolf, and Agree (1990) found that it is primarily the simple availability of adult children, rather than the number and type, that determines whether an older unmarried woman will live alone and require formal services. With regard to the effect of health on living arrangement, older persons who live alone, as compared to those who live with others, were consistently found to have fewer medical problems and less functional and cognitive impairment (Lawton, Moss, & Kleban, 1984; Mui & Burnette, 1994; Worobey & Angel, 1990b). Health was found to be most important in explaining institutionalization (Mutchler & Burr, 1991; Worobey & Angel, 1990b).

In addition to affordability, availability of kin, and health status, race/ethnicity is a significant determinant of elderly's living arrangement. Because a lower proportion of African American and Hispanic elders are married (due in part to their higher rate of widowhood between ages 65 and 75), these minority elders are much less likely than White elders to live with a spouse. It has also been found that unmarried African American and Hispanic elders, especially women, were more likely than their White counterparts to coreside with their children or other relatives regardless of their financial resources and health status (Angel, Angel, & Himes, 1992; Choi, 1991; 1995; 1996; Hays, Fillenbaum, Gold, Shanley, & Blazer, 1995; Thomas & Wister, 1984; Wolf, 1984).

Because unmarried African American and Hispanic elders are on average much more likely to be poor than their White counterparts, many of them may not be economically able to sustain independent living arrangements. But African American and Hispanic elderly on average are also more likely to have lived in multigenerational or extended families throughout their lives (Ruggles & Goeken, 1992; Sotomayer & Applewhite, 1988). The cultural norms regarding cohesive familism and kinship responsibilities for elderly family members may thus explain the higher likelihood of minority elders to coreside with kin and receive assistance from the younger generation (Chatters & Taylor, 1990; Markides & Mindel, 1987; Mitchell & Register, 1984; Watson, 1990). Because of the higher birthrate and larger families among Hispanics, their elders are especially likely to have opportunities to live with their children (Bean & Tienda, 1987; Burr & Mutchler, 1992). The higher proportion of Hispanic elders who are immigrants also contributes to the higher likelihood that they will live with their adult children, because immigrants are less likely than the native born to have economic resources and more likely to have social/structural barriers to independent living (e.g., English-language proficiency) (Angel, Angel, McClellan, & Markides, 1996).

Studies have also illustrated that cultural norms of mutual assistance among African Americans and Hispanics motivate older persons to take in their children and grandchildren to help them with child care and household chores and to provide economic resources (Gratton, 1987; Mutran, 1985; Ruggles & Goeken, 1992). The analysis of data from the 1984 Survey on Aging shows that unmarried African American and Hispanic elderly women were nearly three times as likely as their non-Hispanic White counterparts to live with children as the head of the household (Worobey & Angel, 1990a). Choi's study (1996) of the composition of unmarried women's households between 1971 and 1991 also found that one of the most striking changes was the increasing proportion of African Americans and Hispanics who coreside with relatives (including children) as head of the household.

## RELATIONSHIP BETWEEN INFORMAL AND FORMAL SUPPORT: LIVING ARRANGEMENT AS SOURCE OF CARE?

As mentioned, married older persons, regardless of race/ethnicity, are most likely to receive care from their spouse and thus may not need to change their living arrangements even when their health starts to deteriorate. However, in the event of serious declines in functional and/or cognitive capacity, a single older person who is living alone may have to continue to live alone, move in with others who can provide instrumental assistance with ADL, or enter an institution, depending on the availability of informal support. An analysis based on the 1986 Longitudinal Study of Aging shows that a decline in functional capacity greatly increases the likelihood that an elderly person will move in with others or be institutionalized. Nevertheless, the study also found that, even when they experience significant decline in health, most single elderly persons who lived alone—African Americans more likely than Whites—continued to do so two years later (Worobey & Angel, 1990b).

Stephens and Christianson (1986) found that on average people living alone or with a spouse had fewer caregivers than those living with a child or others. For those living alone, this may be because they are less likely to have living children than are those who live with others; 37% of African American and 26% of White elders living alone have no children (Kasper, 1988).

If elders who live alone have fewer caregivers, are they more likely than those who live with others to utilize formal services to meet their care needs? To date, the relationship between living arrangement and the likelihood of utilization of formal service has not been extensively analyzed. But the relationship between informal support and formal service utilization has been a topic of numerous previous studies. We would like to apply the conceptual framework concerning the relationship between informal support and formal service utilization in our attempt to examine the association between living arrangement and formal service utilization. Existing research on a reciprocal relationship between informal and formal support has usually tested two competing hypotheses and a third one that is, in some respects, a compromise of the two hypotheses: (1) the hierarchical compensatory or substitution hypothesis, which posits a negative reciprocal relationship between the two types of support, (2) the linking hypothesis, which posits a positive reciprocal relationship, and (3) the task-specific hypothesis, which posits that there are different domains of care appropriate for informal and formal support.

The hierarchical compensatory model (Cantor, 1981; Shanas, 1979) argues that a preferential ordering of or ranks in caregiving both within kin relations and a primacy of kin over nonkin relations exist (spouse, followed by children, followed by other relatives, followed by friends and neighbors, followed by formal sources of care). So, in this model the interplay between informal and formal sources of care is determined primarily by the extent of informal sources of care. Only when informal sources of help are unavailable are formal services brought in. In the same vein, when formal services are available, family members decrease their support, which leads to more reliance on formal support and less reliance on informal support (thus, substitution effect) (Miner, 1995).

In contrast to the compensatory or substitution hypothesis, the linking hypothesis argues that the levels of informal and formal support are positively associated with each other, because the informal network connects older people to formal sources of care and continues to be highly involved even when the formal sources of care are being actively utilized by the older relatives (Stoller, 1989). In turn, formal services may link frail elders to informal networks for support that may not be available through the formal service system.

The task-specific model (Litwak, 1985) views certain caregiving tasks as being more appropriately provided by the informal network and others as being more suitable for formal sources of care. Thus, frail elderly in need of caregiving will end up resorting to both informal and formal sources of care for specific tasks. So, informal and formal sources of care complement each other for an ideal as well as practical care arrangement. Litwak also argues that the task-specific caregiving model applies within the informal support network in which specific needs of older persons are matched to the composition and structural characteristic of each group in the network. For example, the spouse or coresiding daughter is most likely to be responsible for daily caregiving chores for the severely impaired elderly spouse/parent. But elders who need minimal assistance or do not have proximate kin may receive caregiving from friends and/or neighbors.

Some study findings show that spouses are more likely to provide caregiving for greater disability and illness and for a longer period of time (Hess & Soldo, 1985; Montgomery & Kosloski, 1994). But other empirical studies on living arrangements and sources of caregiving do not support the hierarchical compensatory model: Cafferata (1987) found that living in the same household rather than marital status per se is what ensures informal support; Chappell (1991) confirmed that spouses are the primary caregivers for married older persons, but found that when an older person lives with someone else, that someone else, irrespective of relationship to the older person, becomes the primary caregiver. Thus, it is the structural characteristic of living arrangement—living with someone versus living alone—that determines the receipt of informal support. Based on the data from AHEAD, Norgard and Rodgers (1997) also confirmed that coresidence, as opposed to kinship ties, may be a more important factor in determining care patterns; for example, those who live with a spouse or child use less formal care than those who live alone.

In regard to substitution effects, however, Miller and McFall (1991) found a greater use of formal in-home personal care and home-maintenance services among older adults experiencing a decline in access to informal helpers. Penning (1995) found that utilization of formal home care was negatively correlated with high informal instrumental support. Miner (1995), based on the 1984 Supplement on Aging, also supports the substitution hypothesis fully for older Whites, but only partially for older African Americans. Among African Americans, receiving formal services was not associated with lower use of informal support, but informal support reduced the likelihood of formal support. Logan and Spitze (1994) also found support for the compensatory (as well as linking) hypothesis from their study of the relationship between informal and formal support among predominantly White elders.

On the other hand, Stoller (1989) found from her upstate New York sample of elder-caregiver dyads that informal helpers did not withdraw their support when formal substitutes were available. In fact, formal services were most frequently used by more functionally impaired elderly whose informal caregivers had already been providing personal care. Informal helpers who were employed elsewhere reported heavier reliance on formal services, but being employed did not depress the level of informal support the caregiver provided. Shapiro (1986) also reported a positive relationship between contact with relatives and the utilization of formal home care services.

## RACIAL DIFFERENCE IN THE RELATIONSHIP BETWEEN LIVING ARRANGEMENT AND FORMAL SERVICE USE

As just reviewed, findings from existing studies do not agree on the exact relationship between informal and formal support and do not shed much light on the relationship between living arrangements and the likelihood of formal service utilization. With respect to the effect of race/ethnicity as an intervening variable in the relationship between informal and formal support, studies also present inconsistent findings, possibly due to differences in sampling and other research methodology.

At least one study (Miner, 1995) indicated that race/ethnicity may be a significant intervening variable, because Whites and African Americans showed a different reciprocal pattern in utilizing informal and formal services. On the other hand, Miller, McFall, and Campbell (1994) found that race was not a major influence on changes in sources of care (from informal only to mixed informal and formal) when other variables such as socioeconomic and health statuses were controlled. But compared to Whites, African Americans were less likely to use mixed sources of help and more likely to shift to strictly informal help two years later. The authors further reported that the socioeconomic and health characteristics distinguishing those with informal help from those with mixed informal and formal help were similar for African Americans and Whites. Norgard and Rodgers (1997) also found that race (White versus African American) is not a significant explanatory variable for utilization of any formal help. They found that formal service use is significantly positively correlated with living alone (as opposed to living with spouse or others) and the level of functional impairment.

Unfortunately, few studies have explored the difference between Hispanics and Whites in the relationship between informal and formal service use. Hispanic elders, in spite of higher rates of disease and disability, are less likely to utilize nursing homes than their white counterparts, and they are also less likely to use other types of formal services. Hispanics' lower rate of nursing home use is often attributed to their higher rate of residing in multigenerational households (Talamantes, Cornell, Espino, Lichtenstein, & Hazuda, 1996). With the same logic and in support of the compensatory hypothesis or substitution hypothesis, their living arrangement patterns may also reduce the likelihood of them utilizing other formal in-home and community-based services. In other words, family members are a significant component of social support and the source of most informal support and care for frail elders (Stone, Cafferata, & Sangl, 1987). Thus, frail elders who live with kin (including spouse) may be more likely than those who live alone to depend on informal help. On the other hand, it is also possible that relatives shouldering the heavy burden of home care for elders who have serious health problems link those elders to supplemental services from formal sources to ease their own caregiving burden and continue to keep the elders at home.

For Hispanics, another confounding variable may be national origin (e.g., Mexican, Puerto Rican, Cuban, and Central or South American). Talamantes et al. (1996) found no significant national-origin difference per se in perceived caregiver availability. But because national origin has been found to have a differential effect on living arrangements of older Hispanics (Burr & Mutchler, 1992; Zsembik, 1992), it may thus be a significant antecedent variable for formal service use.

In summary, race/ethnicity is an unequivocally significant factor in elderly's living arrangement. Our question is, Do different living arrangements among White, African American, and Hispanic frail elders condition the influence of predisposing, enabling, and need factors that are associated with their utilization of in-home and community-based formal services? In the remainder of this chapter, we analyze within-group differences among White, African American, and Hispanic elders in the relationship between living arrangements and the utilization of in-home and community-based formal services. Among Hispanics, we conduct separate analyses for Mexican Americans, Puerto Ricans, and Cuban Americans.

## METHODOLOGY

### Data Sources and Sample

The sources of data for this chapter are the 1982 Long-Term Care Channeling Demonstration, 1982–1984, and the National Survey of Hispanic Elderly People, 1988. The Long-Term Care Channeling Demonstration survey was used to compare within-group differences among White, African American, and Hispanic frail elders, and the National Survey of Hispanic Elderly People was used to compare differences within subgroups of Hispanic elders—Mexican Americans, Puerto Ricans, and Cuban Americans. A detailed description of the data sets is found in Chapter 2.

### Analytical Framework, Measurement of Variables, and Methods of Analysis

For comparison among White, African American, and Hispanic frail elders, we present results of descriptive bivariate analysis of sociodemographic (age, gender, marital status, and level of education), economic (level of income and SSI recipiency), and health (number of difficulties with ADL and IADL, number of physical illnesses, and number of depressive symptoms) characteristics for each racial group by living arrangement. Living arrangement is dichotomized into living with others versus living alone, because earlier studies indicated the significance of coresidence itself rather than kinship ties (Chappell, 1991; Norgard & Rodgers, 1997). We also present results of bivariate analysis of formal and informal support for each racial group by living arrangement. Formal support is also dichotomized into in-home and community-based services. In-home services, which are delivered to elders at home, include home health care and Meals on Wheels. Community-based services that are offered away from the elders' homes include congregate meals, health programs, social center and church programs, and counseling services. The numbers of total in-home and community-based services used by the elders are noted. In addition, whether the elders had been in a nursing home in the preceding six months or two months, and whether they had applied for nursing home admission were also noted. Informal social support is illustrated by the number of informal helpers. The number of unmet needs, in conjunction with the number of difficulties with ADL and IADL, is also recorded.

For bivariate comparison among subgroups of Hispanic elders—Mexican Americans, Cuban Americans, and Puerto Ricans—in addition to sociodemographic, economic, and health characteristics, self-rated English-language skills and length of stay in the United States (in years) are analyzed. In-home services include homemaker, visiting nurse, home health aide, and Meals on Wheels services. Community-based services include transportation services, senior centers, congregate meals, telephone checks, and church programs. The numbers of in-home and community-based services used by the elders and the number of their unmet need are also noted. Informal social support is measured by the number of children and the number of weekly contacts with the children.

In continuation of the preceding chapter, we adopted the Andersen–Newman model as the analytic tool for separate parallel multivariate logistic regression analyses for each racial/ethnic group. The multivariate analyses aim at determining the effect of living arrangement on formal service use, controlling for other independent variables. The dependent variable for Model I is whether an elder has used any in-home service, and the dependent variable for Model II is whether an elder has used any community-based service. The use of any service was coded dichotomously with 1 indicating users and 0 denoting nonusers. Explanations for independent variables for comparison among White, African American, and Hispanic elders and those for comparison among Mexican Americans, Cuban Americans, and Puerto Ricans are provided under the separate headings that follow.

## Comparison among White, African American, and Hispanic Elders

Predisposing factors are age and gender; enabling factors are income, living arrangement, attitude toward nursing home use, sense of control in life, contact with family and friends, number of informal helpers, and use of community-based services (Model I) or use of in-home services (Model II), and use of nursing home service; and need factors include cognitive impairment, ADL impairment, number of physical illnesses, and perceived unmet ADL and IADL needs.

The predisposing factors were measured as follows: Sex and age groupings were coded dichotomously, with male and age 80 and over coded 1 and female and under age 80 coded 0. As for the enabling factors, income and living arrangements were dichotomized, with monthly income of $1,000 or more and living alone coded 1, and monthly income less than $1,000 and living with others coded 0. Attitude toward nursing home placement was coded 1 for positive and 0 for negative.

The sense-of-control-in-life variable was a composite score based on five questions with three Likert-type responses ranging from (1) "very much" to (2) "somewhat" to (3) "not at all": (1) "In general, how satisfying do you find the way you're spending your life these days?" (2) "Day to day, how much choice do you have about what you do and when you do it?" (3) "How confident are you of figuring out how to deal with you problems?" (4) "How much do you worry about not knowing whom to turn to for help?" (5) "How confident are you of getting services when you need them?" To summarize the data and to avoid problems of multicollinearity, a principal components analysis with varimax rotation was performed that yielded one component. The five items were highly correlated, with factor loadings ranging from .56 to .71. Their summed scores thus yielded a composite measure of sense of control in life (alpha coefficient = .74).

Social contacts were measured as the self-reported frequency of both face-to-face and telephone contacts with relatives and friends during the preceding week. Responses were categorized as (1) once or more daily, (2) two to six times a week, (3) once a week, and (4) none. Number of informal caregivers was a self-report of all family and friends who provided unpaid help. Use of community-based (Model I) or in-home (Model II) services was included in the regression model to control for the role of other contacts with the service-delivery system when use of a particular type of service was being examined. Thus, in assessing the likelihood of any in-home (home health care and Meals on Wheels) service use, the number of community-based services used (congregate meal program, social center/church programs, and counseling services) was included; in examining use of any community-based service, the number of in-home services used was included. Nursing home service use was included for the same reason.

For need factors, cognitive impairment was assessed by means of the SPMSQ (Pfeiffer, 1975); (1) Mild or no impairment was indicated by 9 to 10 correct answers, (2) moderate by 6 to 8, and (3) severe by 5 or fewer. Test–retest reliability was greater than .80 (Kane & Kane, 1981). The number of ADL impairments was determined by asking respondents if they had needed help during the preceding week with eating, bathing, dressing, toileting, and/or getting out of bed or chair (alpha coefficient for entire sample = .79; Whites = .79; African Americans = .76; Hispanics = .82).

Physical illnesses included self-reported anemia, high blood pressure, heart disease, stroke, diabetes, arthritis, cancer, Parkinson's disease, respiratory problems, skin problems, paralysis, orthopedic conditions, vision or hearing problems, and other health conditions. Finally, the number of unmet needs was determined by asking respondents if they needed additional help with ADL and IADL.

## Comparison among Mexican Americans, Cuban Americans, and Puerto Ricans

Predisposing factors were age and gender and length of stay in the United States; enabling factors were education, receipt of public assistance, living arrangement, English-language proficiency, number of children, frequency of contact with children per week, and use of community-based services (Model I) or use of in-home services (Model II); and need factors included ADL impairment, IADL impairment, self-rated health, doctor visits, hospital use, psychological distress, and unmet service need.

The predisposing variables were measured as follows: gender and age groupings were coded dichotomously, with male and age 80 and over coded 1 and female and younger than age 80 coded 0. Length of stay in the United States represents actual years. As for the enabling factors, missing data on income were excessive, so education (categorical variable, with higher score denoting more education/training) is used as a measure of social class standing, and the receipt of public assistance (food stamps, SSI, and/or Medicaid) is used as a rough measure of economic standing. Living arrangements were dichotomized, with living alone coded 1 and living with others coded 0. English-language proficiency refers to ability to speak, read, or write English, each coded 1 denoting the ability to do so, and 0 denoting a lack of such ability. The number of children and frequency of contact with them do not require further explanation. The numbers of community-based (Model I) or in-home (Model II) services were included in the regression model to control for the role of other contacts with the service-delivery system when examining use of a particular type of service. Thus, in assessing the likelihood of using any in-home service, the number of community-based services (congregate meals, senior center, transportation, church, and telephone assurance) used was included; in examining use of any community-based service, the number of in-home services (Meals on Wheels, visiting nurse, homemaker, and home health aide) used was included.

For need factors, the numbers of ADL and IADL impairments refer to actual numbers of difficulties with ADL and IADL. Self-rated health was assessed on a scale of 1 (excellent) to 4 (poor). Doctor visits refer to the actual number of visits in the preceding 12 months, and hospital use denotes whether the elder stayed at a hospital overnight in the preceding 12 months (1 = yes; 0 = no). Psychological distress was assessed by self-reported experience in the preceding few weeks of feeling restless, lonely, bored, depressed, and/or upset (each coded dichotomously). A principal components analysis with varimax rotation was performed, and the five items were summed to create a composite score of psychological distress (alpha coefficient = .71). Number of unmet service needs refers to the total number of in-home and community-based services needed.

## RESULTS

### Comparison among African American, White, and Hispanic Elders

Data in Table 9.1 show that 32% of African American frail elders ($n = 1,272$), 45% of White frail elders ($n = 4,133$), and 23% of Hispanic frail elders ($n = 211$) lived alone, while 68% of the African Americans, 55% of the Whites, and 77% of the Hispanics lived with others. African American and White elders who lived with others were not different from their peers who lived alone in terms of age distribution, but Hispanic elders who lived with others included a larger proportion of relatively younger people (65 to 74 years) as compared with those who lived alone. For all three racial groups, the living alone had a significantly higher proportion of females than did the living with others. It was fully expected that a significant portion of the living with others group would consist of married elders. More than half of both White and Hispanic elders who lived with others were married, indicating that they were most likely to be living with their spouse. But only 38.3% of African American elders who lived with others were married, indicating that almost two-thirds of them were living with someone other than a spouse. The living alone and the living with others did not differ in level of education across all three racial groups. As for income, African Americans did not differ by living arrangement, whereas the living-alone Whites and Hispanics had significantly lower incomes than their peers who lived with others. Across all three racial groups, a significantly higher proportion of those who lived alone than those who lived with others received SSI.

In terms of health status, those living with others had significantly more problems with ADL, IADL, and physical health than did those living alone. Despite their worse health status, African American and White elders who

**Table 9.1**
**Background Characteristics of Frail Elders by Ethnicity by Living Arrangement**

| Characteristics | African American n = 1,272 | | White[a] n = 4,133 | | Hispanic n = 211 | |
|---|---|---|---|---|---|---|
| | Living with others (68%) | Living alone (32%) | Living with others (55%) | Living alone (45%) | Living with others (77%) | Living alone (23%) |
| **Age (%)** | | | | | | |
| 65 to 69 years | 14.1 | 16.0 | 11.2 | 9.9 | 11.7 | 4.1[b] |
| 70 to 74 years | 17.9 | 19.1 | 15.8 | 14.9 | 17.9 | 12.2 |
| 75 to 79 years | 20.0 | 21.9 | 22.2 | 21.7 | 9.3 | 14.3 |
| 80 to 84 years | 22.8 | 21.9 | 22.4 | 24.6 | 28.4 | 36.7 |
| 85 to 89 years | 14.4 | 12.5 | 17.9 | 18.9 | 16.7 | 28.6 |
| >=90 | 10.7 | 8.6 | 9.9 | 9.9 | 16.1 | 4.1 |
| **Gender (%)** | | | | | | |
| Female | 66.6 | 79.6[b] | 64.9 | 82.7[b] | 66.1 | 79.6[b] |
| **Marital status (%)** | | | | | | |
| Married | 38.3 | 1.0[b] | 53.9 | 1.4[b] | 53.1 | 0.0[b] |
| **Education (%)** | | | | | | |
| None or elementary | 71.7 | 69.7 | 59.4 | 54.8 | 75.9 | 73.5 |
| Some secondary | 13.7 | 14.8 | 13.2 | 15.1 | 1.8 | 4.1 |
| High school | 8.3 | 7.6 | 16.3 | 17.3 | 12.4 | 12.2 |
| College | 5.3 | 6.9 | 9.1 | 10.2 | 6.8 | 2.0 |
| Postcollege | 0.9 | 1.0 | 1.9 | 2.6 | 3.1 | 8.2 |
| **Income (monthly) (%)** | | | | | | |
| < $500 | 66.7 | 88.5 | 23.9 | 56.1[b] | 50.0 | 100.0[b] |
| $500 to $999 | 23.1 | 7.7 | 51.1 | 31.6 | 30.0 | 0.0 |
| >= $1000 | 10.2 | 3.8 | 25.0 | 12.3 | 20.0 | 0.0 |
| **SSI Receipt** | 25.8 | 37.1[b] | 9.1 | 16.4[b] | 52.5 | 56.3[b] |
| | **Mean (SD)** | | **Mean (SD)** | | **Mean (SD)** | |
| **ADL problems** | 2.2(1.2) | 1.1(1.2)[b] | 2.3(1.3) | 1.1(1.2)[b] | 2.5(1.4) | 1.0(1.3)[b] |
| **IADL problems** | 3.3(2.0) | 3.1(1.7)[b] | 3.4(1.9) | 2.8(1.8)[b] | 3.2(2.1) | 2.7(1.5)[b] |
| **No. of illnesses** | 5.1(2.2) | 4.4(1.9)[b] | 5.1(2.2) | 4.3(2.0)[b] | 5.8(2.4) | 4.5(2.2)[b] |
| **Depressive symptoms** | 2.9(2.1) | 3.3(2.2)[b] | 3.5(2.1) | 4.0(2.1)[b] | 4.2(2.3) | 3.9(2.0)[b] |

*Data Source*: National Long-Term Care Channeling Demonstration, 1982–1984.
[a]None was of Hispanic origin.
[b]Within group differences were significant at less than 0.05 level or better.
Chi-square and *t* statistics were used.
*p < 0.05; **p < 0.01; ***p < 0.001; ****p < 0.0001.

lived with others reported fewer depressive symptoms than their living alone peers. But, for Hispanic elders, those living with others reported more depressive symptoms.

Data in Table 9.2 show descriptive statistics regarding formal and informal support by living arrangement. A higher proportion of African Americans and Whites who lived with others used home health care than their living alone peers. But the proportion of Hispanics who used home health care did not differ by living arrangement. A significantly higher proportion of those living alone than those living with others used Meals on Wheels across all three racial groups. The same was true of congregate meals and social center services. Although the proportion of elders who used a nursing home did not differ by

**Table 9.2**
**Formal and Informal Support of Frail Elders by Ethnicity by Living Arrangement**

| Characteristics | African American n = 1,272 | | White[a] n = 4,133 | | Hispanic n = 211 | |
|---|---|---|---|---|---|---|
| | Living with others | Living alone | Living with others | Living alone | Living with others | Living alone |
| **In-home service** (%) | | | | | | |
| Home health care | 29.4 | 25.3[b] | 33.6 | 25.3[b] | 26.5 | 20.8 |
| Meals on Wheels | 7.2 | 21.8[b] | 11.3 | 27.0[b] | 13.7 | 28.6[b] |
| **Community-based service** | | | | | | |
| Congregate meals | 2.1 | 5.3[b] | 2.7 | 6.5[b] | 3.9 | 8.5[b] |
| Use health program | 0.7 | 0.9 | 2.0 | 2.0 | 1.5 | 2.2 |
| Social center | 13.5 | 21.2[b] | 8.4 | 17.3[b] | 8.1 | 16.3[b] |
| Counseling | 3.4 | 4.0 | 4.8 | 5.4 | 9.1 | 7.7 |
| **Nursing home service** | | | | | | |
| Nursing home use in preceding 6 months | 3.5 | 5.4 | 9.9 | 10.5 | 4.3 | 2.0 |
| Nursing home use in preceding 2 months | 43.5 | 40.0 | 60.0 | 65.2 | 50.0 | 0.0[b] |
| Nursing home application | 4.6 | 3.0[b] | 6.9 | 5.4[b] | 6.5 | 0.0[b] |
| | Mean (SD) | | Mean (SD) | | Mean (SD) | |
| **Social support** | | | | | | |
| Informal helpers | 2.4(1.2) | 1.7(1.0)[b] | 2.2(1.1) | 1.5(1.0)[b] | 2.1(1.0) | 1.5(1.0)[b] |
| No. of services used | 1.5(0.7) | 1.6(0.8)[b] | 1.6(0.7) | 1.7(0.8)[b] | 1.5(0.7) | 1.6(0.9)[b] |
| Unmet needs | 4.5(2.8) | 5.0(2.8)[b] | 3.7(2.7) | 4.2(2.7)[b] | 3.3(2.7) | 3.6(2.9)[b] |

*Data Source*: National Long-Term Care Channeling Demonstration, 1982–1984.
[a]None was of Hispanic origin.
[w]Within group differences were significant at less than 0.05 level or better.
[b]Chi-square and *t* statistics were used.
*p < 0.05; **p < 0.01; ***p < 0.001; ****p < 0.0001.

living arrangement for African Americans and Whites, those living with others were significantly more likely to have applied for nursing home admission than those living alone across all three racial groups.

Considering their worse health conditions, it is not surprising that a higher proportion of those who lived with others used home health care and applied for nursing home admission. Because of the level of frailty among these elders, the coresiding informal support system appears to have not been adequate to meet all their needs, although those who lived with others naturally had more informal helpers and fewer unmet needs than those who lived alone. Those who lived alone appeared to have used more formal services (e.g., Meals on Wheels, congregate meals, and social centers), at a statistically significant level, than have those who lived with others; however, the real difference was in fact miniscule.

Logistic regression coefficients for in-home service use are presented in Table 9.3. When other predisposing, enabling, and need factors were controlled for, living alone was a significant predictor of in-home service use for African American and White frail elders, but not for their Hispanic counterparts. African Americans and Whites younger than age 80 were less likely, but those who had previously used a nursing home were more likely to use in-home services. Age is included as a predisposing factor, but it is in fact an indicator of need because older persons are more likely to have health limitations. Thus, the significance of age underscores the importance of need as a determinant. Previous experience with nursing home use also indicates serious health problems, and may also be interpreted as an established link to the formal service system. For Whites, the number of illnesses was positively associated with in-home service use, but the use of community-based services was negatively associated with it. For Hispanic elders, only two variables were significant predictors: The number of informal helpers was negatively associated and the number of ADL impairments was positively associated with the likelihood of in-home services.

Logistic regression coefficients for community-based service use are presented in Table 9.4. Other things being equal, living alone was also a significant predictor of the likelihood of community-based service use for African Americans and Whites, but not for Hispanics. African Americans and Whites with more social contact (lower scores represent more frequent contact) and more illnesses were also more likely to have used community-based services. (The positive association between social contact and community-based service use may be tautological, because elders who use congregate meals and social centers have more contact with their peers at meal sites and at social centers.) In addition, White elders with more ADL impairments were less likely to have used community-based services. For Hispanic elders, more illness was positively associated with the likelihood of community-based service use, but the number of in-home service uses was negatively associated with the likelihood of community-based service use. Given that the sample members

**Table 9.3**
**Logistic Regression Analysis of Use of In-Home Service by Ethnicity**

| Variables | Unstandardized logit coefficients (SE)[a] | | |
|---|---|---|---|
| | African-American | White[b] | Hispanic |
| **Predisposing factors** | | | |
| Sex (male=1) | -0.14(0.20) | 0.18(0.11) | -0.48(0.50) |
| Age (≥80=1) | -0.49(0.18)** | -0.39(0.09)**** | 0.46(0.54) |
| **Enabling factors** | | | |
| Income (>$1000=1) | 0.00(0.00) | 0.00(0.00) | 0.00(0.00) |
| Living alone (alone=1) | 0.30(0.19)** | 0.38(0.10)*** | 0.09(0.06) |
| Nursing home attitude | | | |
| (positive=1) | 0.06(0.08) | 0.01(0.04) | 0.22(0.30) |
| Sense of control in life | 0.02(0.03) | 0.00(0.01) | -0.12(0.10) |
| Social contact | -0.09(0.09) | -0.03(0.05) | -0.49(0.33) |
| Informal helpers | 0.10(0.07) | -0.02(0.04) | -0.52(0.26)** |
| Community-based service use | -0.08(0.13) | -0.18(0.06)* | -0.33(0.32) |
| Nursing home service use | 0.12(0.05)** | 0.18(0.03)**** | -0.15(0.11) |
| **Need factors** | | | |
| Cognitive impairment | -0.17(0.14) | -0.17(0.06)* | 0.00(0.00) |
| ADL impairment | 0.06(0.09) | 0.01(0.02) | 0.50(0.27)** |
| No. of illnesses | 0.07(0.05) | 0.13(0.03)**** | 0.00(0.10) |
| Unmet needs | 0.00(0.03) | -0.02(0.01) | -0.01(0.10) |
| Intercept | -1.30(0.65)** | -0.76(0.33)* | 1.65(0.20) |
| Model chi square | 27.37**** | 119.18**** | 18.58* |

*Data Source*: National Long-Term Care Channeling Demonstration, 1982–1984.
[a]Standard error.
[b]None was of Hispanic origin.
*$p < 0.05$; **$p < 0.01$; ***$p < 0.001$; ****$p < 0.0001$.

were frail elders, many of whom have functional impairment, it is likely that they were mobility impaired and thus homebound. So those who depended on in-home service may have not been able to utilize services that were accessible in the community.

Overall, bivariate analyses present a similar picture in terms of differences, by living arrangement, in health status, and in informal and formal support of all three racial groups of frail elders. The results of multivariate analyses indicate that African Americans and Whites are more similar to each other, but these two racial groups are different from Hispanics in terms of predictors of formal service use. For one thing, African American and White frail elders who lived alone were more likely than their peers who lived with others to have used both in-home and community-based formal services; it is likely that they did so to compensate for their lack of informal support. But Hispanic frail elders who lived alone were not more likely to have used formal services.

**Table 9.4**
**Logistic Regression Analysis of Use of Community-Based Service by Ethnicity**

| Variables | Unstandardized logit coefficients (SE)[a] | | |
|---|---|---|---|
| | African-American | White[b] | Hispanic |
| **Predisposing factors** | | | |
| Sex (male=1) | -0.04(0.04) | -0.13(0.11) | -0.34(0.20) |
| Age (≥80=1) | -0.24(0.17) | -0.14(0.09) | 0.06(0.02) |
| **Enabling factors** | | | |
| Income (>$1000=1) | 0.00(0.00) | 0.00(0.00) | 0.00(0.00) |
| Living alone (alone=1) | 0.25(0.09)** | 0.09(0.10)* | 0.24(0.22) |
| Nursing home attitude (positive=1) | -0.02(0.08) | 0.07(0.04) | 0.30(0.30) |
| Sense of control in life | 0.02(0.03) | 0.02(0.02) | -0.10(0.10) |
| Social contact | -0.19(0.09)** | -0.10(0.05)** | -0.33(0.31) |
| Informal helpers | 0.02(0.07) | -0.08(0.04) | -0.01(0.01) |
| In-home service use | -0.06(0.12) | -0.07(0.07) | -0.60(0.38)** |
| Nursing home service use | 0.05(0.05) | 0.00(0.01) | -0.09(0.08) |
| **Need factors** | | | |
| Cognitive impairment | 0.12(0.11) | -0.09(0.06) | 0.05(0.09) |
| ADL impaired | -0.15(0.09) | -0.14(0.05)** | -0.30(0.24) |
| No. of illnesses | 0.14(0.05)*** | 0.12(0.03)** | 0.46(0.11)** |
| Unmet needs | 0.03(0.03) | -0.02(0.01) | -0.01(0.02) |
| Intercept | 1.07(0.62)** | 0.09(0.07) | 1.78(0.20) |
| Model chi square | 29.74**** | 52.39** | 10.91* |

*Data Source*: National Long-Term Care Channeling Demonstration, 1982–1984.
[a]Standard error.
[b]None was of Hispanic origin.
*$p < 0.05$; **$p < 0.01$; ***$p < 0.001$; ****$p < 0.0001$.

Those who had fewer informal helpers, regardless of their living arrangements, were more likely to use in-home services. As for the utilization of community-based services by Hispanic frail elders, however, neither living arrangement nor number of informal helpers was significantly associated. Thus, it is safe to say that the utilization of some types of formal services by Hispanic frail elders may be determined by factors that are dissimilar to those determining formal service use among their African American and White peers.

### Comparison among Mexican Americans, Cuban Americans, and Puerto Ricans

According to Table 9.5, of the three nationality groups of Hispanic elders, Puerto Ricans stood out as containing the highest proportion of those who lived alone: 37% of Puerto Rican ($n = 368$), as compared to 22% of Mexican

## Table 9.5
## Background Characteristics of Hispanic Elders by Living Arrangement

| Characteristics | Mexican American n = 773 | | Cuban American n = 714 | | Puerto Rican n = 368 | |
|---|---|---|---|---|---|---|
| | Living with others (78%) | Living alone (22%) | Living with others (79%) | Living alone (21%) | Living with others (63%) | Living alone (37%) |
| **Age (%)** | | | | | | |
| 65 to 69 | 41.0 | 25.7[b] | 33.5 | 28.0 | 40.3 | 39.3[b] |
| 70 to 74 | 22.6 | 24.6 | 23.1 | 27.3 | 25.3 | 22.2 |
| 75 to 79 | 18.6 | 18.7 | 21.3 | 28.0 | 16.7 | 24.4 |
| 80 to 84 | 11.1 | 22.8 | 12.8 | 12.7 | 9.9 | 8.9 |
| >=85 | 6.6 | 8.2 | 9.4 | 4.0 | 7.7 | 5.2 |
| **Gender (%)** | | | | | | |
| Female | 57.5 | 80.1[b] | 59.2 | 74.7[b] | 57.9 | 81.5[b] |
| **Marital status (%)** | | | | | | |
| Married | 65.3 | 1.2[b] | 66.5 | 2.7[b] | 53.7 | 0.7[b] |
| **Education (%)** | | | | | | |
| Grade school | 81.4 | 82.5 | 57.9 | 64.0 | 81.9 | 87.4 |
| High school level | 15.0 | 15.8 | 23.8 | 20.0 | 12.9 | 11.1 |
| College level | 3.5 | 1.8 | 18.3 | 16.0 | 5.2 | 1.5 |
| **Financial condition (%)** | | | | | | |
| Medicaid | 31.4 | 45.0[b] | 41.3 | 64.0[b] | 45.5 | 66.7[b] |
| Food Stamps | 12.1 | 26.9[b] | 34.0 | 63.3[b] | 21.5 | 61.5[b] |
| SSI | 10.8 | 17.0[b] | 11.4 | 20.0[b] | 16.3 | 17.0 |
| Income below poverty line | 41.7 | 50.9[b] | 30.9 | 58.7[b] | 39.1 | 58.5[b] |
| **English-language skills (%)** | | | | | | |
| Able to speak | 46.3 | 46.2 | 36.5 | 37.3 | 52.4 | 18.2 |
| Able to read | 55.5 | 59.1 | 43.3 | 44.0 | 54.9 | 46.7 |
| Able to write | 43.9 | 48.5 | 34.9 | 32.7 | 44.2 | 35.6 |
| | **Mean (SD)** | | **Mean (SD)** | | **Mean (SD)** | |
| ADL problems | 1.2(1.2) | 1.0(1.5) | 0.9(1.3) | 0.6(1.2) | 1.5(1.4) | 1.3(1.4) |
| IADL problems | 1.4(1.7) | 1.3(1.4) | 1.0(1.0) | 0.8(1.1)[b] | 1.5(1.3) | 1.3(1.5) |
| Perceived health | 2.6(0.9) | 2.6(0.8) | 2.4(0.8) | 2.3(0.9) | 2.7(0.8) | 2.8(0.8) |
| Depressive symptoms | 1.1(1.3) | 1.4(1.6)[b] | 0.9(1.1) | 1.3(1.0)[b] | 1.5(1.0) | 1.6(1.5) |
| Length of stay in the United States | 46(21) | 53(20)[b] | 24(13) | 24(11) | 37(15) | 40(13) |

*Data Source*: National Survey of Hispanic Elderly People, 1988.
[b]Within group differences were significant at less than 0.05 level or better.
Chi-square and *t* statistics were used.

American ($n$ = 773) and 21% of Cuban American ($n$ = 714) elders, lived alone. In terms of age distribution, it appears that Puerto Rican elders who lived alone were more likely than those who lived with others to contain people in the 75-to-79-year-old group; for Mexican Americans, those who lived alone were significantly more likely than those who lived with others to be 80 years old or over. Cuban Americans did not differ in age distribution by living arrangement. For all three nationalities, the living-alone group was comprised of significantly more females, but was not different from the living-with-others group in level of education, although Cuban Americans on average were much better educated than Mexican Americans and Puerto Ricans. Mexican Americans who lived alone had lived in the United States significantly longer than their peers who lived with others, whereas Cuban Americans and Puerto Ricans did not differ in length of stay by living arrangement. Self-rated English-language skills did not differ by living arrangement for all three nationality groups. But those living alone were significantly more likely to have income below the poverty line and receive Medicaid, food stamps, and SSI (with the exception of Puerto Ricans, who did not differ by living arrangement in SSI receipt).

Those living alone did not differ from those living with others in terms of health status (ADL/IADL and perceived health status); although Cuban Americans who lived alone were a little better off than their peers who lived with others, the real difference appears to be insubstantial. Mexican Americans and Cuban Americans who lived alone reported more depressive symptoms than did those who lived with others, but Puerto Ricans did not differ by living arrangement. (Because the sample members of the National Survey of Hispanic Elderly People were representative of elderly persons with all levels of health status, their average health status was not as frail as the sample members of the Long-Term Care Channeling Demonstration Survey.)

As shown in Table 9.6, a significantly higher proportion of those who lived alone appeared to have used at least two or more of the in-home services of the four about which they were asked (home maker, visiting nurse, home health aide, and Meals on Wheels). The living-alone groups were also significantly more likely to have used at least three or more community-based services (transportation, senior center programs, congregate meals, telephone checks, and church programs). As for the informal support network, the living-alone groups had significantly fewer children than the living with others group, but with the exception of Cuban Americans, they did not differ from those who lived with others in the frequency of contact with their children. That may be the reason that only Cuban Americans who lived alone had significantly more unmet needs than their peers who lived with others.

Unlike bivariate results, results of multivariate logistic regression analyses (see Table 9.7) show that living alone was a significant predictor of in-home service use for Mexican Americans only, when other variables were controlled for.

**Table 9.6**
**Formal and Informal Support of Hispanic Elders by Living Arrangement**

| Characteristics | Mexican American n = 773 | | Cuban American n = 714 | | Puerto Rican n = 368 | |
|---|---|---|---|---|---|---|
| | Living with others (78%) | Living alone (22%) | Living with others (79%) | Living alone (21%) | Living with others (63%) | Living alone (37%) |
| **In-home service use** | | | | | | |
| Home maker service | 3.7 | 17.5[a] | 3.7 | 8.7[a] | 12.5 | 22.2[a] |
| Visiting nurse | 7.5 | 14.0[a] | 9.9 | 8.0 | 13.7 | 25.2[a] |
| Home health aides | 2.7 | 9.7[a] | 6.0 | 4.7 | 5.6 | 8.9 |
| Meals on Wheels | 6.5 | 15.8[a] | 2.3 | 7.3[a] | 2.6 | 5.2 |
| **Community-based service use** | | | | | | |
| Transportation | 7.1 | 15.2[a] | 15.6 | 27.3[a] | 18.9 | 28.9[a] |
| Senior center | 10.3 | 18.1[a] | 7.5 | 16.7[a] | 15.5 | 27.4[a] |
| Congregate meals | 12.6 | 22.8[a] | 7.1 | 22.0[a] | 11.2 | 23.7[a] |
| Telephone checks | 2.7 | 11.7[a] | 3.4 | 4.0 | 3.0 | 5.9 |
| Church programs | 7.8 | 10.5 | 2.8 | 2.0 | 5.2 | 5.9 |
| | **Mean (SD)** | | **Mean (SD)** | | **Mean (SD)** | |
| **No. of in-home services** | 0.2(0.5) | 0.6(0.9)[a] | 0.2(0.3) | 0.3(0.6) | 0.3(0.8) | 0.6(1.0)[a] |
| **No. of community-based services used** | 0.4(0.8) | 0.8(0.9)[a] | 0.4(0.7) | 0.7(1.0)[a] | 0.5(0.8) | 0.9(1.0)[a] |
| **Unmet service needs** | 2.2(2.8) | 2.0(2.4) | 1.3(2.2) | 1.7(2.0)[a] | 2.2(2.4) | 2.0(2.3) |
| **Informal support network** | | | | | | |
| No. of children | 4.9(3.2) | 3.6(3.2)[a] | 2.1(1.6) | 1.7(1.6)[a] | 4.0(2.9) | 3.4(2.6)[a] |
| Children contact (per week) | 2.7(1.6) | 2.6(1.8) | 1.6(1.7) | 1.5(1.2) | 1.2(1.0) | 1.4(1.0)[a] |

*Data Source*: National Survey of Hispanic Elderly People, 1988.
*Note:* Within-group differences were significant at less than 0.05 level or better; chi-square and *t* statistics were used.

Of the predisposing factors, only age was negatively associated with in-home service use for Puerto Ricans. Of the enabling factors, higher education, ability to write English, and a higher number of community-based services used were significant predictors for Mexican Americans; frequency of contact with children was significant for Cuban Americans; and inability to speak English and a higher number of community-based services used were significant for Puerto Ricans. Of need factors, none was significant for Mexican Americans; more ADL impairments, lower self-rated health, more hospital use, and more unmet service needs were significant for Cuban Americans; and more IADL impairments were significant for Cuban Americans.

**Table 9.7**
**Logistic Regression Analysis of In-Home Service Use by Nationality Groups**

| Variables | Mexican American | Cuban American | Puerto Rican |
|---|---|---|---|
| | Unstandardized Logit Coefficients (SE)[a] | | |
| **Predisposing factors** | | | |
| Age (≥80=1) | 0.92(0.98) | -0.01(0.02) | -0.23(0.10)** |
| Gender (Male=1) | -0.08(0.10) | 0.11(0.40) | 0.44(0.45) |
| Length of stay in U.S. | -0.01(0.02) | 0.02(0.01) | -0.03(0.02) |
| **Enabling factors** | | | |
| Education | 0.13(0.08)** | -0.57(0.35) | -0.75(0.80) |
| Living alone | 0.20(0.08)** | 0.69(0.48) | -0.09(0.08) |
| Able to speak English | 0.05(0.08) | 0.81(0.62) | -1.21(0.70)** |
| Able to read English | -0.95(1.00) | -0.31(0.30) | 0.10(0.90) |
| Able to write English | 0.27(0.13)** | -0.45(0.34) | -0.38(0.82) |
| No. of children | -0.20(0.12) | -0.09(0.14) | -0.02(0.12) |
| Frequency of children contact | 0.12(0.20) | 0.26(0.10)** | 0.23(0.22) |
| On public assistance[b] | 0.56(0.46) | 0.16(0.21) | 0.33(0.38) |
| Community-based service use | 0.12(0.40)*** | 0.02(0.20) | 1.28(0.35)*** |
| **Need for care factors** | | | |
| ADL impairment | 0.35(0.25) | 0.45(0.17)*** | 0.30(0.22) |
| IADL impairment | 0.39(0.30) | 0.23(0.22) | 0.49(0.27)** |
| Self-rated health | 0.21(0.40) | -0.58(0.29)** | 0.46(0.42) |
| Doctor visits | 0.05(0.05) | 0.02(0.02) | 0.03(0.02) |
| Hospital use | 0.86(0.77) | 0.43 (0.47)*** | 0.76(0.58) |
| Psychological distress | -0.13(0.25) | -0.03(0.10) | -0.05(0.20) |
| Unmet service needs | 0.19(0.13) | 0.26(0.09)** | -0.11(0.10) |
| Intercept | -9.41**** | -2.91**** | -3.48 |
| Model chi square | 57.42**** | 90.62**** | 70.12** |

*Data Source*: National Survey of Hispanic Elderly People, 1988.
[a]Standard error.
[b]Recipients of either food stamps, SSI, and/or Medicaid.
*$p < 0.05$; **$p < 0.01$; ***$p < 0.001$; ****$p < 0.0001$.

As shown in Table 9.8, results of multivariate logistic regression analyses of the likelihood of community-based service use show that living alone was a significant predictor for Puerto Ricans only. As for the other significant predictors of the likelihood of community-based service use, a longer length of stay was the only significant predisposing factor for Mexican Americans only. For enabling factors, more in-home services used was significant for Mexican Americans; more children, receipt of public assistance, and more in-home services used were significant for Cuban Americans; and ability to write English and more in-home services used were significant for Puerto Ricans. Thus, for all three groups, in-home services used was a consistently significant predictor, indicating that it could have been a link to community-based services

**Table 9.8**
**Logistic Regression Analysis of Community-Based Service Use by Nationality Groups**

| | Unstandardized Logit Coefficients (SE)[a] | | |
|---|---|---|---|
| Variables | Mexican American | Cuban American | Puerto Rican |
| **Predisposing factors** | | | |
| Age (≥80=1) | 0.11(0.52) | 0.40(0.36) | -0.19(0.10) |
| Gender (Male=1) | 0.42(0.40) | -0.06(0.29) | 0.64(0.46) |
| Length of stay in U.S. | 0.02(0.01)* | 0.01(0.01) | -0.02(0.02) |
| **Enabling factors** | | | |
| Education | 0.43(0.57) | 0.24(0.20) | -0.40(0.53) |
| Living alone | 0.36(0.37) | 0.35(0.32) | 0.78(0.44)** |
| Able to speak English | 0.21(0.20) | 0.13(0.12) | 0.51(0.48) |
| Able to read English | 0.58(0.40) | -0.16(0.20) | 0.78(0.71) |
| Able to write English | -1.17(0.63) | -0.31(0.34) | 1.21(0.69)* |
| No. of children | 0.01(0.02) | 0.24(0.09)*** | 0.06(0.08) |
| Frequency of children contact | 0.27(0.21) | 0.07(0.08) | 0.29(0.25) |
| On public assistance[b] | 0.02(0.02) | 0.48(0.13)*** | 0.18(0.23) |
| In-home service use | 0.91(0.42)*** | 0.64(0.28)** | 0.92(0.30)*** |
| **Need for care factors** | | | |
| ADL impairment | 0.10(0.21) | 0.16(0.14) | 0.10(0.12) |
| IADL impairment | -0.45(0.24)* | 0.08(0.12) | 0.21(0.20) |
| Self-rated health | 0.21(0.30) | 0.11(0.19) | 0.12(0.25) |
| Doctor visits | 0.06(0.04) | 0.04(0.02) | 0.03(0.02) |
| Hospital use | 0.33(0.56) | 0.47(0.38) | 0.07(0.13) |
| Psychological distress | 0.42(0.16)** | 0.12(0.10) | -0.24(0.20) |
| Unmet service needs | -0.19(0.09)** | 0.02(0.06) | -0.03(0.09) |
| Intercept | -3.32**** | -2.92**** | -1.42 |
| Model chi square | 35.59** | 44.78*** | 41.21** |

*Data Source*: National Survey of Hispanic Elderly People, 1988.
[a]Standard error.
[b]Recipients of either food stamps, SSI, and/or Medicaid.
*$p < 0.05$; **$p < 0.01$; ***$p < 0.001$; ****$p < 0.0001$.

or vice versa (see Table 9.7 for the significance of community-based services used as predictor of in-home service use). For need factors, fewer IADL impairments, more psychological distress, and fewer unmet needs were significant for Mexican Americans; and none was significant for Cuban Americans and Puerto Ricans.

Despite different sample selection criteria, these results regarding the association between living arrangement and formal service use among Hispanic elders confirm those we obtained for Hispanic frail elders based on the Long-Term Care Channeling Survey: Living arrangement was a significant predictor for formal service use of only one nationality group out of three, when other predisposing, enabling, and need factors were controlled for. The multivariate analyses show that a predictor of formal service use that was consistently significant for all nationality groups was other type of service use. Hispanic elders connected to one formal support system are more likely to use another formal support system, apparently using one system as a gateway to another.

The findings also indicate some inter-nationality group difference in terms of the significance of other enabling or need factors. Cuban American elders on average had fewer children as compared to Mexican American and Puerto Rican elders, and that may be the reason the number of children and frequency of contact with children as proxy for informal support was significant for Cuban Americans only. Mexican Americans comprised the only group for whom both education and ability to write English were significant enabling factors for in-home services, although their length of stay in the United States was, on average, the longest of all three nationality groups. This may indicate that recent immigrants who tend to have insufficient education and English-language skills face tougher barriers than native-born persons or long-time immigrants. Ability to write English was also a significant factor for community-based service use among Puerto Ricans, suggesting the dearth of service providers who cater to Spanish-speaking elders.

## DISCUSSION

The findings confirm that elders who live alone, regardless of their race and degree of frailty, are on average still in better functional and physical condition than their peers who live with others. Frail elders who are in really bad shape may have moved in with someone if they had the opportunity. The findings also confirm that frail elders who live alone have significantly fewer informal helpers than their peers who coreside with someone, and as a result, they report more unmet needs. At least for African American and White frail elders who live alone, the lack of informal support vis-à-vis their health needs may have been a contributing factor to their higher likelihood of utilizing formal services.

The positive association between living alone and the likelihood of formal service use among African American and White frail elders thus supports the "compensatory" rather than the "linking" hypothesis, meaning that formal services are used to fill the needs gap left by an insufficient informal support network among those who live alone. For Hispanic frail elders, living arrangement per se was not a predictor of formal service use. Nevertheless, because of the significant negative association between the number of informal helpers and the likelihood of using in-home (but not community-based) services, we may also conclude that there is limited support for the compensatory hypothesis among Hispanic frail elders when it comes to in-home services.

As for the utilization of community-based services, the compensatory hypothesis was not supported for Hispanic frail elders either.

Also deserving mention is the significance of need factors as determinants of formal service use for all three racial/ethnic groups of frail elders. Other things being equal, physical and functional impairments are predictors of both in-home and community-based service use, which is not a new finding. A more important finding is that regardless of their living arrangements, frail elders of all races report a significant number of unmet needs, ranging from 3.3 to 5.0 per person. This apparently means that both informal and formal service networks are not adequately meeting the needs of these elders. Many of them may not have been properly connected to the helping networks, or the helping networks may have been overloaded and therefore unable to serve all those needing assistance.

The findings from the analyses of the three nationality groups of Hispanic elders also confirm that those who lived alone had fewer children than those who lived with someone. So, in addition to the absence of a spouse (as shown by their marital status), number of children is apparently a determinant of living alone versus living with others. Unlike the subjects of the Long-Term Care Channeling Survey, the sample members of the National Survey of Hispanic Elderly People were randomly selected from all age groups and thus, on average, had few health problems. Nevertheless, it is still notable that there were few significant differences in functional limitations and perceived health status by living arrangement among these Hispanic elders. Only Cuban American elders who lived alone were a little better off functionally than their peers who lived with others. Cuban American elders who lived alone also comprised the only group who had significantly more unmet needs than did their peers who lived with others.

But the living arrangements of Cuban American elders were not associated with the likelihood of their formal service use. Regardless of their living arrangements, it appears that Cuban American elders who had more children or kept more frequent contact with them were more likely to use formal services. Thus, these positive relationships support the linking hypothesis for them. For Mexican Americans, the positive relationship between living alone and in-home service use renders limited support for the compensatory hypothesis. For Puerto Ricans, the positive relationship between living alone and community-based service use renders limited support for the compensatory hypothesis. As mentioned, the source of this internal heterogeneity between Cuban Americans and Mexican Americans/Puerto Ricans may be the fact that Cuban Americans had fewer children.

But one aspect that was homogenous to all nationality groups was the positive relationship between the two types of formal services. Thus, it appears that access to one type of service functions as a bridge to another type of service, indicating that a link to one system is a significant enabling factor for the use of other services by Hispanic elders. But the other side of this statement is that Hispanic elders can be placed into two groups, one using both types of services and the other not using any. Apparently, Hispanic elders and their relatives, like all elders, are more likely to obtain information on available services through services that they are already connected to. It is also likely that service providers, rather than the elders themselves or their relatives, act as advocates and connect the elders to other available services. In either case, the findings underscore the importance of connecting Hispanic elders to an existing formal service system as a first step to breaking their isolation.

The findings also underscore the significance of the inability to speak English as a barrier to utilizing formal services among Mexian and Puerto Rican elders. In other words, connecting Hispanic elders to any existing formal service system may not be a sufficient condition. To ensure their service use, Spanish-speaking service providers and services that cater to Hispanic elders are needed to serve those who need the services most.

## REFERENCES

Angel, R. J., Angel, J. L., & Himes, C. L. (1992). Minority group status, health transitions, and community living arrangements among the elderly. *Research on Aging, 14,* 496–521.

Angel, J. L., Angel, R. J., McClellan, J. L., & Markides, K. S. (1996). Nativity, declining health, and preference in living arrangements among elderly Mexican Americans: Implications for long-term care. *The Gerontologist, 36,* 464–473.

Bean, F. D., & Tienda, M. (1987). *The Hispanic population of the United States.* New York: Russell Sage.

Burr, J. A., & Mutchler, J. E. (1992). The living arrangements of unmarried elderly Hispanic females. *Demography, 29,* 93–112.

Cafferata, G. L. (1987). Marital status, living arrangements, and the use of health services by elderly persons. *Journal of Gerontology, 42,* 613–618.

Cantor, M. H. (1981). Factors associated with strain among family, friends, and neighbors caring for the frail elderly. Paper presented at the 34th annual meeting of the Gerontological Society of America, Toronto, Ontario.

Chappell, N. L. (1991). Living arrangements and sources of caregiving. *Journal of Gerontology, 46,* S1–S8.

Chatters, L. M., & Taylor, R. J. (1990). Social integration. In Z. Harel, E. A. McKinney, & M. Williams (Eds.), *Black aged: Understanding diversity and service needs* (pp. 82–99). Newbury Park, CA: Sage.

Choi, N. G. (1991). Racial differences in the determinants of living arrangements of widowed and divorced elderly women. *The Gerontologist, 31,* 496–504.

Choi, N. G. (1995). Racial differences in the determinants of the coresidence of and contacts between elderly parents and their adult children. *Journal of Gerontological Social Work, 24*(1/2), 77–95.

Choi, N. G. (1996). Changes in the composition of unmarried elderly women's households between 1971 and 1991. *Journal of Gerontological Social Work, 27*(1/2), 113–131.

Gratton, B. (1987). Familism among the black and Mexican-American elderly: Myth or reality? *Journal of Aging Studies, 1,* 19–32.

Hays, J. C., Fillenbaum, G. G., Gold, D. T., Shanley, M. C., & Blazer, D. G. (1995). Black–White and urban–rural differences in stability of household composition among elderly persons. *Journal of Gerontology, 50B,* S301–S311.

Hess, B., & Soldo, B. J. (1985). Husband and wife networks. In W. J. Sauer & R. T. Coward (Eds.), *Social support networks and the care of the elderly* (pp. 67–92). New York: Springer.

Himes, C. L., Hogan, D. P., & Eggebeen, D. J. (1996). Living arrangements of minority elders. *Journal of Gerontology, 51B,* S42–S48.

Kane, R. A., & Kane, R. L. (1981). *Assessing the elderly: A practical guide to measurement.* Lexington, MA: Lexington Books.

Kasper, J. D. (1988). *Aging alone: Profiles and projections. A report of the Commonwealth Fund Commission on Elderly People Living Alone.* New York: The Commonwealth Foundation.

Lawton, M. P., Moss, M., & Kleban, M. H. (1984). Marital status, living arrangements, and the well-being of older people. *Research on Aging, 6,* 323–345.

Litwak, E. (1985). *Helping the elderly: The complementary roles of informal networks and formal systems.* New York: Guilford Press.

Logan, J. R., & Spitze, G. (1994). Informal support and the use of formal services by older Americans. *Journal of Gerontology, 49,* S25–S34.

Macunovich, D. J., Easterlin, R. A., Schaeffer, C. M., & Crimmins, E. M. (1995). Echoes of the baby boom and bust: Recent and prospective changes in living alone among elderly widows in the United States. *Demography, 32,* 17–28.

Markides, K. S., & Mindel, C. H. (1987). *Aging and ethnicity.* Newbury Park, CA: Sage.

Michael, R. T., Fuchs, V. R., & Scott, S. R. (1980). Changes in the propensity to live alone, 1950–1976. *Demography, 17,* 39–53.

Miller, B., & McFall, S. (1991). The effect of caregiver's burden on change in frail older persons' use of formal helpers. *Journal of Health and Social Behavior, 32,* 165–179.

Miller, B., McFall, S., & Campbell, R. T. (1994). Changes in sources of community long-term care among African and White frail older persons. *Journal of Gerontology, 49,* S14–S24.

Miner, S. (1995). Racial differences in family support and formal service utilization among older persons: A nonrecursive model. *Journal of Gerontology, 50B,* S143–S153.

Mitchell, J., & Register, J. C. (1984). An exploration of family interaction with the elderly by race, socioeconomic status, and residence. *The Gerontologist, 24,* 48–54.

Montgomery, R. J. V., & Kosloski, K. (1994). A longitudinal analysis of nursing home placement for dependent elders cared for by spouse versus adult children. *Journal of Gerontology, 49,* S62–S74.

Mui, A. C., & Burnette, J. D. (1994). A comparative profile of frail elderly persons living alone and those living with others. *Journal of Gerontological Social Work, 21,* 5–26.

Mutchler, J. E. (1990). Household composition among the nonmarried elderly: A comparison of Black and White women. *Research on Aging, 12,* 487–506.

Mutchler, J. E. (1992). Living arrangements and household transitions among the unmarried in later life. *Social Science Quarterly, 73,* 565–580.

Mutchler, J. E., & Burr, J. A. (1991). A longitudinal analysis of household and nonhousehold living arrangements in later life. *Demography, 28*, 375–390.

Mutran, E. (1985). Intergenerational family support among Blacks and Whites: Response to culture or to socioeconomic differences. *Journal of Gerontology, 40*, 382–389.

Norgard, T. M., & Rodgers, W. L. (1997). Patterns in in-home care among elderly Black and White Americans. *Journal of Gerontology, 52B*, 93–101.

Penning, M. J. (1995). Health, social support, and utilization of health services among older adults. *Journal of Gerontology, 50B*, S330–S339.

Pfeiffer, E. (1975). A short portable mental status questionnaire for the assessment of organic brain deficit in elderly patients. *Journal of the American Geriatric Society, 23*, 433–441.

Ruggles, S., & Goeken, R. (1992). Race and multigenerational family structure, 1900–1980. In S. J. South & S. E. Tolnay (Eds.), *The changing American family* (pp. 15–42). Boulder, CO: Westview.

Santi, L. L. (1988). The demographic context of recent change in the structure of American households. *Demography, 25*, 509–519.

Shanas, E. (1979). The family as a social support system in old age. *The Gerontologist, 19*, 169–174.

Shapiro, E. (1986). Patterns and predictors of home care use when need is the sole basis for admission. *Home Health Care Services Quarterly, 7*, 29–44.

Soldo, B. J., Wolf, D. A., & Agree, E. M. (1990). Family, households, and care arrangements of frail older women: A structural analysis. *Journal of Gerontology, 45*, S238–S249.

Sotomayer, M., & Applewhite, S. R. (1988). The Hispanic elderly and the extended multigenerational family. In S. R. Applewhite (Ed.), *Hispanic elderly in transition* (pp. 121–133). New York: Greenwood.

Spitze, G., Logan, J. R., & Robinson, J. (1992). Family structure and changes in living arrangements among elderly nonmarried parents. *Journal of Gerontology, 47*, S289–S296.

Stephens, S. A., & Christianson, J. B. (1986). *Informal care of the elderly.* Lexington, MA: Lexington Books.

Stoller, E. P. (1989). Formal services and informal helping: The myth of service substitution. *Journal of Applied Gerontology, 8*, 37–52.

Stone, R., Cafferata, G. L., & Sangl, J. (1987). Caregivers of the frail elderly: A national profile. *The Gerontologist, 27*, 616–626.

Talamantes, M. A., Cornell, J., Espino, D. V., Lichtenstein, M. J., & Hazuda, H. P. (1996). SES and ethnic difference in perceived caregiver availability among young–old Mexican Americans and non-Hispanic Whites. *The Gerontologist, 36*, 88–99.

Thomas, K., & Wister, A. (1984). Living arrangements of older women: The ethnic dimension. *Journal of Marriage and the Family, 48*, 67–77.

Watson, J. F. (1990). Family care, economics, and health. In Z. Harel, E. A. McKinney, & M. Williams (Eds.), *Black aged: understanding diversity and service needs* (pp. 50–68). Newbury Park, CA: Sage.

Wolf, D. A. (1984). Kin availability and the living arrangement of older women. *Social Science Research, 13*, 72–89.

Wolf, D. A. (1990). Household patterns of older women: Some international comparisons. *Research on Aging, 12,* 463–486.

Worobey, J. L., & Angel, R. J. (1990a). Poverty and health: Older minority women and the rise of the female-headed household. *Journal of Health and Social Behavior, 31,* 370–383.

Worobey, J. L., & Angel, R. J. (1990b). Functional capacity and living arrangements of unmarried elderly persons. *Journal of Gerontology, 45,* S95–S101.

Zsembik, B. A. (1992). Determinants of living alone among older Hispanics. *Research on Aging, 15,* 449–464.

# Chapter Ten

# Ethnicity, Informal Caregiving, and Caregiver Burden

Notwithstanding the emergence and availability of professional formal services for disabled and dependent elders under public policy auspices, families and friends are still the main providers of instrumental as well as emotional supports for them. It is estimated that between 70% and 80% of all care for frail elders in the United States is given by the informal, not the formal, service sector (Brody & Brody, 1989; Select Committee on Aging, 1987; Stone, Cafferata, & Sangl, 1987). Brody (1985) and Brody and Brody (1989) underscore the fact that despite the alleged fragmentation of traditional families into nuclear units, there is far more family and intergenerational caring and more difficult caring today than in preceding generations.

Caring for a frail, dependent older person, however, can be an overwhelming and all- absorbing experience of almost indefinite duration. The tasks involved are not easy to endure, as chronic fatigue, anger, depression, and increased mental problems often end up afflicting the caregivers (George & Gwyther, 1986; Monk, Lerner, McCann-Oakley, & Cox, 1989; Rabins, Mace, & Lucas, 1982). Other researchers point to related psychosocial problems such as isolation, frustration, and the increased use of psychotropic medications (Barnes, Raskind, Scott, & Murphy, 1981; Chenoweth & Spencer, 1986; George & Gwyther, 1986). In addition, the worsening of a caregiver's own health, including negatively perceived health status and increased stress-related medical conditions, has been reported as a frequent consequence of caregiving (Aronson & Gaston, 1986).

Family caregiving has received much attention in recent social gerontological inquiries, but more empirical work is needed, specifically on the differing caregiving experiences of African Americans, Hispanics, and Whites. In this chapter, we analyze overall caregiving network characteristics and demographic profiles of, and the extent of caregiving involvement by primary caregivers of African American, Hispanic, and White frail elders. We then analyze, in a multivariate framework, how the tasks of caring for frail, impaired elderly persons impact primary caregivers in the three main ethnic groups. In this multivariate analysis, we focus on emotional, physical, and financial strains that befall caregivers of different racial/ethnic groups.

## SIZE AND COMPOSITION OF INFORMAL CAREGIVING NETWORKS

The size and composition of informal caregiving networks represent the range and depth of resources that can be tapped for assistance. A large network with additional helpers may alleviate the burden on a primary caregiver, provide a greater variety of tasks for frail elders, and thus enable caregivers to continue their help for a longer period (Burton et al., 1995).

Studies of caregiving networks have documented racial differences in their size and composition. Gibson (1982), based on two national data sets from 1957 and 1976, found that African Americans select from a more varied pool of helpers to deal with the distress associated with the aging process, substituting one type of helper for another. Gibson suggested that this flexibility in source of support may prepare African American elders for losses, making adaptation in support sources more of a transition than a crisis. Thornton, White-Means, and Choi's (1993) analysis of the 1982 National Long-Term Care Survey and the companion Informal Caregiver Survey (ICS) also found that African American elders had marginally larger informal caregiving networks than Whites of English, Irish, and German descent, and that they were more likely to include relatives outside the immediate family than their white counterparts. The study also found that African American caregivers contributed signficantly more caregiving hours than did their White counterparts. Examining the 1982 and 1984 waves of the National Long-Term Care Survey and the ICS, Miller and McFall (1991) also found that (predominantly Black) non-Whites not only had more helpers initially, but also were more likely than Whites to expand informal helper networks in size and intensity (amount of help provided) in response to changes in the frail older person's health and functional status.

Based on a more recent (1989) wave of the National Long-Term Care Survey, Burton et al. (1995) found that level of functional disability, cognitive impairment, age, and poverty, but not race, were significant predictors of the size of caregiving networks. There was, however, a difference in composition of the network by race: Consistent with findings of previous studies, older disabled African Americans had a greater likelihood of having at least one caregiver from outside the immediate family.

These racial differences in the size, composition, and/or intensity of caregiving networks are attributable to cultural differences between African

Americans and Whites. Research on African American and White families in general indicates that kinship ties among African Americans are stronger than those among Whites, as indicated by joint residency, visiting, and the exchange of mutual aid among kin (Hays & Mindel, 1973). The African American family system is described as highly integrated, serving as an important resource for its members' survival and social mobility (McAdoo, 1978; Scanzoni, 1977; Stack, 1974). African Americans of all ages are more likely than Whites to live in an extended family household (Allen, 1979; Angel & Tienda, 1982; Hofferth, 1984). Compared to Whites, African Americans demonstrate greater reliance on family than on formal care and have lower formal service utilization (Mindel & Wright, 1982a). Other studies have found that African Americans are more likely than Whites to regard elderly persons with respect and to feel that children should help their older relatives (Mutran, 1985; Wylie, 1971). Reciprocal obligations of help from kin are more salient among African Americans (Mutran, 1985). Most African Americans also have active, ongoing friendships; on the periphery of any kinship system, relationships between kin and friends commonly become blurred, and distant relatives and friends often serve as alternative family members (Johnson & Barer, 1990). Furthermore, African American women may be better able than their white counterparts to cope with psychological distress (Gibson, 1982) because they have had to learn to cope with more trying circumstances in their lives (Rodgers-Rose, 1980; Spurlock, 1984).

Few studies specifically compared the size and composition of Hispanic elders' informal caregiving networks to those of African Americans and Whites. Nevertheless, quite a few studies have provided insights into the social support networks of Hispanic elders. In a study of family support among Hispanic elders, Cantor (1979) found that they consistently reported higher levels of interaction and support from their children than either African American or White elders. In their comparative study of social networks of White, African American, Chinese American, and Mexican American elders, Lubben and Becerra (1987) found that Mexican Americans were three times more likely to live with one of their children than were Whites and that they reported the highest frequency of weekly contact with children and grandchildren of all the ethnic groups studied. Mexican American children were also more likely than White children to help with laundry, housework, meals, and shopping. Studies show that the extended family remains one of the most structural components of Hispanic culture, and multigenerational living arrangements and active interaction among generations based on cultural values stressing respect and responsibilities for older family members are common among all Hispanics regardless of country of origin (Cantor & Little, 1985; Queralt, 1984).

But for Hispanic elders, more than 50% of whom according to the 1980 Census came from abroad (Biafora & Longino, 1990), immigration histories and the degree of acculturation to majority norms may compound patterns of family support and service use (Linn, Hunter, & Perry, 1979; Markides & Mindel, 1987; Vaux, 1985). For one thing, a study based on the 1993–1994 Hispanic Established Population for the Epidemiological Studies of the Elderly shows that immigrant Mexican American elders are less likely to live alone and more likely to live with children than are native-born Mexican American elders and that they state that they would like to continue living with their children in the event that they can no longer care for themselves (Angel, Angel, McClellan, & Markides, 1996). This living arrangement preference among the immigrant population may have been partly motivated by their lower economic status than that of the native born. Immigrants are also more likely to depend on adult children for assistance because they lack English-language skills and familiarity with formal helping systems. But adherence to traditional values from the Old World may also be stronger among immigrants.

## CAREGIVER BURDEN: THEORETICAL FRAMEWORKS

The scarcity hypothesis of role theory, which includes the concepts of role strain, role demand overload, and role conflict, provides a useful framework for conceptualizing the experience of primary caregivers who, along with many other role demands, assist frail elderly relatives. According to this hypothesis, people do not have enough time or resources to adequately fulfill their multiple role obligations. Therefore, multiple role commitments produce a strong tendency toward role strain as a consequence of role demand overload and role conflict (Goode, 1960).

As prescribed by societal and cultural norms, a middle-aged caregiver typically has a variety of relational, marital, vocational, and/or social obligations in addition to caregiving responsibilities (Scharlach, 1987). When the demands of these other social roles conflict with his or her caregiving duties, a caregiver is likely to experience a sense of role strain, which is defined as felt difficulty in the fulfillment of caregiving role obligations (Goode, 1960). One source of role strain is role demand overload, which refers to the lack of sufficient time, energy, and personal resources to fulfill the responsibilities of all the roles that a person engages in (Wallace & Noelker, 1984). Role demand overload may be appropriate to describe a middle-aged woman who serves as the primary caregiver for an elderly relative while juggling her other roles as a spouse, parent and/or grandparent, and employee. Another source of role strain is role conflict, which refers to incompatibilities among role expectations (Wallace & Noelker, 1984). In the caregiving context, a caregiver may need to deal with conflicting expectations from his or her elderly relative, spouse, children, and employer.

Initially, caregivers may express satisfaction in providing care to a family member or friend; however, these feelings gradually dissipate as the caregiving demands are progressively intensified. Mindel and Wright (1982b), for instance, report that caregivers' satisfaction in providing assistance declines as the demand begins to require additional functions that the caregiver may not have initially anticipated. This is consistent with Zarit, Reever, and Bach-Peterson's (1980) findings, which established that beside the stress associated with direct care, caregivers may also experience stress as a result of "practical frustrations" from difficulties in locating community programs, from social isolation, or from realistic anxieties stemming from the fear that back-up services may not be available in a crisis situation. A different perspective is offered by Motenko (1989), who observed that the duration of caregiving or severity of the illness is "relatively unimportant" in predicting the magnitude of stress experienced by the caregiver.

It has often been assumed that specific interventions may act to strengthen the caregiver's coping abilities and ease the burden of care. Particularly significant is the presence of other informal supports, usually another family member or friends, upon whom the caregiver can call and rely when additional assistance and social support are needed. These persons can play a decisive role as they provide both concrete assistance and emotional help. Zarit et al. (1980) reported that having available informal supports is associated with reduced feelings of burden, and with more effective functioning on the caregiver's part. On the other hand, in a study of respite services for caregivers of people with Alzheimer's disease, Lawton, Brody, and Saperstone (1989) found that while the caregivers were satisfied with such services, they were not effective in reducing their sense of burden and mental stress.

In the literature, the emotional cost or negative psychological effect of caregiving has been conceptualized as caregiver burden (Morycz, Malloy, Bozich, & Martz, 1987; Zarit et al., 1980), caregiver strain (Cantor, 1983; Morycz, 1985; Scharlach & Boyd, 1989), and caregiver stress (Lieberman & Kramer, 1991; Stephens, Kinney, & Ogrrocki, 1991). Building on these earlier conceptual frameworks and theories of stress and coping, more fully developed models of caregiver burden were presented in the early 1990s. These models posit that the combinations of stressors and resources influence the caregiver's cognitive and affective appraisal of and reaction to caregiving stress (see Lawton, Moss, Kleban, Glickman, & Rovine, 1991; Pearlin, Mullan, Semple, & Skaff, 1990).

In Pearlin et al.'s model (1990), which was developed from their study of Alzheimer's caregivers' stress, caregiver burden or stress—depression, anxiety, irascibility, cognitive disturbance, physical health, and yielding of role—is an outcome of a caregiving process that is influenced by the following domains: (1) background and context of stress (sociodemographic and economic characteristics of caregivers, including race/ethnicity, caregiving history, family network composition, and availability of formal programs); (2) primary stressors (objective indicators of care recipient's disability such as cognitive status, problem behaviors, and functional dependencies; and subjective indicators of role overload or burnout and relational deprivation felt by caregivers); (3) secondary role strains (family conflict, job-caregiving conflict, economic strains, constriction of social life); (4) secondary intrapsychic strains (self-esteem, mastery, loss of self, role captivity, competence, and gain); and (5) mediators (coping and social support) that reinforce or attenuate the strength of the relationship between a stressor and an outcome.

One critique of Pearlin et al.'s model is that caregiving activities are not included as stressors, although these factors might increase caregiver stress through fatigue, lack of time for other activities, and emotional burden resulting from supervising a relative with cognitive impairment (Fredman, Daly, & Lazur, 1995).

In Lawton et al.'s model (1991), caregiving outcomes include both positive and negative affect in the sense that, on the one hand, caregiving is an activity that the caregiver "is committed to and is therefore positively affirming," while on the other hand, "it is a demand that competes with other needs of the person and has the capacity to exceed the person's resources" (p. P182). Stressors and resources include severity of the care recipient's symptoms, the caregiver's health and help received from other sources, and help given by the caregiver. These factors are directly and indirectly correlated with caregiving satisfaction and caregiving burden, which in turn effect positive affect or negative outcomes such as depression. Thus, unlike Pearlin et al.'s linear model, Lawton et al.'s model posits two parallel processes and outcomes that may be more congruent with mixed valence of caregiving. But a weakness of the model may be its omission of socioeconomic variables, including race, that may be strong mediators of the appraisal process.

Together, however, these two models have contributed to expanding the parameters of caregiver stress. That is, caregiver burden, strain, or stress include not only the emotional cost or negative psychological effect of caregiving but also the negative physical and economic effects of caring for an impaired person (Fredman et al., 1995), because reaction to stress is likely to encompass all aspects of life.

For the multivariate analysis of caregiver burden in this chapter, we have adopted a combination of these theoretical frameworks. That is, we define caregiving burden as, in the context of role theory, the emotional, physical, and financial role strains that the caregivers experience in the process of fulfilling caregiver role obligations. In terms of stressors and resources, we use indicators specified in Pearlin et al.'s (1990) and Lawton et al.'s (1991) models.

## RACIAL DIFFERENCES IN THE IMPACT OF CAREGIVING ON PRIMARY CAREGIVERS

Attending to the needs of an elderly relative can restrict the caregiver's personal and social life, as well as employment and vocational opportunities. These limitations, together with the concurrent emotional, physical, and financial effects of the helping relationship can create a very stressful environment, especially for primary caregivers (Archbold, 1983; Brody, 1981; 1985; Cantor, 1983; Horowitz, 1985b; Young & Kahana, 1989).

Caring for a disabled elderly relative may thus exact health, social, and financial costs and even sacrifices, but the effectiveness and perseverance of the primary caregivers largely depend on the circumstances in which the care is provided. Schulz (1990) affirms that the reaction to the "objective stressors," that is, the frail patient's illness, disability, cognitive impairment, and illness-related behavioral problems, is affected by "contextual" variables, including the sociodemographic and personality characteristics of the informal caregivers, as well as their values, attitudes, and beliefs, and the extent to which they can count on a social network of additional, or secondary, caregivers. Pearlin et al. (1990) also stress that virtually everything about caregiving and its consequences is potentially influenced by key characteristics of the caregiver, which "signify where people stand within stratified orders having unequal distribution of rewards, privileges, opportunities, and responsibilities" (p. 585). They emphasize that "the kinds and intensities of stressors to which people are exposed, the personal and social resources available to deal with stressors, and the way stress is expressed are all subject to the effects of these statuses" (p. 585). Essentially, no two caregivers or no two care recipients, for that matter, are identical.

For instance, one important such contextual variable or key characteristic that has been studied a great deal is the caregiver's gender. The emotional strain, in particular, appears to be felt most acutely by women caregivers (Horowitz, 1985b; Morycz et al., 1987; Stoller, 1983; Young & Kahana, 1989); men seem to be better able to distance themselves emotionally from their care recipient when providing informal care. In addition, Horowitz (1985b) found that women providing care to an older relative frequently minimize the involvement of their husbands in the caregiving process, even when significant (Horowitz, 1985a; Stoller, 1983). It may also be that men more often distance themselves emotionally from the caregiving process, possibly because their male identity is less tied to success in nurturing.

Barnett and Baruch (1985), studying middle-aged women's involvement in multiple roles, as well as the relationship of role demand overload and role conflict with anxiety, found that the number of roles a woman occupies is significantly related to both role demand overload and role conflict. Female caregivers with competing obligations and responsibilities struggle with setting priorities and deciding how to divide their time, energy, and financial resources between their older relatives and their families. Furthermore, studies indicate that employed women who face these competing demands do not reduce the extent of relative care. Rather, they sacrifice their leisure activities so that they can take on the additional burden (Brody & Schoonover, 1986; Horowitz, 1985b).

Another important contextual variable or key characteristic in the United States is the ethnic extraction of the caregiver. Unlike the effect of gender, that of ethnicity or race on caregiving stress has not been extensively researched. Yet available studies show that ethnicity, as an indication of distinctive social and cultural heritage, plays a significant role in the stress and coping process as a result of (1) a differential risk for specific health disorders and disability; (2) variation in the caregiver's appraisal of stress events and potential stressors; (3) differential perception and mode of family support and coping behavior; and (4) especially for racial and ethnic minorities, their generally low socioeconomic status and minority status itself (Aranda & Knight, 1997).

One available study (Morycz et al., 1987)) reports no racial differences in the amount of burden experienced by Black and White caregivers ($n = 80$) of functionally disabled elders and in their desire to institutionalize a nondemented family member. But the predictors of burden varied between the two groups. Among Black caregivers, being unmarried and the elder's ADL impairments predicted burden; among White caregivers, the elder's diagnosis of a dementia and IADL impairments were predictors.

Most other studies of caregiver burden generally report significant racial differences. For example, based on the 1982 National Long-Term Care Survey and the companion ICS, Fredman et al. (1995) found that Black caregivers performed more caregiving activites and cared for persons with greater functional and cognitive impairment. However, White caregivers reported significantly more burden. The authors also found that Black caregivers received more support with caregiving activities than did their White counterparts. Miller, Campbell, Farran, Kaufman, and Davis's (1995) study of 215 caregivers recruited from diverse health and social service programs and churches also found that African American caregivers were less likely to report caregiver depression (measured by the Center for Epidemiological Studies Depression Scale [CES-D]) and global role strain (measured by Caregiver Global Role Strain scale) than were White caregivers, before and after differences in sociodemographics, stressors, and resource variables were controlled for, although there was no racial difference in the process influencing caregiver distress.

Another study of a small sample ($n = 152$) of Black and White dementia caregivers recruited from New York-area dementia-evaluation clinics, physician referrals, and a social service program reported similar findings: Black caregivers, who are more likely to be adult children with their own parenting needs and to occupy lower social class positions, evidence fewer differences in their adaptation to dementia caregiving than their White counterparts. Although Black caregivers are likely to voice more unmet needs than their White counterparts, they report less burden and less desire to institutionalize their relatives (Hinrichsen & Ramirez, 1992). Lawton, Rajagopal, Brody, and

Kleban's study (1992) of primary caregivers ($n = 629$) of dementia patients recruited in the Philadelphia area also found that, after socioeconomic and background differences were accounted for, Black caregivers expressed a greater sense of traditional caregiving ideology and caregiving mastery and satisfaction then White caregivers. Black caregivers also reported less subjective burden and depression and a lower perception of intrusion on their lives due to caregiving.

A recent review and analysis (Connell & Gibson, 1997) of the empirical studies published since 1985 that have examined the impact of race, culture, and/or ethnicity on dementia caregiving experience sums up its findings as follows: Compared to White caregivers of dementia patients, Black caregivers reported lower levels of caregiver stress, burden, and depression, endorsed more strongly held beliefs about filial support, and were more likely to use prayer, faith, or religion as coping mechanisms. Black caregivers were also more likely to be adult children, friends, or other family members; White caregivers were more likely to be spouses. (Included in the review are Cox, 1993; 1995; Haley, West, Wadley, Ford, White, Barrett, Harrell, & Roth, 1995; Hinrichsen & Ramirez, 1992; Lawton et al., 1992; Macera et al., 1992; Miller et al., 1995; Morycz et al., 1987; Wood & Parham, 1990; and Wykle & Segal, 1991, for comparison between Black and White caregivers; Mintzer, Rubert, & Herman, 1994, for comparison between Hispanic and White caregivers; and Cox & Monk, 1990, for comparison between Black and Hispanic caregivers.)

Methodological limitations stemming from the fact that most of the studies reviewed used nonrandom, volunteer samples restricted to limited geographic areas may serve to undermine their generalizability. But the consistent findings they report indicate that there are indeed differences in caregiver burden felt by Black and White caregivers. Explanations for lower burden and depression reported by Black caregivers as compared to those of their White counterparts have yet to be advanced. Among the probable explanations suggested are that the distress of caregiving may be viewed by Black caregivers as relatively minor in light of the continual struggle that they face in this society, that they may be more likely to view the symptoms of dementing illnesses as part of the normal aging process (Miller et al., 1995), and that they receive more help from other informal social support systems (Fredman et al., 1995).

Studies of Hispanic caregivers have been scant. However, available research findings indicate that they tend to react more negatively to caregiving situations than do their Black counterparts. Cox and Monk's (1990) study of 31 Black and 19 Hispanic caregivers in New York and Baltimore reported that the two groups were similar in sociodemographic, health, and social support profiles and that they had similar burden scores and similarly strong support for filial responsibilities. But the Hispanic caregivers reported much higher levels of depression (measured by CES-D). In a review of research on Hispanic caregivers of dementia patients, Aranda and Knight (1997) also found that

Hispanic caregivers reported a level of psychological burden or depression that was similar to (Mintzer et al., 1994) or higher than (Valle, Cook-Gait, & Tazbaz, 1993) that of White caregivers. In Valle et al.'s study, Hispanics (mainly Mexican Americans) were more likely than Whites to report feeling bothered or upset by specific caregiving tasks (such as instrumental support with ADL) and by care recipients' "problem" behaviors (cited in Aranda & Knight, 1997). Again, generalizability of these findings is limited because of the small number of studies, nonrandom sampling, and small sample sizes. In addition, possible cultural bias of the CES-D may have resulted in exaggerated scores among Hispanics, especially among groups characterized as poor, less educated, Spanish-speaking, and female (see Aranda & Knight, 1997).

Considering the general socioeconomic and health status of the Hispanic population, Hispanic caregivers, as compared to their White counterparts, are likely to be poorer and in poorer health, as well as more likely to juggle multiple role responsibilities of family, work, and caregiving activities, which all contribute to greater psychological distress. Aspects of Hispanic culture discussed in Aranda and Knight (1997) as possible explanations of the higher level of distress among Hispanic caregivers also provide valuable insights. That is, Hispanics greatly value extended social support networks and are more sensitive to crises and disruption of them. In that context, they may be more likely than Whites to experience the relative's illness as distressing when it disrupts the family system and requires its reorganization or relocation. Moreover, Hispanic caregivers are less prone to talk about their situation or share their private feelings.

Overall, although there has not been an abundance of empirical data regarding the differential experiences of African American, Hispanic, and White caregivers to date, it seems reasonable to hypothesize that the sources of caregiver role strain are different for African Americans, Hispanics, and Whites because of the differences in filial norms, values, role expectations, degree of extended family support, and patterns of formal service utilization. This chapter aims to contribute to filling the void in information in question. It first examines the size and composition of informal caregiving networks, and then the impact and correlates of such impact of elderly caregiving on primary caregivers in the African American, Hispanic, and White communities.

## METHODOLOGY

### Data Source and Sample

Data were obtained from the informal caregiver survey portion of the National Long-Term Care Channeling Demonstration conducted from 1982 to 1984. Detailed information on the database is discussed in Chapter 2. The baseline informal caregiver survey was conducted with 451 African American,

1,409 White, and 69 Hispanic caregivers who were providing care for frail elders referred to the Channeling Demonstration.

## Measurement of Variables

As dependent variables, caregiver role strains were operationalized as the caregiver's subjective evaluation of emotional, physical, and financial response to caregiver role obligations. The interviewer asked each caregiver, "We would like to get some idea of the amount of stress or strain that caring for your older relative places on you." The interviewer then asked the caregiver to rate the amount of emotional, physical, and financial strain on a five-point scale, where 1 meant he or she experienced little or no emotional, physical, and financial strain and 5 meant a great deal of emotional, physical, and financial strain. Thus, unlike previous studies where caregiver role strain was usually conceptualized as a unidimensional concept (Cantor, 1983; Morycz, 1985; Sainsbury & Grad de Alarcon, 1970; Scharlach & Boyd, 1989), in this chapter role strain is conceptualized multidimensionally, encompassing emotional as well as physical and financial domains.

Using role theory, four sets of predictor variables—role demand overload variables, role conflict variables, elders' impairment and caregivers' sociodemographic variables, and resources variables—were identified and hypothesized to be associated with the caregiver role strain experienced by the primary caregivers. The frail elder's impairment characteristics, caregiver demographic characteristics, and the availability of social resources were control variables, serving as background or context of caregiving and mediators of caregiving stressors (e.g., Bromberg, 1983; Cantor, 1983; Deimling & Bass; 1986; Lawton et al., 1991; Pearlin et al., 1990; Poulshock & Deimling, 1984; Pratt, Schmall, Wright, & Cleland, 1985).

*Role demand overload* was measured by three conceptually different components. First, caregiving role demand, which was a composite measure (alpha = .82), included three items: (1) the average number of caregiving days per week, (2) the average number of caregiving hours per day, and (3) the total number of ADL tasks and IADL tasks that the caregiver provided for the elderly relative. Second, other competing role demands, which comprised a composite measure (alpha = .58), included two items: (1) the total number of other social roles (which included being married, being the mother of children under age 15, and being the caregiver of another chronically impaired person), and (2) the number of hours of paid work per week. The third component was the duration of the caregiving, representing the tenure of caregiving in years. These measures quantitatively indicate the extent to which a primary caregiver was involved in multiple roles.

*Role conflict* was operationally defined by using six items: caregiving effects on other relationships, limits on time with family, limits on personal privacy, limits on social life, perceived time conflict in caring for the elderly relative, limits on social life, perceived time conflict in caring for the elderly relative, and work conflict. Work conflict was defined as being present when a primary caregiver turned down a job, refused a more demanding job, decreased working hours, or was unable to look for work when desired because of the caregiving responsibilities. The primary caregivers were asked to rate their perceptions in these areas on a three-point scale: (1) not a problem, (2) a problem but not serious, and (3) a serious problem. Principal component analysis with varimax rotation of the six measures of role conflict revealed two components. Component I contained the first five items and represented perceived conflict between caregiving and the caregiver's personal and social life. The raw scores of the five items were summed to create a composite score (alpha coefficient = .83). Only work conflict, another dimension of competing demands, loaded on component II; it was treated as a separate independent variable. Zero-order correlations between role demand overload, role conflict, and other predictor measures ranged from .09 to .32, indicating that multicollinearity was not a problem.

The level of ADL and IADL impairments, the number of unmet ADL and IADL needs, and the number of behavioral problems manifested by the elderly relative were included in the analysis to control for their effects, if any, on the caregiver role strain score. The level of ADL impairment was measured by asking elderly respondents if they had been helped during the preceding week in the following five areas: eating, bathing, dressing, toileting, and getting out of bed or a chair. The level of IADL impairment was measured by asking elderly persons if they had needed help during the preceding week in the following nine areas: meal preparation, housekeeping, shopping, taking medicine, indoor mobility, outdoor mobility, transportation, money management, and telephone use. Perceived unmet needs with ADL and IADL were assessed by asking elderly persons if they needed more help in those ADL and IADL areas. The number of the elderly person's behavioral problems was a number count, from the caregivers' perspective, of such problems as embarrassment, forgetting/confusion, and yelling. This variable was used instead of the cognitive impairment variable in the multivariate analysis to avoid multicollinearity problems.

The age, income, and gender of the caregiver and the living arrangement of the care recipient were also included in the analyses so that the effects of role overload, role conflict, and race could be assessed after the effects of relative impairment as well as those of the sociodemographic and economic variables were taken into account in the multiple regression analyses. Age and income are ordinal variables, and gender and living arrangements are dichotomous variables (see Table 10.1).

Resources of the primary caregiver were defined as both internal and external (nonmaterial) resources available to him or her. Because the resources available may moderate the effect of role overload and role conflict on

**Table 10.1**
**Demographic Characteristics of Primary Caregivers of Frail Elders**

| Characteristics | African American n = 451 (%) | White n = 1,409 (%) | Hispanic n = 69 (%) |
|---|---|---|---|
| **Age** | | | |
| <= 40 | 13.5 | 9.9 | 11.6 |
| 41 to 50 | 13.3 | 15.1 | 13.0 |
| 51 to 60 | 22.2 | 22.6 | 20.3 |
| 61 to 70 | 24.6 | 24.3 | 30.4 |
| 71 to 80 | 21.1 | 19.5 | 18.8 |
| >= 80 | 5.3 | 8.6 | 5.8 |
| **Gender** | | | |
| Female | 76.3 | 72.6 | 66.7 |
| **Income (monthly)****** | | | |
| < $500 | 30.8 | 13.8 | 32.8 |
| $500 to $999 | 24.7 | 22.9 | 28.4 |
| >= $1000 | 44.5 | 63.3 | 38.8 |
| **Education****** | | | |
| None | 1.6 | 1.9 | 2.9 |
| Elementary | 28.4 | 20.2 | 30.4 |
| Some secondary | 25.1 | 13.7 | 11.6 |
| Completed high school | 25.5 | 33.7 | 18.8 |
| Some post high school | 9.8 | 17.5 | 10.1 |
| Completed college | 4.7 | 7.1 | 15.9 |
| Postcollege | 5.1 | 5.8 | 10.1 |
| **Marital status****** | | | |
| Married | 48.3 | 66.3 | 60.9 |
| Not married | 51.7 | 33.7 | 39.1 |
| **Employment status** | | | |
| Employed | 31.5 | 34.9 | 36.2 |
| Unemployed | 68.5 | 65.1 | 63.8 |
| **Living arrangement*** | | | |
| With elderly | 60.3 | 54.9 | 63.8 |
| Apart | 39.7 | 45.1 | 36.2 |
| **Other caregiving duty** | 14.2 | 17.3 | 21.7 |

*Data Source*: National Long-Term Care Channeling Demonstration, 1982–1984.
**$p < 0.01$; ****$p < 0.0001$.

after the effect of resources was taken into account. Indicators of internal resources included the perceived health status of the caregiver and the quality of the relationship between the caregiver and the care recipient. The perceived health status was rated by the primary caregivers on a four-point scale ranging from (1) excellent health to (4) poor health. The primary caregivers rated the quality of the relationship with their relatives on a three-point scale ranging from (1) very good to (3) not very good. External resources include the availability of respite support and the number of formal service uses. The availability of respite was measured by the question, "If you were unable to help the elderly person, is there someone (including all friends, family members, and paid workers) who would do the things that you do?" The number of formal service uses included those of in-home, community-based, and institutional services used by the elderly relative.

### Methods of Analysis

Bivariate analyses compared the following among African American, White, and Hispanic frail elders: (1) size and composition of the caregiving networks, (2) sociodemographic and economic characteristics of primary caregivers and their relationship to the elderly care recipient, (3) extent of the primary caregivers' caregiving activities and role strains, and (4) patterns of frail elders' formal service utilization and perceived unmet needs.

For multivariate analysis, separate parallel hierarchical regression analyses were used for African American, White, and Hispanic caregivers to find the determinants of caregivers' role strain in emotional, physical, and financial domains. Our hypothesis is that some of the independent variables have differential effects on three domains of role strain for the three racial/ethnic groups of caregivers. Therefore, for each domain of role strain (emotional, physical, and financial), separate regressions were conducted for African American, Hispanic, and White caregivers. The regression models were simple additive ones, in which role demand overload and role conflict variables would have an additive effect on the dependent variables, controlling for elder impairment, caregiver sociodemographic, and resource variables.

Because of the small sample size of Hispanic caregivers, we caution that the multivariate findings pertaining to Hispanics may be unstable and thus need to be interpreted only in an advisory capacity.

### RESULTS
### Size, Composition, and Characteristics of Sample

When examining the size, composition, and characteristics of the informal caregiving networks (Table 10.2), it can first be observed that the three racial/ethnic groups were not statistically different in the size of their caregiver

Table 10.2
Caregiving Network Characteristics of Frail Elders by Racial/Ethnic Groups

| Characteristics | African American n = 451 (%) | White n = 1,409 (%) | Hispanic n = 69 (%) |
|---|---|---|---|
| **Network category** | | | |
| Only primary caregiver | 38.1 | 42.1 | 39.1 |
| Two caregivers | 32.6 | 30.9 | 42.0 |
| Three or more | 29.3 | 27.0 | 18.8 |
| **Network relationship**** | | | |
| Related to elder | 86.7 | 91.3 | 94.2 |
| Not related to elder | 13.3 | 8.7 | 5.8 |
| **Network composition***** | | | |
| Spouse only | 9.8 | 13.3 | 14.5 |
| Spouse and children | 5.5 | 7.8 | 7.3 |
| Spouse and other | 4.7 | 2.8 | 2.9 |
| Children only | 20.2 | 33.9 | 37.7 |
| Children, spouse, and other | 2.2 | 2.0 | 0.0 |
| Children and other | 20.8 | 17.3 | 18.8 |
| Other only | 36.8 | 22.9 | 18.8 |
| **Primary caregivers' relationship to elders***** | | | |
| Spouse | 20.2 | 23.4 | 24.6 |
| Daughter | 25.9 | 32.9 | 31.9 |
| Son | 8.7 | 11.6 | 17.4 |
| Sibling | 9.7 | 6.5 | 1.5 |
| Daughter-in-law | 2.0 | 5.4 | 1.5 |
| Grandchildren | 6.4 | 2.6 | 5.8 |
| Other relative | 10.7 | 7.3 | 10.2 |
| Friend | 16.4 | 10.3 | 7.1 |

*Data Source*: National Long-Term Care Channeling Demonstration, 1982–1984.
**$p < 0.01$; ****$p < 0.0001$.

networks and that the caregiving tasks tend to be shared by more than a single caregiver in about 60% of the cases. Second, and in terms of caregiver composition, Whites and Hispanics rely mostly on immediate kin, whereas African Americans incorporate a wider range of nonfamily acquaintances, such as friends and neighbors. In fact, reliance on these unrelated, nonkin caregivers is proportionally twice as high among African Americans as among Hispanics (37% versus 19%). Finally, children assume a more dominant caregiving role among Hispanic participants.

As for primary caregivers, African American elders were again distinctive because more than one-fourth of them had primary caregivers who were not immediate family members. Hispanic primary caregivers were more likely to be sons (17.4%) than their African American (8.7%) and White (11.6%) counterparts. Grandchildren were at least twice as likely to be primary caregivers of both African American and Hispanic frail elders as White frail elders.

Table 10.2 shows the sociodemographic and economic characteristics of the primary caregivers. It points to a modal age of 61 to 70 years, with nearly three-fourths exceeding age 50; it is, indeed, a middle-aged and older population. Furthermore, two-thirds are women: wives, daughters, daughters-in-law, sisters, and other female relatives. As expected, White caregivers reported a higher monthly income than their African American and Hispanic counterparts. White and Hispanic primary caregivers are mostly married (66.3% and 60.9%, respectively), but this is the case of slightly less than half of the African American primary caregivers. About two-thirds of all caregivers were not employed at the time of the study, and the majority, ranging from 55% among Whites to 63.8% among Hispanics, lived in the same premises as the dependent frail older person. For many, it appeared, their caregiving was an exclusive commitment. Moreover, 14.2% of African Americans, 17.3% of Whites, and 21.7% of Hispanics appeared to have additional, and probably competing, caregiving responsibilities.

According to data in Table 10.3, the average duration of the caregiving responsibilities of the three ethnic groups was similar, ranging from 3.2 to 3.4 years. There was also uniformity across the ethnic divide concerning the average number of hours required daily for these tasks, ranging from 4.4 to 4.7 hours, as well as the number of both ADL and IADL assisted by caregivers. Considering that the ADL scale consists of five items, the 4.3 and 4.2 scores indicate that, on average, help was needed for practically all of them; the same applies for the IADL scale (nine items, with 6.4 and 6.3 scores).

Descriptive levels of role strain show that African American caregivers reported lower emotional-strain scores than White and Hispanic caregivers and that the latter two groups did not differ from each other. For physical strain, African Americans again reported the lowest score, followed by Hispanics and then by Whites. Despite their income, which was lower than that of Whites, African Americans also reported lower financial-strain scores than did Whites. Hispanics were not different from African Americans.

The utilization rates of formal services varied from group to group (Table 10.4). Hispanics resorted more often to outpatient visits to doctors' offices, as well as to home-delivered meals, but were lower consumers of social and formal home care services and were the least inclined toward placement of their frail elders in institutional, nursing home settings. Among Whites, the reverse tended to hold true: They resorted more often to home care and social services, and a higher proportion of them applied and were wait-listed for institutional care.

**Table 10.3**
**Involvement of and Impact on Primary Caregivers of Frail Elders**

| Characteristics | African American $\underline{n}$ = 451 | White $\underline{n}$ = 1,409 | Hispanic $\underline{n}$ = 69 |
| --- | --- | --- | --- |
| Caregiving duration (year) | 3.2[a] | 3.2[a] | 3.4[a] |
| Caregiving hours/day | 4.4[a] | 4.6[a] | 4.7[a] |
| ADL tasks provided | 4.2[a] | 4.3[a] | 4.3[a] |
| IADL tasks provided | 6.3[a] | 6.4[a] | 6.3[a] |
| Emotional strain (1 to 5) | 2.9[a] | 3.6[b] | 3.7[b] |
| Physical strain (1 to 5) | 2.5[a] | 3.3[b] | 2.9[c] |
| Financial strain (1 to 5) | 2.1[a] | 2.5[b] | 2.0[a] |

*Data Source*: National Long-Term Care Channeling Demonstration, 1982–1984.
*Note*: ANOVA statistics with post hoc multiple comparisons were used to test the differences among means.
[a,b,c]Means with different letters are significantly different at less than 0.05 level in the same variable.

African Americans were more frequent participants in community-based recreational services, but on the whole, they were less intensive users of formal services. The greater availability of informal helpers to them did not seem to compensate or reduce the need for community-based formal services. African American elders had a mean of 2.3 informal helpers, as compared to 2.1 for Whites and 2.0 for Hispanics, but they also perceived that a higher number of their ADL and IADL needs remained inadequately met. It would appear, in consequence, that the informal supports, even if more extensive numerically, could not properly cope with the greater incidence of disability evidenced among the African American frail elderly. In other words, the numerical advantage of 0.3 in the number of informal helpers may not be substantial enough to cover the greater incidence of disability. At the other end, Hispanics could count on fewer informal helpers, and yet their use of the formal service system was sporadic or restrained. In a way this could be rationalized by their admission of a lower rate of perceived unmet needs, a fact that does not seem consistent with their higher rates of ADL and cognitive impairment, bedbound state, and incontinence (as reported in Table 3.1). It may be assumed in this case that caregivers who adhere to more categorical norms of filial or spousal commitment also subscribe to the idea that their family unit must be self-sufficient and must stand by its frail and dependent loved ones, regardless of the physical and emotional costs involved. Applying for services outside the family boundaries would therefore be regarded as morally reprehensible or an abdication of the noted imperatives of spousal or filial responsibility.

**Table 10.4**
**Formal Service Utilization Patterns and Perceived Unmet Needs of Frail Elders by Racial/Ethnic Group**

| Characteristics | African American $\underline{n} = 451$ | White $\underline{n} = 1,409$ | Hispanic $\underline{n} = 69$ |
|---|---|---|---|
| **Medical care services** | | | |
| Regular medical care | 91.4% | 92.8% | 86.1% |
| In hospital in preceding 2 months | 72.0% | 72.0% | 67.6% |
| Hospital days in preceding 6 months | 19.8ᵃ | 18.5ᵃ | 15.2ᵃ |
| Average doctor visits in preceding 2 months | 1.7ᵃ | 1.7ᵃ | 2.3ᵇ |
| Social service use (mean) | 1.5ᵃ | 1.6ᵃ | 1.3ᵇ |
| **In-home services** | | | |
| Regular home care* | 27.8% | 29.8% | 13.9% |
| Meals on Wheels* | 10.7% | 16.5% | 16.7% |
| **Community-based services** | | | |
| Congregate meals | 2.8% | 4.1% | 4.1% |
| Social center participation** | 16.6% | 11.5% | 8.5% |
| Respite support | 29.3% | 26.4% | 18.8% |
| **Institutional service use** | | | |
| In nursing home in preceding 6 months**** | 3.3% | 9.0% | 2.8% |
| Nursing home application** | 2.9% | 6.2% | 2.9% |
| Nursing home wait-listed** | 2.2% | 5.4% | 1.4% |
| **Perceived unmet ADL and IADL needs** | 4.6ᵃ | 3.8ᵇ | 2.8ᶜ |
| **Informal helpers (mean)** | 2.3ᵃ | 2.1ᵇ | 2.0ᵇ |

*Data Source*: National Long-Term Care Channeling Demonstration, 1982–1984.
*Note*: ANOVA statistics with post hoc multiple comparisons were used to test the differences among means.
ᵃ,ᵇ,ᶜMeans with different letters are significantly different at less than 0.05 level in the same variable.
$*p < 0.05$; $**p < 0.01$; $****p < 0.0001$.

## Factors Associated with Caregiver Role Strain

*Emotional Strain.* The results of the emotional-strain regression models for three ethnic/racial caregiver groups are presented in Table 10.5. The standardized regression coefficients of a series of predictor variables proved to be different for the three groups in reference. For the African American respondents they were (1) the increase in behavioral problems of their elderly charges; (2) their own perceived decline in health; (3) the lack of respite support, to alleviate the continuous caregiving chores; (4) caregiving role demands; and

**Table 10.5**
**Sources of Caregiving Emotional Strain among Caregivers of Different Ethnic Groups**

| Predictor variables | Standardized regression coefficients (SE) | | |
| --- | --- | --- | --- |
| | African American | White | Hispanic |
| **Sociodemographic variables** | | | |
| Elder ADL impairment | -- | 0.06(0.04)* | -- |
| Elder unmet ADL and IADL needs | -- | -- | -- |
| Elder behavioral problems | 0.15(0.06)** | 0.14(0.04)**** | -- |
| Caregiver age | -- | 0.08(0.03)** | -- |
| Caregiver income | -- | -- | -- |
| Caregiver gender (female=1) | -- | 0.29(0.08)**** | -- |
| Living arrangement (alone=1) | -- | -- | -- |
| **Resource variables** | | | |
| Quality of relationship | -- | 0.23(0.07)** | -- |
| Caregiver's perceived health | 0.12(0.07)** | 0.14(0.04)**** | -- |
| Respite support | -0.11(0.14)* | -- | -0.37(0.20)** |
| Formal service use | -- | -- | -- |
| **Role demand overload variables** | | | |
| Caregiving duration | -- | -- | -- |
| Caregiving role demand | -0.13(0.00)* | -- | -0.39(0.01)* |
| Competing demands | -- | -- | -- |
| **Role conflict variables** | | | |
| Conflict in life | 0.38(.0.03)**** | 0.37(0.01)**** | 0.32(0.05)*** |
| Work conflict | 0.11(0.17)* | 0.32(0.09)** | -- |
| $R^2$ | 0.31 | 0.32 | 0.41 |
| Adjusted $R^2$ | 0.28 | 0.31 | 0.24 |

*Data Source*: National Long-Term Care Channeling Demonstration, 1982–1984.
*Note*: Standard errors are in parentheses.
*$p < 0.05$; **$p < 0.01$; ***$p < 0.001$; ****$p < 0.0001$.

(5) caregiving conflicts with both their personal life and their work responsibilities. The inverse relationship between emotional strain and caregiving role demand may signify that their high expectations of self in the assumed role of caregiver exceeds the demands placed upon them by their dependents.

For Hispanic caregivers, factors associated with high emotional strain were unavailability of respite support, caregiving role demand, and resulting life conflicts. Finally, with the White majority, the number of predictors ran almost the total range of variables. Emotional strain thus increased with (1) the number of functional impairments of the dependent elders; (2) the behavioral problems evidenced by the dependent charges; (3) the caregiver's own age; (3) the caregiver's being female; (4) poor quality of the relationship with the care recipient; (5) the caregiver's own perceived poor health; (6) conflicts between caregiving and the caregivers' personal and social life; and (7) conflict with the caregiver's work responsibilities.

*Physical Strain.* Table 10.6 presents the results of the regression model on physical strain. For African American caregivers, predictors of physical strain were the high levels of perceived unmet ADL and IADL needs of the elderly care recipients, the caregivers' age, the caregivers' own perceived poor health, the emerging conflict between caregiving tasks and the caregivers' personal and social life, and conflicts with the caregivers' occupational duties. For Hispanic caregivers, care recipients' perceived unmet ADL and IADL needs and conflict between caregiving and the caregivers' personal and social life were significant predictors. For White caregivers, factors associated

**Table 10.6**
**Sources of Caregiving Physical Strain among Caregivers of Different Ethnic Groups**

| Predictor variables | Standardized regression coefficients (SE) | | |
|---|---|---|---|
| | African American | White | Hispanic |
| **Sociodemographic variables** | | | |
| Elder ADL Impairment | -- | 0.08(0.04)*** | -- |
| Elder unmet ADL and IADL needs | 0.11(0.02)** | -- | 0.22(0.07)* |
| Elder behavioral problems | -- | 0.08(0.03)** | -- |
| Caregiver age | 0.21(0.06)**** | 0.12(0.03)**** | -- |
| Caregiver income | -- | -- | -- |
| Caregiver gender (female=1) | -- | 0.40(0.08)**** | -- |
| Living arrangement (alone=1) | -- | -- | -- |
| **Resource variables** | | | |
| Quality of relationship | -- | -- | -- |
| Caregiver's perceived health | 0.15(0.08)** | 0.23(0.04)**** | -- |
| Respite support | -- | -- | -- |
| Formal service use | -- | -- | -- |
| **Role demand overload variables** | | | |
| Caregiving duration | -- | -- | -- |
| Caregiving role demand | -- | 0.14(0.00)**** | -- |
| Competing demands | -- | -- | -- |
| **Role conflict variables** | | | |
| Conflict in life | 0.33(0.03)**** | 0.30(0.01)*** | 0.51(0.05)**** |
| Work conflict | 0.38(0.18)* | -- | -- |
| $R^2$ | 0.31 | 0.35 | 0.41 |
| Adjusted $R^2$ | 0.28 | 0.34 | 0.24 |

*Data Source*: National Long-Term Care Channeling Demonstration, 1982–1984.
*Note*: Standard errors are in parentheses.
*$p < 0.05$; **$p < 0.01$; ***$p < 0.001$; ****$p < 0.0001$.

with high physical strain were the elders' ADL impairment and behavioral problems; the caregivers' being older, being female, and having perceived poor health; high levels of caregiving role demand; and conflict between caregiving and the caregivers' life.

*Financial Strain.* Table 10.7 shows that the three common predictors of financial strain for the three groups were caregivers' lower income levels, the care recipients' living alone, and the perceived conflict between caregiving and the caregivers' personal and social life. For African American caregivers, the unique predictors of financial strain were the care recipients' perceived unmet ADL and IADL needs, and the conflict between caregiving and the caregivers' personal and social life. For Hispanic caregivers, the only unique

### Table 10.7
### Sources of Caregiving Financial Strain among Caregivers of Different Ethnic Groups

| Predictor variables | Standardized regression coefficients (SE) | | |
| --- | --- | --- | --- |
| | African American | White | Hispanic |
| **Sociodemographic variables** | | | |
| Elder ADL Impairment | -- | -- | -- |
| Elder unmet ADL and IADL needs | 0.11(0.02)* | -- | -- |
| Elder behavioral problems | -- | -- | -- |
| Caregiver age | -- | 0.10(0.03)** | -- |
| Caregiver income | -0.20(0.09)* | -0.08(0.05)* | -0.29(0.03)** |
| Caregiver gender (female=1) | -- | -- | -- |
| Living arrangement (alone=1) | 0.23(0.04)*** | 0.15(0.05)**** | 0.39(0.02)** |
| **Resource variables** | | | |
| Quality of relationship | -- | -- | -- |
| Caregiver's perceived health | -- | 0.16(0.04)*** | 0.26(0.24)** |
| Respite support | -- | -- | -- |
| Formal service use | -- | -- | -- |
| **Role demand overload variables** | | | |
| Caregiving duration | -- | 0.06(0.01)* | -- |
| Caregiving role demand | -- | -- | -- |
| Competing demands | -- | 0.08(0.00)* | -- |
| **Role conflict variables** | | | |
| Conflict in life | 0.26(0.03)*** | 0.19(0.09)**** | 0.26(0.01)** |
| Work conflict | -- | 0.49(0.09)**** | -- |
| $R^2$ | 0.25 | 0.19 | 0.49 |
| Adjusted $R^2$ | 0.22 | 0.18 | 0.33 |

*Data Source*: National Long-Term Care Channeling Demonstration, 1982–1984.
*Note*: Standard errors are in parentheses.
*$p < 0.05$; **$p < 0.01$; ***$p < 0.001$; ****$p < 0.0001$.

predictor of financial strain was the caregivers' perceived poor health. Finally, for White caregivers, their sense of financial strain was affected uniquely by their age, their own perceived deteriorating health, the duration of caregiving, other competing role demands, and work conflict.

## DISCUSSION

This chapter addresses ethnic differences in family caregiving and the extent to which African Americans, Hispanics, and Whites experience a sense of stress when providing those caregiving tasks. African Americans have more extensive support networks, drawn from both kin and nonkin relations, while Hispanics have more limited networks, confined for the most part to their immediate family. For African Americans, caregiving is therefore more of an open, community affair, whereas for Hispanics and, for that matter, also for Whites, caregiving tends to be a more private or intrafamilial concern; yet neither the size nor the composition of the networks seems to be a determinant of the level of stress felt in each ethnic group.

As for caregiver burden, which was operationalized as caregiver role strain in emotional, physical, and financial domains, bivariate findings corroborate the findings of previous studies, which indicated the overall lower caregiving burden felt by African American as compared to White caregivers. This racial difference was evident even though the two groups did not differ in the duration and intensity of caregiving activities. As observed in Table 10.3, African Americans had the lowest mean (2.9), equivalent to a low or moderate stress level. Whites and Hispanics shared almost the same mean value—3.6 and 3.7, respectively—which indicates a higher but not acute level of stress. The analysis of variance confirmed the statistical significance in the differences between the African American mean, on the one hand, and those of Whites and Hispanics, on the other. Although Hispanic caregivers reported emotional strain at a level similar to that of White caregivers, they also reported lower physical-strain and financial-strain scores than Whites.

The differential level of role strain identified among the three caregiver groups in this chapter offers preliminary support for a cultural interpretation. Due to cultural differences in filial norms, values, role expectations, extended family support, patterns of formal service use, and ways of coping, it is understandable that African American, Hispanic, and White caregivers would perceive and react to the caregiving responsibilities in different ways. There are two possible explanations for the African American caregivers' report of lower caregiver role strain than the White caregivers'. First, it is possible that racial differences are variances in self-reporting or expression, rather than real differences. African American caregivers may be unwilling to admit the concerns surrounding their caregiving role because they experience a stronger sense of obligation (Mui, 1992; 1993). On the other hand, this difference may reflect the African American caregivers' acceptance of caregiving as a fact of life (Morycz et al., 1987). It may be that they are indeed better able to cope in this labor-intensive and time-consuming caregiving work because of more effective lifelong adaptive skills (Gibson, 1982).

In terms of the predictors of the three domains of caregiver role strain, there were both similarities and differences among the three racial/ethnic groups. For all caregivers, regardless of race and ethnicity, role strain in all three domains was associated with the conflict between caregiving and the caregiver's personal and social life. It makes sense that role conflicts would ensue for any caregiver because he or she has to juggle multiple demands and competing role expectations. These role conflicts also mean that there would be lifestyle restrictions imposed by the caregiving role, which tend to frustrate many caregivers. Furthermore, the prevalence of strain among these caregivers supports the contention that caregiving is emotionally, physically, and financially taxing and suggests that a sizeable number of the caregivers in this sample was vulnerable and in obvious need of help if they were to continue their elder care responsibilities indefinitely.

For all caregivers, regardless of ethnicity/race, low income and situations where the elder lived alone and apart from the caregiver were also common predictors of financial strain. It is obvious that fewer financial resources make it difficult to provide elder care. And the situation where the elder lives alone is likely to create an economic burden because of the added expense of maintaining two households. Income and the elders' living arrangement were not predictors of emotional or physical strain for any of the three groups.

Formal service use was not significant in either of the strain models among the three groups, but this finding is consistent with those of other studies (see Stephens & Christianson, 1986). The utilization of formal services among the frail elderly examined in this study actually improved both the elders' and their caregivers' quality of life, largely because it meant that more of the elders' needs were met (Phillips et al., 1986). However, the use of formal services did not have a marked impact on the caregivers' sense of well-being (Mui, 1992; 1993; 1995a).

Inasmuch as there are ethnic/racial similarities in the predictors of role strain, they also appear to reflect differences in cultural values, norms, and role expectations. For example, ethnic differences in expectations of assistance from family members appear to affect the reactions to caregiver role strain among the three ethnic groups. The unavailability of respite support was in this vein a significant predictor of emotional strain for both African American and Hispanic caregivers, but not for Whites. It is unclear why this was so. For the other two ethnic groups, the strain may be due to their higher expectation of support from their extended family, a pattern that appears more pronounced among Hispanic than among African American caregivers. The effect of the lack of respite was stronger (larger beta) for

Hispanics than for African Americans. Furthermore, the unavailability of respite support was not significant among African American and Hispanic caregivers in other role-strain domains (physical and financial).

The findings also suggest that differences exist among the ethnic groups with respect to caregiving role expectations and norms of reciprocity (Mui, 1992). Paradoxically, African American and Hispanic caregivers experienced higher levels of emotional strain when the caregiving role demands diminished. This negative relationship between emotional strain and caregiving role demand is complex and difficult to interpret. It may be due to differences in cultural meanings assigned to caregiving role performance as well as to the sense of obligation experienced by these ethnic families. Because of a possible stronger sense of duty and reciprocity, these families may feel that they never do enough for their elders (Mui, 1992). Again, it is not clear whether this is a real difference or just a self-reporting problem.

The data also suggest ethnic differences in filial norms. White caregivers reported more emotional strain when the quality of the relationship between caregivers and elders was poor, a fact corroborated by the literature (Horowitz & Shindelman, 1983; Mui, 1992; 1995a; 1995b; 1995c; Scharlach & Boyd, 1989). It may also be that problematic or not-so-positive previous elder-caregiver relationships make the necessary and frequent interaction required in caregiving more difficult emotionally. However, the quality of the preceding elder-caregiver relationship was not an issue for either the African American or the Hispanic caregivers. It may be that the latter groups have stronger filial obligations that motivate them to do what they feel they should do regardless of how well they have gotten along with the elders. They may also be less inclined to publicly admit relationship problems because of a stronger respect for elders (Morycz et al., 1987).

Both older African American and White caregivers seemed to experience high levels of physical strain. Older caregivers may have less physical resilience to enable them to continue giving help, a fact bound to increase their perception of strain. Yet caregiving role demand increased physical strain among White caregivers but not among African American and Hispanic caregivers. For African American and Hispanic caregivers, numbers of unmet ADL and IADL needs were positively associated with physical strain. Also, feelings of financial strain were associated with extended caregiving duration and competing demands only for White caregivers, but not for the other two groups. It appears that White caregivers may have more problems coping with long-term caregiving demands and with multiple roles.

## SUMMARY AND IMPLICATIONS

The findings presented in this chapter raise a number of important implications for research, public policy, and the provision of services. Role theory is a useful framework for examining the impact of caregiving on middle-aged caregivers, who are shouldering the major responsibility of caring for their frail elderly relatives, in addition to other personal and social responsibilities. Identification of the specific relationships between role strain and role demand overload, role conflict, and resources clarifies basic theoretical premises. The results also support the conclusion that caregiver strain is multidimensional—emotional, physical, and financial. The findings also confirm that caregivers are a diverse group, not necessarily sharing uniform or even similar experiences.

The findings also point to a need for multifaceted long-term care programs to provide adequate, available, accessible, affordable, and culturally sensitive programs to caregivers of different racial groups and to their frail elderly dependents. The different correlates of role strain of African American, Hispanic, and White caregivers provide new insight into the design of culturally appropriate caregiver interventions. Counseling could center on how to cope with the conflict or tension between caregiving duties and a caregiver's personal and social life.

## REFERENCES

Allen, W. R. (1979). Class, culture, and family organization: The effects of class and race on family structure in urban American. *Journal of Comparative Family Studies, 10,* 301–313.

Angel, J. L., Angel, R. J., McClellan, J. L., & Markides, K. S. (1996). Nativity, declining health, and preferences in living arrangements among elderly Mexican Americans: Implications for long-term care. *The Gerontologist, 36,* 464–473.

Angel, R., & Tienda, M. (1982). Determinants of extended household structure: Cultural pattern or economic model? *American Journal of Sociology, 87,* 1360–1383.

Aranda, M. P., & Knight, B. G. (1997). The influence of ethnicity and culture on the caregiver stress and coping process: A sociocultural review and analysis. *The Gerontologist, 37,* 342–354.

Archbold, P. G. (1983). Impact of parent-caring on women. *Family Relations, 32,* 39–45.

Aronson, M., & Gaston, P. (1986, November). *Excess morbidity in spousal caregivers of patients with Alzheimer's disease.* Paper presented at the 39th annual meeting of the Gerontological Society of America, Chicago.

Barnes, R. F., Raskind, M. A., Scott, M., & Murphy, C. (1981). Problems of families caring for Alzheimer's patients: Use of a support group. *Journal of the American Geriatrics Society, 29,* 80–85.

Barnett, R. C., & Baruch, G. K. (1985). Women's involvement in multiple roles and psychological distress. *Journal of Personality and Social Psychology, 49,* 135–145.

Barusch, A. S., & Spaid, W. M. (1989). Gender differences in caregiving: Why do wives report greater burden? *The Gerontologist, 29,* 667–676.

Biafora, F. A., & Longino, C. F. (1990). Elderly Hispanic migration in the United States. *Journal of Gerontology, 45,* S212–S219.

Brody, E. M. (1981). "Women in the middle" and family help to older people. *The Gerontologist, 21,* 471–480.

Brody, E. M. (1985). Relative care as a normative family stress. *The Gerontologist, 25,* 19–25.

Brody, E. M., & Brody, S. J. (1989). The informal system of health care. In C. Eisdorfer, P. A. Kessler, & A. N. Spector (Eds.), *Caring for the elderly: Reshaping public policy* (pp. 259–277). Baltimore: Johns Hopkins University Press.

Brody, E. M., & Schoonover, C. B. (1986). Patterns of parent-care when adult daughters work and when they do not. *The Gerontologist, 26,* 372–380.

Bromberg, E. M. (1983). Mother–daughter relationships in later life: The effect of quality of relationship upon mutual aid. *Journal of Gerontological Social Work, 6,* 75–92.

Burton, L., Kasper, J., Shore, A., Cagney, K., LaVeist, T., Cubbin, C., & German, P. (1995). The structure of informal care: Are there differences by race? *The Gerontologist, 35,* 744–752.

Cantor, M. H. (1979). The informal support system of New York's inner-city elderly: Is ethnicity a factor? In D. E. Gelfand and A. J. Kutzik (Eds.), *Ethnicity and aging: Theory, research, and policy* (pp. 153–174). New York: Springer.

Cantor, M. H. (1983). Strain among caregivers: A chapter of experience in the United States. *The Gerontologist, 23,* 597–604.

Cantor, M. H., & Little, V. (1985). Aging and social care. In R. H. Binstock & E. Shana (Eds.), *Handbook of aging and the social sciences* (2d ed., pp. 745–782). New York: Van Nostrand Reinhold.

Chenoweth, B., & Spencer, B. (1986). Dementia: The experience of family caregivers. *The Gerontologist, 26,* 267–272.

Connell, C. M., & Gibson, G. D. (1997). Racial, ethnic, and cultural differences in dementia caregiving: Review and analysis. *The Gerontologist, 37,* 354–364.

Cox, C. (1993, May/June). Service needs and interests: A comparison of African American and White caregivers seeking Alzheimer's assistance. *American Journal of Alzheimer's Disease,* 33–40.

Cox, C. (1995). Comparing the experience of Black and White caregivers of dementia patients. *Social Work, 40,* 343–349.

Cox, C., & Monk, A. (1990). Minority caregivers of dementia victims: A comparison of Black and Hispanic families. *Journal of Applied Gerontology, 9,* 340–354.

Deimling, G. T., & Bass, D. M. (1986). Symptoms of mental impairment among elderly adults and their effects on family caregivers. *Journal of Gerontology, 41,* 778–784.

Fredman, L., Daly, M. P., & Lazur, A. M. (1995). Burden among White and Black caregivers to elderly adults. *Journal of Gerontology, 50B,* S110–S118.

George, L. K., & Gwyther, L. P. (1986). Caregiver well-being: A multidimensional examination of family caregivers of demented adults. *The Gerontologist, 26,* 253–259.

Gibson, R. C. (1982). African-Americans at middle and later life: Resources and coping. *Annals of the American Academy of Political and Social Science, 464,* 79–90.

Goode, W. J. (1960). A theory of role strain. *American Sociological Review, 25,* 483–496.

Haley, W. E., West, C. A. C., Wadley, V. G., Ford, G. R., White, F. A., Barrett, J. J., Harrell, L. E., & Roth, D. L. (1995). Psychological, social and health impact of caregiving: A comparison of Black and White dementia family caregivers and non-caregivers. *Psychology and Aging, 10,* 540–552.

Hays, W. C., & Mindel, C. H. (1973). Extended kinship relations in African-American and White families. *Journal of Marriage and the Family, 35*, 51–57.

Hinrichsen, G. A., & Ramirez, M. (1992). Black and White dementia caregivers: A comparison of their adaptation, adjustment, and service utilization. *The Gerontologist, 32*, 375–381.

Hofferth, S. L. (1984). Kin networks, race, and family structure. *Journal of Marriage and the Family, 46*, 791–806.

Horowitz, A. (1985a). Family caregiving to the frail elderly. In C. Eisdorfer, M. P. Lawton, & G. L. Maddox (Eds.), *Annual review of gerontology and geriatrics* (Vol. 5, pp. 194–246). New York: Springer.

Horowitz, A. (1985b). Sons and caregivers as caregivers to older parents: Differences in role performance and consequences. *The Gerontologist, 25*, 612–617.

Horowitz, A., & Shindelman, L. W. (1983). Reciprocity and affection: Past influences on current caregiving. *Journal of Gerontological Social Work, 5*, 5–50.

Johnson, C. L., & Barer, B. M. (1990). Families and networks among older inner-city Blacks. *The Gerontologist, 30*, 726–733.

Lawton, M. P., Brody, E. M., & Saperstone, A. (1989). A controlled study of respite service for caregivers of Alzheimer's patients. *The Gerontologist, 29*, 8–16.

Lawton, M. P., Moss, M., Kleban, M. H., Glickman, A., & Rovine, M. (1991). A two-factor model of caregiving appraisal and psychological well-being. *Journal of Gerontology, 46*, P181–P189.

Lawton, M. P., Rajagopal, D., Brody, E., Kleban, M. H. (1992). The dynamics of caregiving for a demented elder among Black and White families. *Journal of Gerontology, 27*, S156–S164.

Lieberman, M. A., & Kramer, J. H. (1991). Factors affecting decisions to institutionalize demented elderly. *The Gerontologist, 31*, 371–374.

Linn, M. W., Hunter, K. I., & Perry, P. R. (1979). Differences by sex and ethnicity in the psychological adjustment of the elderly. *Journal of Health and Social Behavior, 20*, 273–281.

Lubben, J. E., & Becerra, R. M. (1987). Social support among Black, Mexican, and Chinese elderly. In D. E. Gelfand & C. M. Barresi (Eds.), *Research and ethnic dimensions of aging* (pp. 130–144). New York: Springer.

Macera, C. A., Eaker, E. D., Goslar, P. W., Deandrade, S. J., Williamson, J. S., Cornman, C., & Jannarone, R. J. (1992, September/October). Ethnic differences in the burden of caregiving. *American Journal of Alzheimer's Disease*, 4–7.

Markides, K. S., & Mindel, C. H. (1987). *Aging and ethnicity.* Newbury Park, CA: Sage.

McAdoo, H. P. (1978). Factors related to stability in upwardly mobile African-American families. *Journal of Marriage and the Family, 40*, 761–776.

Miller, B., & McFall, S. (1991). Stability and change in the informal task support network of frail older persons. *The Gerontologist, 31*, 735–745.

Miller, B., Campbell, R. T., Farran, C. J., Kaufman, J. E., & Davis, L. (1995). Race, control, mastery, and caregiver distress. *Journal of Gerontology, 50B*, S374–S382.

Mindel, C. H., & Wright, R. (1982a). The use of social services by African-American and White elderly: The role of social support systems. *Journal of Gerontological Social Work, 4*(3/4), 107–125.

Mindel, C. H., & Wright, R. (1982b). Satisfaction in multigenerational households. *Journal of Gerontology, 37*, 483–489.

Mintzer, J. E., Rubert, M. P., & Herman, K. C. (1994). Caregiving for Hispanic Alzheimer's disease patients: Understanding the problem. *American Journal of Geriatric Psychiatry, 2*, 32–38.

Monk, A., Lerner, J., McCann-Oakley, A., & Cox, C. (1989). *Families of African-American and Hispanic dementia patients: Their use of formal and informal support services.* Final report to the AARP-Andrus Foundation. New York: The Institute on Aging, Columbia University, School of Social Work, 220 pp.

Morycz, R. K. (1985). Caregiving strain and the desire to institutionalize family members with Alzheimer's disease. *Research on Aging, 7*, 329–361.

Morycz, R. K., Malloy, J., Bozich, M., & Martz, P. (1987). Racial differences in family burden: Clinical implications for social work. *Journal of Gerontological Social Work, 10*, 133–154.

Motenko, A. K. (1989). The frustrations, gratifications, and well-being of dementia caregivers. *The Gerontologist, 29*, 166–176.

Mui, A. C. (1992). Caregiver strain among Black and White daughter caregivers: A role theory perspective. *The Gerontologist, 32*, 203–212.

Mui, A. C. (1993). The effects of caregiving on the emotional well-being of American older caregivers. *Hong Kong Journal of Gerontology, 7*, 14–20.

Mui, A. C. (1995a). Caring for frail elderly parents: A comparison of adult sons and caregivers. *The Gerontologist, 35*, 86–93.

Mui, A. C. (1995b). Multidemensional predictors of caregiver strain among older persons caring for their frail spouses. *Journal of Marriage and the Family, 57*, 733–740.

Mui, A. C. (1995c). Determinants of perceived health and functional limitations in elderly caregivers of frail spouses. *Journal of Aging and Health, 7*, 283–300.

Mutran, E. (1985). Intergenerational family support among Blacks and Whites: Response to culture or socioeconomic differences. *Journal of Gerontology, 40*, 382–389.

Pearlin, L. I., Mullan, J. T., Semple, S. J., & Skaff, M. M. (1990). Caregiving and the stress process: An overview of concepts and their measures. *The Gerontologist, 30*, 583–594.

Phillips, B. R., Stephens, S. A., Cerf, J. J., Ensor, W. T., McDonald, A. E., Moline, C. G., Stone, R. T., & Wooldridge, J. (1986). *The evaluation of the national long-term care demonstration survey data collection design and procedures.* Princeton, NJ: Mathematica Policy Research, Inc.

Poulshock, S. W., & Deimling, G. T. (1984). Families caring for elders in residence: Issues in the measurement of burden. *Journal of Gerontology, 39*, 230–239.

Pratt, C. C., Schmall, V. L., Wright, S., & Cleland, M. (1985). Burden and coping strategies of caregivers to Alzheimer's patients. *Family Relations, 34*, 27–33.

Queralt, M. (1984, March/April). Understanding Cuban immigrants: A cultural perspective. *Social Work, 29*, 115–121.

Rabins, P., Mace, N., & Lucas, M. (1982). The impact of dementia on the family. *Journal of the American Medical Association, 248*, 333–335.

Rodgers-Rose, L. F. (1980). The African-American women: A historical overview. In L. F. Rodgers-Rose (Ed.), *The African-American women.* Newbury Park, CA: Sage.

Rogler, L. H. (1978). Help patterns, the family, and mental health: Puerto Ricans in the United States. *International Migration Review, 12*, 248–259.

Sainsbury, P., & Grad de Alarcon, J. (1970). The psychiatrist and the geriatric patient: The effects of community care on the family of the geriatric patient. *Journal of Geriatric Psychiatry, 1,* 23–41.

Scanzoni, J. H. (1977). *The African-American family in modern society: Patterns of stability and security.* Chicago: University of Chicago Press.

Scharlach, A. E. (1987). Role strain in mother–daughter relationships in later life. *The Gerontologist, 27,* 627–631.

Scharlach, A. E., & Boyd, S. L. (1989). Caregiving and employment: Results of an employee survey. *The Gerontologist, 29,* 382–387.

Schulz, R. (1990). Theoretical perspectives on caregiving: Concepts, variables, and methods. In D. E. Biegel and A. Blum (Eds.), *Aging and caregiving—theory, research and policy* (pp. 27–52). Newbury Park, CA: Sage.

Select Committee on Aging, U.S. House of Representatives. (Stone, R.) (1987). Exploding the myths: Caregiving in America (One-hundredth Congress, First Session. Comm. Pub. No. 99-611). Washington, DC: U.S. Government Printing Office.

Spurlock, J. (1984). African-American women in the middle years. In G. Baruch and J. Brooks-Gunn (Eds.), *Women in midlife.* New York: Plenum.

Stack, C. B. (1974). *All our kin: Strategies for survival in an African-American community.* New York: Harper & Row.

Stephens, M. A. P., Kinney, J. M., & Ogrrocki, P. K. (1991). Stressors and well-being among caregivers to older adults with dementia: The in-home versus nursing home experience. *The Gerontologist, 31,* 217–223.

Stephens, S. A., & Christianson, J. B. (1986). *Informal care of the elderly.* Lexington, MA: Lexington Books.

Stoller, E. P. (1983). Parental caregiving by adult children. *Journal of Marriage and the Family, 45,* 851–858.

Stone, R., Cafferata, G., & Sangl, J. (1987). Caregivers of the frail elderly: A national profile. *The Gerontologist, 27,* 616–626.

Thornton, N. C., White-Means, S. I., & Choi, H. K. (1993). Sociodemographic correlates of the size and composition of informal caregiver networks among frail ethnic elderly. *Journal of Comparative Family Studies, 24,* 235–250.

Valle, R., Cook-Gait, H., & Tazbaz, D. (1993). *The cross-cultural Alzheimer/dementia caregiver comparison study.* Paper presented at the 46th annual scientific meeting of the Gerontological Society of America, New Orleans.

Vaux, A. (1985). Variations in social support associated with gender, ethnicity, and age. *Journal of Social Issues, 41,* 89–110.

Wallace, R. W., & Noelker, L. S. (1984, November). *Conceptualizing family caregiving: An application of role theory.* Paper presented at the 37th annual scientific meeting of the Gerontological Society of America, San Antonio, Texas.

Wood, J. B., & Parham, I. A. (1990). Coping with perceived burden: Ethnic and cultural issues in Alzheimer's family caregiving. *Journal of Applied Gerontology, 9,* 325–339.

Wykle, M., & Segal, M. (1991). A comparison of black and white family caregivers with dementia. *Journal of National Black Nurses Association, 5,* 28–41.

Wylie, F. M. (1971). Attitudes toward aging and the aged African-American Americans: Some historical perspectives. *Aging and Human Development, 2,* 66–70.

Young, R. F., & Kahana, E. (1989). Specifying caregiver outcomes: Gender and relationship aspects of caregiving strain. *The Gerontologist, 29,* 660–666.

Zarit, S. H., Reever, K. E., & Bach-Peterson, J. (1980). Relatives of the impaired elderly: Correlates of feelings of burden. *The Gerontologist, 20,* 649–655.

# Conclusion: Practice and Policy Implications

In recent years, social gerontological research focusing on ethnic and cultural differentiation has been emerging as a promising discipline that has potential to impact and shape public policies as well as health and social service programs. But the volume and depth of such research has not yet reached the point of critical mass where a firmly established knowledge base could be used to engineer changes in existing policies and programs to improve their effectiveness and to promote and create services for newly identified needs. Lack of such a knowledge base notwithstanding, American society is at a critical juncture where policy makers, practitioners, families, and individuals of all ethnic backgrounds are forced to face the common, difficult issue of long-term care of frail elders. We began this book with the goal of filling the gap in knowledge about long-term care for ethnic/racial minority elders by analyzing and comparing between-group and within-group differences in psychological, physical, and functional health statuses; applications for nursing home admission; in-home and community-based service use; the relationship between informal social support and formal service utilization; informal caregiving; and caregiver burden. Although we would very much like to state that we have achieved our goals, we also admit there is much more to be done. At minimum, we hope our findings provide a reference point for further studies by interested scholars and students of minority aging and long-term care. In the remainder of the chapter, we provide a brief summary of research findings, discuss policy and practice implications of the findings, and recommend directions for future research.

## SUMMARY OF RESEARCH FINDINGS

In Chapter 3, we compared African American, White, and Hispanic frail elders in terms of their psychological well-being, as measured by self-reported depressive symptoms, and analyzed its correlates with respect to life-strain and coping resources. Hispanic frail elders reported the highest mean score of depressive symptoms, and African American frail elders reported the lowest mean score. Female gender, poor objective and subjective health status, and perceived unmet needs with ADL and IADL were common predictors of low psychological well-being for all three groups of elders. But fewer informal helpers for Hispanics, living alone for Whites, and fewer formal care providers for African Americans were unique racial/ethnic predictors.

In Chapter 4, we analyzed internal heterogeneity among three national-origin Hispanic elder groups—Mexican Americans, Puerto Ricans, and Cuban Americans—in their health status, financial strain, and psychological distress. Cuban American elders were healthier and financially better off than Mexican American and Puerto Rican elders. But the three national-origin groups were common in that health indicators, family stress, low income, and unmet needs were predictors of problems in all three domains of well-being. Neither national origin nor English-language ability was a significant predictor of psychological distress.

In Chapter 5, within the framework of an expanded Andersen-Newman model, frail elders who had applied for nursing home admission and those who had not were compared to examine factors associated with such an application. White frail elders were 73% more likely than African American and Hispanic frail elders to have applied for nursing home admission. In addition to race, other predictors of such an application included advanced age, cognitive and functional impairments, low income, number of formal services used, living alone, and number of unmet needs. Availability of informal support was not a significant factor.

In Chapter 6, we analyzed the determinants of nursing home application within the sample of African American and White frail elders. Cognitive impairments, a positive attitude toward nursing home placement, and a high number of formal services used were common predictors for both groups. In addition, advanced age as well as a high number of functional impairments and of unmet needs were predictors unique to Whites.

In Chapter 7, we analyzed racial differences in the rate of utilization of in-home and community-based services for long-term care, as well as the determinants of such utilization, among African American, White, and Hispanic frail elders. The utilization rates of both in-home services (home health care and Meals on Wheels) and community-based services (congregate meals, social center/church programs, and counseling services) were low for all three ethnic groups. Need factors such as physical illness, ADL impairments, previous use of a nursing home, and living alone were predictors of use of in-home services. But fewer difficulties with ADL, fewer informal helpers, and living alone were predictors of use of congregate meals and social center/church programs; and a lower sense of control in life and fewer ADL problems were predictors of use of counseling services. White elders were more likely to use Meals on Wheels than Hispanics, African Americans were more likely to use social center/church programs than Whites, and Hispanics were more likely to use counseling services than Whites and African Americans. There was no racial difference in the likelihood of using home health care and congregate meal services, when all the other predisposing, enabling, and need factors are controlled for.

Chapter 8 compared the three national-origin groups of Hispanic elders in terms of predictors of their in-home and community-based service use. Need factors again had the most predictive power for home health care use followed by enabling factors, advanced age, and living alone. National origin and English-language ability did not have any independent effect. However, the likelihood that elders would use Meals on Wheels service was associated with their ability to read English, and Mexican Americans were more likely than Cuban Americans to use the service. The length of stay in the United States and the ability to read English, in addition to fewer problems with ADL, were also predictors of congregate meal service use. Also, in-home and community-based service use were positively associated with each other, indicating that connecting Hispanic elders to one type of service may increase the odds of their using others.

In Chapter 9, as an extension of Chapters 7 and 8, we focused on the relationship between living arrangement and in-home and community-based service use within each ethnic/racial group. Although a bivariate analysis showed that a higher proportion of African American and White frail elders who lived with someone used home health services than did their living-alone counterparts, multivariate analysis showed that, other things being equal, African American and White frail elders who lived alone were more likely to use both in-home and community-based services than those who lived with others. For Hispanics, however, the number of informal helpers, not living arrangement per se, was a significant predictor. Among the three national-origin groups of Hispanic elders, living alone was a significant predictor of in-home service use for Mexican Americans only, and it was a significant predictor of community-based service use for Puerto Ricans only. For both Mexican Americans and Puerto Ricans, ability to write English was also a predictor. Also in confirmation of the findings in Chapter 8, a consistently significant factor of service use for all three national-origin groups was the other type of service used.

In Chapter 10, we analyzed racial differences in the size and composition of informal support systems and caregiving burden of the primary caregiver.

The three ethnic/racial groups were not significantly different in the size of their caregiver networks. In terms of caregiver composition, Whites and Hispanics rely mostly on immediate kin, whereas African Americans incorporate a wider range of nonfamily acquaintances such as friends and neighbors. Among the primary caregivers, African Americans complained that many of their needs were not met, and yet their stress level was the lowest. Hispanics and Whites both reported high levels of stress. As to physical, emotional, and financial strain from caregiving, the findings point to a rather complex host of factors that acquire a specific configuration for each ethnic group. African Americans and Whites share many of the same predictors, especially the role conflicts with both their personal life and occupational obligations. For Hispanics, it is the lack of rest or opportunities to find respite, and a sheer sense of being crushed by the weight of these responsibilities. Like African Americans and Whites, Hispanics had limited informal supports but denied that their needs were not being properly met—they seemed to implicitly affirm that everything was under control—and, as a consequence, they did not need to seek out formal services. By the same token, Hispanic caregivers were the least inclined to place their elders in nursing homes, whereas White caregivers were less hesitant to pursue the placement of their frail relatives in long-stay institutions.

In summary, the findings, ranging from psychological well-being to nursing home application to in-home and community-based formal service use to informal support of frail elders, present some commonalities transcending the racial/ethnic line. That is, physical, functional, and/or cognitive impairments and unmet needs in regard to these impairments are found to be common determinants of quality of life, institutional application, and other formal service use. Besides affirming the significance of need factors, the findings also present singular and divergent paths, resulting partly from cultural differences, for each racial/ethnic group. Of the three groups, Hispanic elders were the most likely to be affected by informal helping networks. Specifically, the number of informal helpers was a predictor of their psychological well-being as was formal service use, indicating their higher level of attachment and dependence on informal support networks than the other two groups. The strong adherence to cohesive familism and filial obligation being the core Hispanic cultural values, its overriding effect on frail elders is not surprising. English-language ability posing as a barrier to formal service use was also distinctive to Hispanics. Compared to Hispanics and African Americans, Whites appeared to be less inhibited about choosing an institution as a long-term care arrangement. African Americans were more like Whites than Hispanics in terms of factors affecting in-home and community-based service use. But African Americans, despite their health status, which was the lowest of all three racial/ethnic groups, reported the lowest depression score. They also distinctively differed from both Whites and Hispanics in the composition of their informal support network; specifically, African American elders drew their informal support from more varied sources. Although African American caregivers were the most likely to perceive unmet needs, they also reported the lowest caregiving stress.

## PRACTICE AND POLICY IMPLICATIONS

Health and social service providers need to be aware of these racial/ethnic differences when serving diverse groups of elderly clients and their families. Given the high attachment of Hispanic elders to their informal support system, composed mostly of immediate family members, service providers working with them need to strengthen their informal support system by linking the family members to health and social service programs as well. Long-term care for Hispanic elders needs to be a family and community affair, in which both the frail elders and their family members are provided services to meet the care needs of the elders and help the family member cope with the family's stress and other problems associated with caregiving. First, service providers need to be trained to understand personal and familial stresses and problems related to an elder's disability and dependence as well as the impact of such stresses and problems on the quality of life among Hispanics. Second, family caregivers must be supported by the formal service system, which can supplement their caregiving chores and help alleviate their psychological, physical, and financial strains. Specifically, service providers must reach out to Hispanic elders and their families to draw them in and connect them to appropriate services—respite, counseling, and mutual support groups for caregivers as well as in-home and community-based services.

Because our findings indicate that, particularly for Hispanics, access to one service apparently functions as a gateway to accessing other types of service, outreach to those who are not connected to the existing service systems is especially important. The findings imply that lack of knowledge about the availability of services may be a significant barrier for Hispanic elders. Such lack of knowledge may be due to the limited English-language ability of many of them; this was in fact found to be a factor determining the likelihood of their using some in-home and community-based services. Outreach to Hispanic frail elders and their families thus requires bilingual service providers and programs to remove their language barrier to accessing necessary services. For example, Spanish-language flyers, ethnic food, and Spanish-speaking site managers, dietitians, social workers, and/or volunteers would certainly encourage more participation by Hispanic elders in programs such as Meals on Wheels and congregate meals. Similarly, recruitment of Spanish-speaking visiting nurses and home health aides is also important to encourage participation in in-home service programs. In urban areas, where the

Hispanic population is concentrated, it is also important for the service providers to locate in the Hispanic community and incorporate Hispanic cultural heritage in the programs. Locating the services in their own neighborhood is especially important not only for Hispanic elders who have difficulty with the English language, but also for all low-income minority elders who lack transportation or have other mobility problems. In designing effective long-term care services, it may be more convenient and cheaper for service providers to bring services to the locations where these elders are instead of trying to bring the elders to the service location.

In the future, long-term care services for frail elders, regardless of their ethnicity/race, will need to be designed with coordinated access to service or case management as the core mechanism to promote efficiency and effectiveness. Once an elderly client is identified as needing long-term care, his or her needs and eligibility for different types of services should be evaluated by a case manager or a similar system. Based on the comprehensive evaluation, all necessary referrals for coordinated care can be made and services can be provided accordingly. The coordinated care system will help elders and their families of all races, but it will especially help ease the burden of long-term care among the minority groups whose access to long-term care services is more likely to be impeded by lack of information and the bureaucracy of the complex long-term care system. It will also promote quality and encourage cost saving because it can cut overlapping procedures and services.

African American elders and their extended informal support systems are not much more likely than Hispanics to utilize formal services. However, our findings indicate that those who use the services are apparently benefiting from them and that they are more likely than their Hispanic or White counterparts to perceive their need for formal services, except institutional services. To reiterate, despite their significantly worse health conditions, African American elders and their caregivers are much less likely than their White counterparts to use a nursing home as a long-term care setting regardless of the size of their informal support system. But African Americans apparently regard formal in-home and community-based services as an acceptable and even desirable supplement to informal caregiving. Although it is not clear specifically why a large majority of them do not use the services, in spite of their desire to do so, the barriers may pertain to accessibility, availability, and/or acceptability of the services: waiting lists in urban areas, lack of programs in rural areas, transportation problems, and cultural insensitivity. In fact, part of the reason nursing home application rates among African Americans (and Hispanics) are so much lower than those of Whites may be that they perceive nursing homes as institutions dominated by a White majority. Their attitude toward institutionalization might in fact become more favorable if they were given a choice of nursing homes catering primarily to African Americans.

Unlike Hispanics, whose informal support system consists largely of immediate kinship (grandchildren, siblings, and godparents included), African Americans draw their informal support from a larger circle—neighbors, friends, and most importantly, churches. Thus, to improve the availability of and access to in-home and community-based services for African American elders and their caregivers, service providers may need to bring services to churches and other neighborhood social and cultural centers. As community resources, churches and these neighborhood organizations can serve as focal points for information dissemination and service delivery. Because African American churches have long functioned as informal helping agencies as well as places of worship, the foundation in terms of visibility and people's trust has been laid. Service providers will have to develop more infrastructure by bringing in more funding, professional staff, and diversified programs to churches. Since the 1996 welfare reform legislation (the Personal Responsibility and Work Opportunity Reconciliation Act) has allowed churches to become direct recipients of social service funding, they can now also function as direct service providers. Being located in the neighborhood and interacting with the residents on a daily basis, these organizations often have the most intimate knowledge of people's needs. Thus, services provided by grassroots organizations such as churches and neighborhood centers can appeal to potential consumers to a greater extent than those offered by traditional, often bureaucratic, service providers because such organizations are more likely to offer a convenient location, flexibility, familiarity, and cultural sensitivity. Because unnecessary bureaucratic layers that are characteristic of the oftentimes hierarchical service-delivery system can be cut down in the grassroots setting, better-quality services may also be provided at the benefit of considerable cost saving.

Extolling the virtues of grassroots organizations for long-term care services, however, must not be equated with the denigration of public interventions. As we have witnessed in the past few decades, the remarkable expansion of private not-for-profit organizations in the social and health services arena is a result primarily of the infusion of public funding. For a social problem of such magnitude as long-term care, federal funding through Medicare, Medicaid, social services, and public health block grants needs to grow further to meet the growing need and to reach those who have not been reached. After all, long waiting lists for home health care, Meals on Wheels, and other in-home and community-based services can be shortened primarily by increased funding for personnel, especially those with training in cultural sensitivity, to serve minority elders, and other necessary resources.

Together with provision of the funding, federal and state governments need to intervene more actively to improve the quality of care in nursing homes and to expand in-home and community-based care through legislative and administrative channels. Especially with the increasing pressure for cost control and the rising tide of capitation payment systems and managed care, governments have the responsibility to balance their regulatory and deregulatory power. On the one hand, the development of innovative in-home and community-based programs needs to be encouraged under continued government waiver programs. On the other hand, the clients' rights and quality of care should be protected from unscrupulous service providers driven by the zeal for cost saving and profit maximization. Public intervention is especially needed to prevent disadvantaged minority groups, who are more likely to be alienated from existing service structures, from being short-changed and pushed further back by the usurping force of privatization and fee-for-service systems.

Given Hispanics' and African Americans' lack of interest in institutional care, development of more accessible in-home and community-based services is especially important to effectively cover these population groups. But our findings also show that a majority of frail elders of all ethnicities/races reject institutional care as a viable alternative. Not only because of consumer preference but also because of the escalating cost of institutional care, long-term care will need to continue its shift toward in-home and community-based service. Innovations for improved accessibility, efficiency, and quality of in-home and community-based services need to continue.

Despite the increasing focus on in-home and community-based services, nursing homes will need to continue to exist. Our findings show that physical, functional, and cognitive impairments are the strongest risk factors for institutionalization of elders of all races. Technology may stretch the limits of the in-home and community-based services in the future and allow more frail elders to remain in the community and avoid institutionalization. Nevertheless, the most impaired of all will still require institutional care. With increasing numbers of the very old and, especially, a growing pool of those with serious cognitive impairments, families and community-based resources will not be able to meet the care needs of these severely disabled elders. Nursing homes are here to stay. Accordingly, access to nursing home beds needs to be facilitated by prompt processing of applications and an adequate supply of beds to prevent long waiting lists; in addition, the quality of nursing home care needs to be improved. We will not be able to do without institutions; therefore, we had better make them more acceptable. To serve minority elders better, nursing homes need to increase their minority staff and provide culturally sensitive care. In addition, on the micro level, service providers working with minority elders and their families may need to take an active role in preparing them to cope with the institutionalization that may become inevitable at some point.

Throughout the book, it is quite clear that families and other informal support systems, regardless of ethnicity/race, were on the front line of long-term care, providing daily assistance to their frail elderly relatives. Care provided at home by family members and other informal helping networks certainly enhances elders' quality of life and reduces the cost of formal services. However, although there were racial differences in the level of caregiving stress experienced by primary caregivers, they—women, disproportionately—all experience physical, emotional, and financial strains because caregiving role demands conflict with their familial and occupational roles. Caregiving for a frail elderly relative frequently compromises a caregiver's well-being. Despite the well-established literature on the value of informal caregiving and caregiver burden, however, little effort has been made to alleviate the burden on close families and other relatives of frail elders. We should not allow a caregiver's love of and commitment to a frail elderly relative result in his or her forsaking of other goals, aspirations, and responsibilities in life. In designing long-term care services, enhancement of caregivers' well-being, or at least prevention of the deterioration of their quality of life, needs to be considered on a par with the quality of life of their frail elderly charges. Support for caregivers has to be an integral part of long-term care services.

It appears that elders who lived alone also frequently received informal care from relatives who were residing apart. Nevertheless, the living alone elders were more likely to be consumers of all types of formal service, apparently because many of them had fewer informal helpers than those who lived with someone else. In other words, these elders lived alone because they lacked an informal support network (no spouse and/or children living nearby). In the future, when childless elders will make up an increasing share of the aged population (since as many as one-fifth of baby boomers are childless), the formal long-term care service system will face the additional challenge of providing care for these childless elders who are likely to end up living alone. The formal service system will need to develop effective methods to identify and target frail elders who live alone, especially those who are low-income minorities, to assure that these elders who lack informal support receive adequate services.

In sum, the challenges the aging American society faces for long-term care are numerous. In this book, we focused on the challenges created by the increasingly diverse aging population. Compared to the White majority, ethnic/racial minority elders and their families on average have more unmet long-term care needs because of their socioeconomic disadvantages, but they often encounter multiple barriers to obtaining quality long-term care services. In this section, we have emphasized the need for increased awareness and acknowledgment of racial/ethnic differences as a beginning step. To improve minorities' access to quality in-home, community-based, and institutional services, we need to provide culturally sensitive and appropriate interventions through both public and private channels. We have also underscored the need to strengthen the informal support system by providing support and relief through complementary partnerships between informal and formal supports.

## LIMITATIONS OF THIS BOOK AND
## DIRECTIONS FOR FUTURE RESEARCH

Although our findings point to the significance of cultural dimensions in long-term care, specific questions related to elders' and their families' attitudes toward receiving formal help, the nature of cultural barriers to using formal services, and the quality and adequacy of informal and formal supports could not be answered due to limitations of the data sets. The effect of discrimination based on race and/or class, both contemporaneous and cumulative, on the elders' and families' psychological well-being and attitude toward and access to formal service systems could not be tested for the same reason. Also, because the data were cross-sectional, longitudinal changes in the elasticity of informal support and formal service use in response to elders' changing health status and the effect of informal and formal support on health status could not be tested. The longitudinal impact of elders' deteriorating health on their own and their caregivers' psychological well-being, and vice versa, also were not tested for the same reason.

Future research needs to fill these knowledge gaps. To achieve this effect, however, longitudinal national surveys with representative minority samples—Asian Americans and native Americans included—large enough for meaningful multivariate analyses of their long-term care needs and service utilization patterns are needed. In these surveys we also need to recalibrate for minority groups the research instruments that were largely designed for use in the majority population. For example, it has been widely suspected that existing standardized measurement tools for psychological symptomatology may not have equivalent validity and reliability with minority populations. Development of research tools that are more adaptable to minorities is needed to reduce systematic measurement errors. Both federal funding and private foundation funding must be provided to ensure collection of accurate data necessary for the formulation of social policies and design of programs that would address special needs of minority elders and their families.

In conjunction with the analyses of national data sets, gerontologists must remember that the numeric averages and coefficients from the statistical analyses need to be reinforced with real voices of the people represented by such numbers. That is, studies of cultural differences, experience and impact of discrimination, and coping strategies adopted by racial/ethnic minorities often require qualitative as well as quantitative methods and information. Standardized scales, inventories, and survey questionnaires are convenient and useful, but they have limited utility when it comes to the presentation of in-depth, subjective accounts of the sample members as real, live human beings who feel and reason. The stories of vulnerability as well as strengths of racial/ethnic minority elders and their families with respect to the elders' long-term care need to be told to supplement and complement quantitative information.

# Index

African American elderly, 1–2, 5–11, 17, 19–23, 61, 68, 202–209; attitudes of, 90–92, 95–96, 100; attitudes towards, 173; and cultural aversion to institutional care, 83–84, 98, 100, 145; disadvantages concerning, 80–81, 87–89, 94–95, 97–98; and greater tolerance of disabilities, 99; and informal caregiving, 171–174, 176–180, 184–194, 204–207; living arrangements of, 143–145, 148–158, 164–166; lower rates of nursing home placements among, 79, 98; and low rate of depression, 204–205; and noninstitutional service use patterns, 104, 106–107, 111–120, 208; and nursing home placement, 79–100; quality-of-life issues among, 27–39; role of churches and social centers among, 83, 111, 117–118, 187, 205, 207

Aging and frail elders, 1–5; depression and psychological distress among, 27–39, 179, 204; need for proper care of, 75; and race/ethnicity, 5–8, 17–19, 27–29, 38–39, 72, 139

American Association of Retired Persons (AARP), 27

Andersen–Newman model, 60–61, 63, 75, 86, 104, 107–108, 119, 126–127, 138, 150

Arabs, 5

Asian American elderly, 1–2, 5–6, 210

Asset and Health Dynamics among the Oldest Old (AHEAD), 107, 147

Civil Rights Act, 6

Cuban American elderly. *See* Hispanic American elderly

First Duke Longitudinal Study of Aging, 79, 106, 145

Hispanic American elderly, 1–2, 5–11, 17, 19–26, 43, 61, 68, 202–209; and Andersen–Newman model, 126–127, 138; church and senior center participation among, 133–134; conclusions regarding noninstitutional service patterns, 135–139; congregate meal service usage, 133–134, 205; coping resources for, 43–

## ABOUT THE AUTHORS

ADA C. MUI is an Associate Professor at the Columbia University School of Social Work. Her professional interests are social gerontology, cross-cultural research methodology, quality of life, mental health, and support systems among frail elders, older persons living alone, and ethnic elderly populations.

NAMKEE G. CHOI is an Associate Professor at the School of Social Work, SUNY at Buffalo, where she teaches social policy, aging policy, and research methods. Her research has been in the areas of racial and gender differences in the elderly's economic status, retirement patterns, living arrangements, and social service utilization.

ABRAHAM MONK is Professor of Social Work and Gerontology at the Columbia University School of Social Work. He has served as consultant or advisor to numerous public and voluntary agencies. He is the author or editor of 10 books, including *The Columbia Retirement Handbook* (1994).

ISBN 0-86569-232-7

90000>

EAN

9 780865 692329

HARDCOVER BAR CODE